KV-568-942

Child Law

A GUIDE FOR COURTS AND PRACTITIONERS

Richard Powell

WATERSIDE PRESS

WINCHESTER

Child Law

CONTENTS

Child Law

Richard Powell is a barrister-at-law and legal team leader in the South Devon Magistrates' Court. He is a member of the Justices' Clerks' Society Human Rights Network and nationwide co-ordinator of the Magistrates' Courts Service Human Rights Web Board. He is co-editor of *Magistrates' Courts Practice* and lectures widely on human rights, criminal law, family law and procedure.

Child Law Richard Powell

Published 2001 by
WATERSIDE PRESS
Domum Road
Winchester SO23 9NN
United Kingdom

Telephone or Fax: 01962 855567
Editorial e-mail: watersidepress@compuserve.com
Orderline e-mail: watersidepress@cs.com
Online catalogue and bookstore: www.watersidepress.co.uk

Copyright: Richard Powell. All rights reserved. No part of this book may be reproduced, stored in any retrieval system or transmitted in any form or by any means, including over the Internet, without prior permission. The 'Youth Court Sentencing Grid' (pp.136-7) is the copyright of Andrew Mimmack and is reproduced by kind permission of *Magistrates' Courts Practice*.

ISBN 1 872 870 92 9

Catalogue-In-Publication Data: A catalogue record for this book can be obtained from the British Library

Printing and binding: Antony Rowe Ltd, Chippenham

Cover design: Waterside Press

Preface

This is a book about rights - primarily the rights of children, but also the rights of parents and the limits on the power of the state to intervene in the way children are brought up in society. It is about the relationship between the conflicting interests of parents to parent, children to thrive and the state to maintain and enforce society's norms.

An emerging system of child specific rights

The text is directed towards everyone with an interest - practically, professionally or theoretically - in the upbringing of children. The book is divided into eleven chapters dealing with children and their interface with the legal system in terms of family proceedings, the criminal justice system, their employment and education. The general premise is that there is an emerging system of child specific rights which is gradually and subtly altering the balance of legal processes. Within this changing picture there exist distinct tensions – such as measures in the Crime and Disorder Act 1998, which on the one hand stigmatise parents for the conduct of their children whilst at the same time imposing severe sanctions on children as young as ten (or under) for 'errant' conduct.

The impact of international law and obligations

In a national context, the book describes a rights-based society striving to provide adequate protection for children while supporting parents in their freedom to bring up children without undue state interference - and in an international context an emerging society where the traditional position of the state is under siege due to an evolution towards 'supranationalism'. In short, the relationship between the individual and the state is now under continual review and scrutiny by international law, obligations and organizations – but with the state generally acting, or seeking to act, in accordance with its responsibilities. Overall, the picture is one of society and state entering a transitional phase in the development of child law and child-related professional practice. In determining the boundaries of the relationship between the community as a whole and the individual - as a member of that community - there emerges a greater sense that both state and citizen have a greater awareness than before of rights and responsibilities, which cannot, of course, operate in a vacuum.

Social engineering

The term social engineering has somewhat sinister overtones, yet as a general description of the purpose of legislative and administrative policy a better one could hardly be found. One of the most important choices society makes is in the prioritising of rights and freedoms. In an autocratic society the rights of individuals are secondary to the needs of the community. In an anarchistic society individual rights are of equal if not greater importance than the general interests of the whole. A rights-based legal system opens up the way to striking the right balance between competing interests and perspectives. Where the rights of an individual come into real conflict with the rights of the whole the controlling institutions of the community may be justified in imposing proportionate sanctions or restraints on an individual.

Changing roles

Social engineering through legislative change is hardly more clearly depicted than by the structural changes wrought by the Criminal Justice and Court Services Act 2000. Under that Act the work of guardians and welfare officers is - for the first time - brought under the auspices of one national organization, the Children and Family Court Advisory and Support Service, CAFCASS for short. By removing the family court welfare function from the National Probation Service the welfare officer's role can no longer be viewed as an adjunct to that service's main responsibilities in the context of its modern, more emphatic, crime prevention-cum-rehabilitation of offenders role within the criminal justice system. Under the 2000 Act both guardians ad litem and court welfare officers were given a name change - becoming 'children's guardians' and 'children and family reporters' respectively - and become more accountable through a dedicated, nationwide organization.

It is sad to reflect that the creation of CAFCASS has led to the loss of many experienced guardians unwilling to accept the change to their employment. In many areas of the country a shortage of guardians and reporters has contributed to an increase in delay in proceedings.

Meanwhile the youth justice system awaits national roll-out of the referral order panel procedure for those children appearing before a youth court for the first time. The scheme - due to come into full operation on 1 April 2002 - will lead to the vast majority of such juveniles being placed, for a period, under the supervision of a referral panel operated under the auspices of a local youth offending team (YOT) and comprising both professional and lay people. The referral panel will work with the juvenile to design an intervention plan, with the overall aim of preventing re-offending (thereby embracing the now statutory principal aim of youth justice). The intervention plan is monitored by the panel. Effectively this shifts the focus of the sentence away from its traditional locus - the youth court - and into a more intensive, immediate and perhaps less remote forum.

I hope that - along with existing practitioners and students interested in the 'bigger picture' - both referral panel members and members of CAFCASS will find something in this book to assist their understanding of the potentially wide range of issues, tensions and conflicts which may be shaping a child's thoughts and his or her attitude to life.

Basic rights – making communities safe

At a basic level the balance of interests between state and citizen can be maintained by using the law to enforce and maintain what are perceived as norms, morals or values. For example, an individual has the power to kill another human being – but unless the life of the community as a whole is threatened (or maybe the life of the perpetrator) such an act is contrary to society's interest and attracts condemnation through prosecution of this deviation from the norm and punishment according to law.

The European Convention On Human Rights describes a number of basic rights and sets a limit on the exercise of those rights by both the state and the individual. A society based on the Rule of Law and on the proper observation of such basic rights has the necessary conditions to develop a further raft of political and social rights. By their very nature such rights and freedoms are essentially reflections of more sophisticated morals and values. They express an objective standard of conduct in the form of duties and responsibilities. Basic rights make communities safe places to live in.

Building children's rights from a sound base

The establishing and enforcement of 'second stage' rights amounts to an exercise in social engineering. The motive behind the exercise can be discerned from the continuing nature of societal evolution, moving on from one stage of existence to the next. In terms of parenting the first stage was the creation of a society in which it was safe to bring up children: a society with a minimum level of healthcare, education and economic prosperity. The second stage is the attempt to establish an objective standard of skill and knowledge supported by the least intrusive measures on behalf of the community as a whole expressed through the state and its institutions.

In the first stage a child has the right to life, health, education and to reasonable economic expectations. In the second stage the child's rights extend to the facility and opportunity to thrive rather than simply to survive, to have a happy childhood and social rights equivalent to those enjoyed by adults. In the transition between the two stages the child's welfare moves from being an equal consideration, alongside other factors, to being a paramount consideration for courts and practitioners.

The society in which these rights evolve through may be in a state of development itself. Throughout history, the manifestation of community has evolved from tribal groupings to empire. In the present state of evolution state communities are characterised by a transitional phase in which nation states transfer a proportion of their substantive and ideological rights to supra-national organizations. For example, the member states of the European Union have voluntarily transferred limited economic and social rights of determination to the wider organization for the good of the nation. In the incorporation of the European Convention On Human Rights into national law the United Kingdom has partly transferred its right to develop a rights-based legal system.

A 'rights-of-the-child-and-responsibilities-of-the-parent' approach

The driver for social engineering in the transitional phase and in stage two rights is found in the concurrent transition from sovereign nation to supra-nationalist nation. There exist many international treaties that describe and promote stage two rights and freedoms. The difficult aspect for observers of the legal system is that during this transitional phase the effect of these international principles is not consistent within the national system. It is possible to identify an emergent rights-of-the-child-and-responsibilities-of-the-parent approach in the policy of the state and in its translation into day-to-day practice - which is reflected throughout this book.

I thus hope that readers will find *Child Law* useful on two levels. Firstly, as a basic guide to the state of the law governing children's rights and parents' rights - and secondly as an analysis of those rights in the context of an evolving society. So many people are involved in the protection of children – as magistrates, members of CAFCASS, YOTs and referral panels and other public sector and private sector services or agencies - that it is sometimes difficult 'to see the wood from the trees'. I hope this book will help answer three fundamental questions:

- What am I doing?
- Why am I doing it?; and
- Why am I doing it in this particular way?

Acknowledgements
My thanks go to the excellent editing skills of Bryan Gibson, the patience and support of my wife, Lesley and to those hardy people able and willing to review the text and to make many useful contributions to its content and layout. On a personal note I also wish to acknowledge the particular encouragement and timely honesty of Fiona Barrie who was also responsible for the majority of the research leading to *Chapter 6*. I am also grateful to Andrew Mimmack for agreeing to the reproduction of his 'Youth Court Sentencing Grid' (which first appeared in *Magistrates Court Practice*) on pp.136-7. Needless to say any omissions and errors remain my own.

Richard Powell

Torquay
October 2001

Table 1.1 *Age-based rights*

Age	Main rights and responsibilities
At any age provided the child is of sufficient age and understanding	To apply for access to personal information held on computer under the Data Protection Act 1984 To apply for access to personal information contained in manual social service's files To access medical reports relating to insurance or employment To baby-sit To change name unless consent is required under a residence order, a care order or from the court To enter into valid contracts for 'necessaries' such as food or clothes To receive a bequest of money or property in a will To be the subject of applications for any order under the Children Act 1989 and to be made the subject of wardship or adoption To be the subject of a Child Safety Order To be the subject of a local Child Curfew Scheme under the Crime and Disorder Act 1998 To give evidence in court. If below 14 years the evidence will be given unsworn To apply for or receive state funded legal representation for criminal proceedings or legal funding for civil proceedings To be represented in court by a lawyer and to seek leave to begin legal proceedings under the Children Act 1989 To sue and be sued through a litigation friend in civil proceedings To make a complaint under the Race Relations Act 1976 and the Sex Discrimination Act 1975 or to make a complaint against the police To give valid consent to medical treatment which can only be overridden by the court and not by those with parental responsibility To refuse to consent to medical treatment although this may be overridden by the court or a person with parental responsibility To seek confidential advice and counselling unless at risk of serious harm To choose own religion To have alcohol confiscated by the police To enter a bar subject to a Children's Certificate if accompanied by an adult To have body pierced provided accompanied by a parent who provides consent To enter but not participate in a bingo club or game To smoke but not purchase tobacco. Tobacco and cigarette papers may be seized by police or park keeper in a public place if under 16 To travel abroad on a passport
5 years	To consume alcohol in private To attend school as a child of compulsory school age To watch a U or PG category film unaccompanied subject to the cinema manager's overriding discretion To rent or buy a U or PG category video subject to the retailer's overriding discretion To pay child fares on trains and buses and tubes in London To retain own seat on a train
7 years	To open and draw money from a National Savings or Trustee Savings Bank Account

10 years	To be held legally capable of committing any sexual offence To be criminally responsible for own actions To be convicted of any criminal offence To be sentenced by a youth court following conviction To be tried and sentenced in the Crown Court for Grave Crimes To be detained in a police station in accordance with the Police and Criminal Evidence Act 1984 To no longer be the subject of an application for a Child Safety Order or a local Child Curfew Scheme
12 years	To be remanded to accommodation provided by the local authority including secure accommodation when charged with a criminal offence To be made the subject of a detention and training order To be trained to participate in dangerous performances subject to licence by the local authority To watch, rent or buy a 12 category film or video To buy a pet To sign passport in own name
13 years	To be held in secure accommodation provided by the local authority otherwise than when charged with a criminal offence
14 years	To enter a bar and buy soft drinks To possess an air weapon under the supervision of a person aged over 21 or for use at a rifle club or shooting gallery To obtain limited employment To ride a horse on a road without protective headgear To be granted a licence to take part in public performances abroad
15 years	To be remanded to a remand centre as a boy charged with a criminal offence in accordance with the Children and Young Persons Act 1969 To watch, rent or buy a 15 category film or video
16 years	To apply for access to school records To accompany another person in the street singing, playing, performing or selling To enter or live in a brothel To give valid consent to surgical, mental or dental treatment To apply for state funded legal representation and be assessed on own means To hold a licence for an invalid carriage or a moped To obtain a commercial pilot's licence to fly a glider or a plane and a flight radiotelephony licence To leave school To receive full-time education free of charge To work full-time subject to limitations in relation to bar work and work in betting shops etc To join the armed forces with parental consent To become a street trader To sell scrap metal To join a trade union To receive an offer of youth training To enter a contract, but not a lease or tenancy for housing To obtain housing from the local authority but only as a priority where the child is vulnerable or his or her welfare is likely to be seriously prejudiced To marry with parental consent To buy premium bonds

	To take part in public performances without a licence To consent to heterosexual intercourse To buy a National Lottery ticket To buy cigarettes etc To consume beer, cider or perry with a meal in a restaurant, hotel or public house To buy liqueur chocolates To be assessed for the purposes of the Child Support Act 1991 To receive income support in certain circumstances To obtain a National Insurance number To pay prescription charges, for sight tests and dental work unless in full-time education To obtain a passport in own name with parental consent. No consent required if the child is married or in the armed forces To pay full train, bus and tube fares in London
17 years	To donate blood without parental consent To no longer be the subject of an application for a care order To be interviewed by the police without an appropriate adult being present To be treated as an adult for the purposes of remands when charged with a criminal offence To hold a driving licence for certain classes of vehicle To obtain a private pilot's licence for a helicopter or balloon To buy or hire any firearm or ammunition To buy or hire a crossbow
18 years *(The age of majority)*	To have access to personal information held by social services To no longer be the subject of an adoption application To apply for a copy of birth certificate after adoption To have name and address placed on the Adoption Contact Register To enter into binding contracts To own land or other forms of property To act as an administrator or executor To ratify contracts made before the age of 18 To ratify loan agreements before the age of 18 To make a will To open a bank account To pawn items To appear in an adult court when charged with a criminal offence To serve on a jury To sue and be sued in own name To no longer be made a ward of court To pay full fees for dental treatment unless pregnant or in full-time education To hold a driving licence for a medium sized goods vehicle To obtain a commercial pilot's licence to fly a glider or plane To receive the national minimum wage To watch, rent or buy an 18 or adults only category film or video To buy fireworks To marry without parental consent To leave home without parental consent To apply for a passport without parental consent To join the armed forces without parental consent To donate body or body parts to science or for transplant without parental consent To vote To take part in a performance of hypnotism To consent to a homosexual act in private between men

	To buy alcohol To enter a betting shop and place bets To take part in gaming To be tattooed To be sentenced to detention in a young offenders institution[1]
19 years	To remain entitled to full-time education
21 years	To adopt a child To be sentenced to imprisonment To supervise a learner driver To obtain a licence to drive a public service vehicle or a heavy goods vehicle To hold a flight navigator's or flight engineer's licence To stand for election to Parliament, the European Parliament or as a local councillor

---

[1] Section 61 Criminal Justice and Courts Services Act 2000 (when in force) abolishes detention in a young offender institution as a sentence (though not in terms of serving as an HM Prison Service establishment). Young people aged 18 to 20 will instead be imprisoned.

CHAPTER 1

Who are 'Children'?

There are a number of definitions of the term 'child' within the legal spectrum. Generally speaking, people are categorised by reference to their biological age rather than their level of maturity. In other circumstances they may be defined by reference to their parents and status at the time of birth. Age-related definitions provide a simple and objective method of identifying children and distinguishing them - in terms of rights, legal treatment and capacity - from adults. Such definitions do not however take into account the level of development or understanding that the individual concerned may - or often more importantly may not - have attained.

LEGAL DEFINITION

A review of statutory definitions of the term 'child' also reveals poor use of language. There is little consistency in the use by Parliamentary draftsmen of certain words or labels applied to people who are of what can be termed 'child age'. This is particularly the case in relation to criminal proceedings and whilst nothing significant should turn on the use of labels it is unfortunate that such inconsistency has crept into legal vocabulary over the years.

Beyond national law, further assistance in understanding the meaning of 'child' can be gleaned from a variety of international treaties to which the UK is a party. Largely speaking, definitions of child in international law follow the various national legal definition in order to maintain respect for differing economic, social and political traditions of collaborating states. The emergence of child specific rights and the extent to which the UK's legal system meets the obligations of nation states under international law is considered in greater detail in *Chapter 3*.

International treaties
Article 1 of the UN Convention On the Rights of the Child provides:

> For the purposes of the present Convention, a child means every human being below the age of 18 years unless under the law applicable to the child, majority is attained earlier.

Paragraph 11 of the UN Rules for the Protection of Juveniles Deprived of their Liberty provides:

> A juvenile is every person under the age of 18. The age limit below which it should not be permitted to deprive a child of his or her liberty should be determined by law.

Rule 2.2 of the UN Standard Minimum Rules for the Administration of Juvenile Justice ('the Beijing Rules') provides:

> A juvenile is a child or young person who, under the respective legal systems, may be dealt with for an offence in a manner which is different from an adult.

Article 1(a) of the European Convention On Recognition and Enforcement of Decisions Concerning Custody of Children provides:

> For the purposes of this Convention, child means a person of any nationality so long as he is under 16 years of age and has not the right to decide on his own place of residence under the law of his habitual residence, the law of his nationality or the internal laws of the state addressed.

The UN Declaration of the Rights of the Child does not contain a separate definition of the term 'child' but recognises that children have the right to be treated differently from adults by reason of their physical and mental immaturity. The European Convention On Human Rights and Fundamental Freedoms provides no child specific rights and accordingly does not contain a definition of child. However the European Court of Human Rights has developed a sophisticated jurisprudence concerning the welfare of the child and similarly recognises the need to treat children differently from adults.

National law
National law – sometimes called 'domestic law' - largely accords with the principles of international law and recognises the special status of children. Various English statutes contain definitions of the term child but there is no single cross-discipline definition.

Civil proceedings
In the context of civil proceedings Rule 21.1(2)(a) of the Civil Procedure Rules 1998 provides: 'A child means a person under 18'.

Child support
In the context of proceedings for the financial support of children under the Child Support Act 1991 section 55 provides:

> 55(1) For the purposes of this Act a person is a child if—
>   (a) he is under the age of 16;
>   (b) he is under the age of 19 and receiving full time education (which is not advanced education)—
>   (i) by attendance at a recognised educational establishment; or
>   (i) elsewhere, if the education is recognised by the Secretary of State; or
>   (c) he does not fall within paragraph (a) or (b) but—
>   (i) he is under the age of 18 and
>   (ii) prescribed conditions are satisfied with respect to him.

(2) A person is not a child for the purposes of this Act if he—
  (a) is or has been married;
  (b) has celebrated a marriage which is void; or
  (c) has celebrated a marriage in respect of which a decree of nullity has been granted.

An additional definition of the term child is provided for the purposes of the Child Support Act 1991 by Schedule 1 to the Child Support (Maintenance Assessment Procedure) Regulations 1992. These regulations expand the meaning of education and enhance the definition of child by reference to age, marital status and education and training being undertaken between the ages of 16 and 19.

Family proceedings

In the context of family proceedings under the Children Act 1989, section 105(1) of that Act provides: 'A child means a person under the age of 18'. This definition is elaborated upon in paragraph 1(2) of the Family Proceedings Court (Children Act 1989) Rules 1991 where child:

(a) means in relation to any relevant proceedings subject to sub-paragraph
  (b) a person under the age of 18 with respect to whom the proceedings are brought
(b) where paragraph 16(1) of Schedule 1 applies, also includes a person who has reached the age of 18.

'Relevant proceedings' has the meaning assigned to it by section 93(3) Children Act 1989 which includes proceedings under the Children Act 1989. Paragraph 16(1) of Schedule 1 includes applications for financial support where the child is over 18 years of age where the Child Support Act 1991 does not otherwise apply.

The Family Proceedings Rules 1991 ascribes the same meaning to the term child as is to be found in section 52(1) Matrimonial Causes Act 1973. For the purposes of family proceedings brought otherwise than under the Children Act 1989 a child is defined by reference to his or her parentage. Section 52(1) provides:

A child in relation to one or both of the parties to a marriage, includes an illegitimate child of that party, or as the case may be, of both parties.

Criminal proceedings

In the context of criminal proceedings a variety of terms have been employed in legislation. For the purposes of section 107(1) Children and Young Persons Act 1933 and section 70(1) Children and Young Persons Act 1969:

A child is a person under the age of 14 years

and

A young person is anyone who has attained the age of 14 years but is under 18.

Both Children and Young Persons Acts and the Criminal Justice Act 1982 use the term 'young offender' to include a person placed under a supervision order or, in the case of the latter Act, people under 21 years of age in the context of detention in a young offender institution (YOI) as opposed to detention in a prison. In April 2000 an order for detention in a YOI for people under the age of 18 was replaced by the detention and training order. Further details of the sentences available in respect of children and young persons are provided in *Chapter 6* which looks at *Safeguards for Children as Offenders.*

Prior to the Criminal Justice Act 1991 the then juvenile court exercised jurisdiction over children and young persons under the age of 17 charged with criminal offences. Section 70 Criminal Justice Act 1991 replaced the juvenile court with the youth court and extended its jurisdiction to include people aged over 17 but under 18. The Crime and Disorder Act 1998 further entrenched the use of the word 'youth' by establishing the Youth Justice Board and youth offending teams (YOTs). However the word juvenile is not entirely redundant - and is yet one more term often used in connection with children. For example the Magistrates' Courts Act 1980 continues to use the word 'juvenile' to describe an accused person or offender under the age of 18. In other contexts juvenile is used to describe young persons who have attained the age of 17. People within such an age group are treated as adults for the purposes of the Bail Act 1976 and in the investigation of crime under the Police and Criminal Evidence Act 1984.

A further term, used by the Magistrates' Courts (Children and Young Persons) Rules 1992 is 'relevant minor', which encompasses both children and young persons in the regulation of youth court proceedings.

Employment
In the context of employment (*Chapter 11*) a child is defined by reference to his or her educational status. Section 558 Education Act 1996 provides:

> For the purposes of any enactment relating to the prohibition or regulation of employment of children or young persons, any person who is not over compulsory school age shall be deemed to be a child within the meaning of that enactment.

In determining whether someone is or is not of 'compulsory school age' it is necessary to look at the separate education provisions outlined below.

Education
In the context of education (*Chapter 11*) a separate definition of child is not essential. The duty of the state is to provide the facility for education to people of compulsory school age. The duty of parents is to ensure that those children of compulsory school age are registered for and attend the educational facilities so provided. Accordingly, whether someone is of compulsory school age operates to define the meaning of a child for the purposes of the Education Act 1996. Section 8 of that Act provides:

8(1) Subsections (2) and (3) apply to determine for the purposes of any enactment whether a person is of compulsory school age.

(2) A person begins to be of compulsory school age—
   (a) when he attains the age of 5, if he attains that age on a prescribed day, and
   (b) otherwise at the beginning of the prescribed day next following his attaining of that age.

(3) A person ceases to be of compulsory school age at the end of the day which is the school leaving date for any calendar year—
   (a) if he attains the age of 16 after that day but before the beginning of the school year next following
   (b) if he attains that age on that day, or
   (c) (unless paragraph (a) applies) if that day is the school leaving date next following his attaining that age.

(4) The Secretary of State may by order—
   (a) provide that such days in the year as are specified in the order shall be, for each calendar year, prescribed days for the purposes of subsection (2);
   (b) determine the day in any calendar year which is to be the school leaving date for that year.

The Education (Start of Compulsory School Age) Order 1998 provides that the prescribed days are August 31, December 31 and March 31 in each year, starting with 31 August 1998.

The Education (School Leaving Date) Order 1997 provides that the school leaving date for 1998 is the last Friday in June.

SAFEGUARDS AS CHILDREN GROW UP

For the purposes of this book 'child' and 'children' refer to people under the age of 18 years unless the contrary is indicated or implied by the statutory definitions described in this chapter. What is soon apparent from considering the limited utility of statutory definitions is that children must be defined by the rights accruing to them at a given age and by the responsibilities imposed upon them by society at that age.

Age and maturity
As a child grows older his or her level of maturity and understanding increases. The law reflects the changes involved in growing up by granting - at various stages - certain rights to the child. At the same time, increased age brings with it a number of responsibilities. The gradual acquisition of these rights and responsibilities defines the objective essence of childhood in society.

As a basic premise it is recognised in the administration of the legal system that children require special safeguards and measures to protect their interests and to promote their welfare. For example the 'welfare principle' is the key feature of the Children Act 1989. In many cases age-based legislation permits the child to partake in conduct otherwise reserved for adults solely on the basis of his or her attaining a given age.

No account is taken of the child's individual and personal ability or capacity to understand the nature of the conduct in question.

In other respects the legal system has developed a sophisticated raft of checks, balances and counter-balances to ensure that some account is taken of the maturity of the child. However, examples of this are largely confined to ascertaining the feelings and wishes of children in family proceedings. Maturity cannot be easily assessed or applied in the granting or withholding of rights to property or in relation to conduct-based rights. Accordingly, age-based rights operate objectively - and therefore without the legal protections otherwise necessary to safeguard the interests and welfare of children.

As a child grows older it becomes both desirable and possible to take into account his or her developing maturity. The extent to which the child's feelings and wishes can be the determinant of particular issues depends on the issue concerned. In *Re P (Minors) (Wardship: Care and Control)* (1992) 2 FCR 625, Butler-Sloss LJ said:

> How far the wishes of children should be a determinative factor in their future placement must of course vary on the particular facts of each case. Those views must be considered and may, but not necessarily must, carry more weight as the children grow older.

As a general rule the older the child and the greater his or her maturity the more important his or her views become but there remains, until he or she attains majority a restriction on the nature of the child's rights of determination. After that age the child becomes an adult and has full and exclusive rights of determination unless qualified through mental incapacity regardless of his or her actual level of understanding or maturity.

'Gillick competence': listening to the child

The legal significance of ascertaining the wishes and feelings of a child can be found in Article 12(1) of the UN Convention On the Rights of the Child. This provides:

> States Parties . . . shall assure to the child who is capable of forming his or her own views the right to express those views freely in all matters affecting the child, the views of the child being given full weight in accordance with the age and maturity of the child.

The minimum that is required of a state is to provide the opportunity for the child to express his or her views. Section 1(3) Children Act 1989 for example requires the court to have regard to the ascertainable wishes and feelings of the child considered in the light of his or her age and understanding. It does not always follow that the court is obliged to give effect to the child's preference. The leading English case on children's views, wishes and feelings is *Gillick v. West Norfolk and Wisbech Area Health Authority* [1986] AC 112 where the House of Lords recognised that a child under the age of 16 years could give valid consent to medical treatment without parental consent or knowledge provided that he or she (in that case she) was of sufficient age and understanding. The situation concerned the provision of advice on contraception but Lord Scarman went on to consider the position in relation to medical treatment generally. He said:

> It will be a question of fact whether a child seeking advice has sufficient understanding of what is involved to give a consent valid in law. Until the child achieves the capacity to consent, the parental rights to make the decision continues save only in exceptional circumstances. Emergency, parental neglect, abandonment of the child, or inability to find the parent are examples of exceptional situations justifying the doctor proceeding to treat the child without parental knowledge and consent, but there will arise, no doubt, other exceptional situations in which it will be reasonable for the doctor to proceed without the parent's consent.

Since this landmark ruling, a child who is of sufficient age and understanding is usually described as being 'Gillick competent'. The principle established by the House of Lords has been applied to a range of other areas of the law so that for example the views of children aged nine and seven were taken into account in *B v. K (Child Abduction)* (1993) Fam Law 17. In cases under the Child Abduction and Custody Act 1985 the issue of Gillick competence has been treated as a question of fact for the judge to decide.

In *Re R (Child Abduction: Acquiescence)* (1995) 1 FLR 716, Balcombe J held that:

> In exercising the [court's] discretion, it was clear that the policy of the Convention, and its faithful implementation by the courts of the countries which have adopted it, should always be a weighty factor to be brought into the scales, whereas the weight to be attached to the objections of the child would clearly vary with his age or maturity; the older the child the greater the weight, the younger the less weight.

The Gillick principle has been further eroded by *Re R (A Minor) (Wardship: Medical Treatment)* (1991) 4 All ER 177 which held that whilst a competent child can give valid consent to medical treatment that did not necessarily mean he or she could withhold consent to necessary treatment. In deciding what order to make the court's primary consideration is the best interests of the child, not whether the refusal to consent is reasonable.[1] However the importance of Gillick remains as the foundation of the rights of the developing child to participate in the determination of issues concerning his or her upbringing.

The age of criminal responsibility

Running in tandem with the child's growing maturity and right to participate in the determination of events is the development of his or her societal responsibilities. The main feature of this concept is the notion

---

[1] *Re T (A Minor) (Wardship: Medical Treatment)* [1997] 1 All ER 906.

that a child capable of asserting rights is also capable of accepting the consequences of his or her actions. The age of criminal responsibility reflects the acquisition of conduct-based rights.

In England and Wales there is a conclusive presumption that children aged under ten are legally incapable of committing crime. Accordingly criminal proceedings cannot be commenced against them and any attempt by the state to intervene or restrict their conduct must be based upon the risk which their lifestyle poses to their welfare. Safeguards are usually achieved through the power of the local authority to take care proceedings under the Children Act 1989.

Prior to the Crime and Disorder Act 1998 there was also a rebuttable presumption that a child under the age of 14 was not legally capable of committing crime. This presumption—known as the *doli incapax* rule — existed on the basis that a child does not know right from wrong unless it can be proved otherwise. The presumption could thus be overturned by the prosecutor adducing evidence to show that the child concerned knew that his or her actions were seriously wrong – sufficient for the court to agree with that evidence. In *JM (A Minor) v. Runeckles* (1984) 79 Cr App Rep 255, Goff LJ said that in order to sustain the conviction of a child under 14 the prosecutor had the burden of proving beyond reasonable doubt the ingredients of the offence and had also to show that the child appreciated that what he or she was doing was seriously wrong, and that his or her act went beyond mere childish naughtiness.

In practice the *doli incapax* rule rendered the prosecution of offenders under 14 relatively rare and complicated. It was abolished by section 34 Crime and Disorder Act 1998. This reflected Parliament's perception that children in the ten to 14 age group no longer require such additional protection. This decision appears to acknowledge the (not unchallenged) view that children are able to fully appreciate the consequences of their actions. At some point in their psychological development they gain a sufficient knowledge of what is behaviourally acceptable and what is unacceptable. At some later point this may be developed through education and exposure to society's norms and values to encompass an appreciation of culpability. But such awareness does not happen overnight. The setting of an age of criminal responsibility at ten years seems to reflect a failure by the state to recognise these crucial maturity milestones and imposes a model of behavioural development which anticipates maturity being reached in a single moment - and which disregards the more easily recognisable gradual move towards maturity and capacity to understand culpability.

Society's treatment of children in the sphere of criminal proceedings has to distinguish between apparent and actual culpability. *Doli incapax* for all of its procedural complexity provided, to a certain extent, the appropriate filter between the age of presumed innocence and the acquisition of adult-like sophistry. The abolition of *doli incapax* also sits at odds with the state's obligations under the UN Standard Minimum Rules for the Administration of Juvenile Justice (the Beijing Rules). Concerning Article 4 of those rules the UN's own commentary runs as follows:

In those legal systems recognising the concept of the age of criminal responsibility for juveniles, the beginning of that age shall not be fixed at too low an age level, bearing in mind the facts of emotional, mental and intellectual maturity.

The minimum age of criminal responsibility differs widely owing to history and culture. The modern approach would be to consider whether a child can live up to the moral and psychological components of criminal responsibility; that is, whether a child, by virtue of his or her individual discernment and understanding, can be held responsible for what is essentially anti-social behaviour. If the age of criminal responsibility is fixed too low or if there is no lower age limit at all, the notion of responsibility would become meaningless. In general, there is a close relationship between the notion of responsibility for delinquent or criminal behaviour and other social rights and responsibilities.

In the English criminal legal system no actual account is taken of a child's emotional, mental and intellectual maturity so far as guilt or innocence is concerned (though it may affect sentence: *Chapter 6*). Instead there is a simple but stark divide between competence to commit a crime and non-competence. The division is based solely on age and fails to reflect the guarantees that are so well provided for by the notion of Gillick competence in family proceedings (above). Why the state should choose to reflect the issue of maturity in one area of the law and not in another is a question of political will and policy-making.

In parallel with the sudden acquisition of responsibility for the consequences of his or her actions runs the gradual acquisition of rights by the child in accordance with age-based legislation. Here the state's granting of rights is characterised by matching the right to do something to an age which equates with an objective measure of maturity.

In *T v. United Kingdom* and *V v. United Kingdom* (1999) 30 EHRR 121 the Court of Human Rights considered whether the very low age of criminal responsibility amounted to inhuman or degrading treatment. The Court considered whether the age of criminal responsibility in the UK was at odds with the age limit as it exists in other member states of the Council of Europe. The Court was unable to find any clear common standard. Whilst most states had adopted an age limit which was higher than that in force in England and Wales, other states attributed criminal responsibility from a younger age, and no clear tendency could be ascertained from examination of the relevant international texts and instruments, for example, the United Nations Convention On the Rights of the Child.

Accordingly the Court said that the age of ten could not be said to be so young as to differ disproportionately to the age limit followed by other European states and did not, therefore, in itself give rise to a breach of Article 3 (prohibition of torture, or inhuman or degrading treatment).

As already explained, rights based on age do not, however, take into account the level of maturity a child may have attained; nor do they distinguish between children who may be in need of special protection. *Table 1.1* on pages *ix* to *xii* sets out the main age-based rights in the UK.

WELFARE

Welfare and human rights generally

Human rights are inherent and inalienable. They are not acquired through status, grant or patronage and are possessed by children to the same extent as adults. The rights described are rights based on the use of property or conduct-based rights. They are not in the nature of fundamental rights and basic freedoms which are guaranteed, as far as the United Kingdom is concerned, by the European Convention and incorporated into English law through the Human Rights Act 1998. These human rights are dealt with in *Chapter 3*.

Many of the responsibilities described in *Table 1.1* require further elaboration and explanation and are dealt with in more detail in later chapters. Of particular importance is the wide range of orders available to a youth court under the Crime and Disorder Act 1998. In dealing with children the youth court is required to take into account the principle set out in section 44(1) Children and Young Persons Act.

> 44(1) Every court in dealing with a child or young person who is brought before it, either as an offender or otherwise, shall have regard to the welfare of the child or young person, and shall in a proper case take steps for removing him from undesirable surroundings, and for securing that proper provision is made for his education and training.

The welfare principle is a common theme, expressed in a variety of ways running through many statutes dealing with children. It appears also as a key feature of international treaties relating to children, and the protection of their rights

Welfare and the Children Act 1989: A paramount consideration

A key principle in national is contained in Section 1 of the 1989 Act which provides:

> 1(1) When a court determines any question with respect to—
> (a) the upbringing of a child; or
> (b) the administration of a child's property or the application of any income arising from it,
> the child's welfare shall be the court's paramount consideration.

The court is also required to consider those issues set out in the welfare checklist in section 1(3) of the 1989 Act and the principles that: delay is prejudicial to the interests of the child; and an order should only be made if it is necessary to promote or protect the child's welfare.[2]

---

[2] See *Chapter 7* for a more detailed consideration of the welfare principle and the welfare checklist.

Welfare in international law

The welfare principle is also recognised in international law.[3] The resolution of disputes between parents over their children should generally be decided in accordance with the best interests of the child under Article 8 of the European Convention On Human Rights. Similar provisions may be found in the UN Convention On the Rights of the Child.[4]

ACCESS TO JUSTICE

Children have a right of access to the courts in international law as an aspect of the general right to a fair trial under Article 6 of the European Convention On Human Rights.[5] In civil proceedings the child's access is through the medium of a litigation friend. In family proceedings the child's access to the court may be exercised either directly by the child seeking the leave of the court to bring proceedings (usually in the High Court) for one of the orders available under the Children Act 1989, or indirectly via the Children and Family Court Advisory and Support Service (CAFCASS) introduced in 2001 and which encompasses the Official Solicitor, the provision of welfare reports and the appointment of a guardian for the child in the proceedings.[6] In criminal proceedings any juvenile has a right to be represented by a solicitor either of his or her own chosing or provided through the state funded legal representation scheme.

---

[3] *Chapter 3.*
[4] See *Whitear v. UK* (1997) EHRLR 291.
[5] *Golder v. UK* (1980) 1 EHRR 524.
[6] *Chapter 2.*

CHAPTER 2

Children and their Parents

Unlike 'family proceedings' the term 'family life' is not used in the Children Act 1989. However the relationship between children and parents inevitably includes the concept of family life.

FAMILY LIFE

No statutory definition exists of 'family life', the usual environment in which children develop and mature. The legal consequences of family life may be found in the description and content of family proceedings but such an approach fails to capture the essence of family life. Article 8 of the European Convention On Human Rights provides protection for the respect of family and private life. Article 8 provides:

> 8(1) Everyone has the right to respect for his private and family life, his home and correspondence.

> 8(2) There shall be no interference by a public authority with the exercise of this right except as is in accordance with the law and is necessary in a democratic society in the interests of national security, public safety or the economic well-being of the country, for the prevention of disorder or crime, for the protection of health or morals, or for the protection of the rights and freedoms of others.

The European Court has been called upon to examine the meaning of family life in a number of cases. The Court's decisions form the major part of the Convention's jurisprudence which must be taken into account by national courts in order to give effect to the basic rights guaranteed under the Convention. It includes the relationships arising from marriage and quasi-marriage, the extended and nuclear family and the form of attachment which may arise between parents and their children when no form of lasting commitment existed between the parents. At present, the definition falls short of according equal rights to same sex couples and the position of transsexuals is not wholly certain. However the protection of basic rights afforded by operation of the Human Rights Act 1998 is as 'a floor and not a ceiling'. This allows for the independent development of rights by the national court to a higher standard than currently reflected by the European Court. In the case of same sex couples the House of Lords has made *obiter* remarks concerning the inclusion of such relationships within the definition of family life. Whilst comments made in this fashion do not establish any principle they are indicative of the development of a trend towards such a principle.[1]

---

[1] *Fitzpatrick v. Sterling Housing Association Ltd* (1999) 2 FLR 1027.

Family proceedings

The Children Act 1989 provides a definition of family proceedings by reference to the classification of legal proceedings rather than by reference to their impact on family life. Accordingly section 8(3) and section 92(2) of the 1989 Act together provide that any of the following proceedings are family proceedings:

(a) those under the inherent jurisdiction of the High Court in relation to children;

(b) any proceedings under the Children Act 1989 dealt with in the magistrates' court; and

(c) proceedings under any of the following provisions:
   (i) Parts I, II and IV of the Children Act 1989;
   (ii) the Matrimonial Causes Act 1973;
   (iii) the Adoption Act 1976;
   (iv) the Domestic Proceedings and Magistrates Courts Act 1978;
   (v) Part III of the Matrimonial and Family Proceedings Act 1984;
   (vi) the Family Law Act 1996; and
   (vii) sections 11 and 12 Crime and Disorder Act 1998.

For the purposes of determining the nature of proceedings any application made under section 25 Children Act 1989 for the use of secure accommodation is also treated as family proceedings.[2]

Subject to certain limitations and a discretion to treat certain enforcement of financial orders as family proceedings set out in section 65 Magistrates' Courts Act 1980, family proceedings in the magistrates' court include proceedings under:

(a) the Maintenance Orders (Facilities for Enforcement) Act 1920;
(b) section 43 National Assistance Act 1948;
(c) section 3 Marriage Act 1949;
(d) section 35 Matrimonial Causes Act 1973;
(e) Part I of the Maintenance Orders (Reciprocal Enforcement) Act 1972;
(f) The Adoption Act 1976, except proceedings under section 34 thereof;
(g) section 18 Supplementary Benefit Act 1976;
(h) Part I of the Domestic Proceedings and Magistrates' Courts Act 1978
(i) section 60 Magistrates' Courts Act 1980;
(j) Part I Civil Jurisdiction and Judgments Act 1982;
(k) the Children Act 1989;
(l) section 106 Social Security Administration Act 1992;
(m) sections 20 and 27 Child Support Act 1991;
(n) Part IV Family Law Act 1996; and
(o) sections 11 and 12 Crime and Disorder Act 1998.

Children and their parents

For those children whose family life has been disrupted through parental conflict which does not engage the duty of the local authority to seek their

---

[2] *R(J) v. Oxfordshire County Council* [1992] 3 All ER 660.

emergency protection, the Children Act contains a number of orders designed to bring stability to their upbringing. The protection of children in public law—that between the state and the individual - and in private law - that between individuals in the case of marital or quasi-marital breakdown - is dealt with in more detail in later chapters.

The Children Act 1989 provides a framework to enable parents to resolve intractable disputes in court. The overreaching principle of the Children Act 1989 is again the welfare principle mentioned earlier in this chapter. The child's welfare is the paramount consideration of any court dealing with questions relating to the child's upbringing. The starting point for the court is the premise that the child has a right to know both of his or her parents. In the case of a contact order[3] Balcombe LJ in *Re H (Minors)(Access)* (1992) 1 FLR 148 approved and cited a passage from a pre-Children Act 1989 case which appeared to him to ably state the approach to be taken. He referred to the headnote of *M v. M (Child: Access)* [1973] 2 All ER 81 which states:

> No court should deprive a child of access to either parent unless it was wholly satisfied that it was in the interests of that child that access should cease, and that was a conclusion at which the court should be extremely slow to arrive. Access was to be regarded as a basic right of the child rather than a basic right of the parent. Save in exceptional circumstances to deprive a parent of access was to deprive a child of an important contribution to his emotional and material growing up in the long-term.

This approach remains valid. The right of a child to know his or her parents takes precedence above the determination of any dispute between them and the child's right may only be limited to the extent that it is contrary to his or her best interests for contact to take place. In an unhappy number of cases the threat to the child posed by violent or absent parents, or a hostile parent having care of the child, can present an overwhelming obstacle to the court's proper facilitation of the child's right. The obligation on the state to ensure that a convenient and meaningful procedure exists for the enforcement of contact orders has been established by the European Court of Human Rights in the case of *Hokkanen v. Finland* (1994) 19 EHRR 139.

The emergence of a child-specific right to know his or her parents is likely to be extended by the wider definition of family life afforded by the Convention so that it may include a right to know the extended family of either parent, through contact or other similarly aimed medium unless contrary to the child's welfare. The extent to which the right can be enforced by a member of the extended family through an application for contact is limited by the need for leave to bring proceedings to be granted by the court.

---

[3] i.e. an order regulating contact between a parent, child and others.

Recent approaches to family life

Over time the common definition of family life has grown to include something wider than the traditional model of the nuclear family. Not only are extended familial relationships encompassed within the meaning of family life but account has also now to be taken of same sex relationships. The demographic increase in the number of single parent families has also led to recent calls by the head of the National Family and Parenting Institute to stress the need to respond to the diversity of family life.

The need to reorganize perceptions and the way society looks at what constitutes family life has also been recognised in national law. In *Fitzpatrick v. Sterling Housing Association* (discussed below) Lord Justice Ward argued strongly for a definition that went beyond the traditional and discriminatory practices inherent in the common usage of the term 'family'. He said:

> I would not define a familial nexus in terms of its structures or components. I would rather focus on familial functions. The question is more what a family does than what a family is. A family unit is a social unit which functions through linking its members closely together. The functions may be procreative, sexual, sociable, economic, emotional. The list is not exhaustive. Not all families function in the same way.

The concept of family life has received substantial judicial attention in the European Court of Human Rights as a result of Article 8 of the European Convention On Human Rights which guarantees the right to respect for family life. The Convention is incorporated into national law by the Human Rights Act 1998 which requires all courts, tribunals and public authorities to give effect to Convention rights.

The existence of family life for the purposes of the Convention is at its most certain where the relationship between people arises out of marriage. The boundaries of the concept have to be determined as an issue of fact in each case. In *K v. UK* (1986) 50 DR 199 the European Commission on Human Rights said:

> The question of the existence or non-existence of 'family life' is essentially a question of fact depending upon the real existence in practice of close personal ties.

Accordingly it does not matter if a child is legitimate or illegitimate. Such a conclusion was reached in *Marckz v. Belgium* (1979) 2 EHRR 330. In *Keegan v. Ireland* (1994) 18 EHRR 342 the Court held that:

> The notion of the 'family' in [Article 8] is not confined solely to marriage-based relationships and may encompass other *de facto* 'family' ties where the parties are living together outside marriage. A child born out of such a relationship is *ipso jure* part of that 'family' unit from the moment of his birth and by the very fact of it. There thus exists between the child and his parents a bond amounting to family life even if at the time of his or her birth the parents are no longer cohabiting or if their relationship has then ended.

Whilst the Court has also emphasised the role of cohabitation in the formation of family life it is clear that the ending of a relationship between the parents does not bring family life to an end; certainly not if such a concession would adversely affect the right of the child to enjoy the benefits of family life. Thus in the case of orders made by a court granting custody of children on divorce to one party and not another:

> The right to respect for family life ... includes the right of a divorced parent, who is deprived of custody following the break-up of marriage, to have access to or contact with his child, and ... the natural link between a parent and a child is of fundamental importance ...

Where there is a pattern of contact between a child and the wider members of his or her extended family the Court has recognised the existence of family life. This is especially so in the case of grandparents (*Marckz v. Belgium* above). As far as other relatives are concerned the existence of family life will depend on the facts of the case.

The duty imposed by the Human Rights Act 1998 on courts and tribunals to take into account the decisions of the Court and the Commission adds a new dimension to the way the concept of family life has to be thought of in the legal system. The national courts are not however bound to follow the lead taken by the Court of Human Rights. Its decisions provide the floor to the protection of rights but not a ceiling. It is therefore open to the national courts to develop an even wider meaning of the term family life than that which is found in the European jurisprudence.

Transsexuals, lesbian and gay couples

In the case of same sex couples the House of Lords may have begun the journey towards the domestic recognition of same sex family life. In *X, Y and Z v. UK* (1997) 24 EHRR 143 the Court of Human Rights recognised that family life under Article 8 included the relationships between transsexuals and their partners. However in the same case the Commission continued:

> Despite the modern evolution of attitudes towards homosexuality the Commission finds that the applicant's relationship does not fall within the scope of respect for family life ensured by the Article.

The position is largely the same under national law. However in *Fitzpatrick v. Sterling Housing Association* (1999) 2 FLR 1027 the House of Lords considered whether the word family as used in the Rent Act 1977 could describe the relationship between two homosexual men. Lord Nicholls said:

> ... the concept underlying membership of a family for present purposes is the sharing of lives together in a single family unit living in one house ... the expression family does not have a single, readily recognisable meaning.

Having concluded that for the limited purposes of the Rent Act 1977 that a stable, long term homosexual relationship was capable of coming within the meaning of the term 'family' Lord Nicholls went on to say:

> ... the decision leaves untouched questions such as ... whether a stable homosexual relationship is within the scope of the right to respect for family life in Article 8 of the Convention.

Although the decision in Fitzpatrick is expressly stated to be without wider impact on the issue of same sex relationships and family life it is clearly an important decision which may be developed over time by the judiciary to provide a greater protection for gay and lesbian families than is currently available under Article 8.

International obligations

The concept of the family is recognised in many other international treaties invariably without definition. The principles set out in them provide a framework for setting the child in the environment most conducive to his or her proper development taking into account the different traditions and social and cultural heritages of the states to the treaties. The Preamble to the UN Convention On the Rights of the Child begins by providing:

> Convinced that the family, as the fundamental group of society and the natural environment for the growth and well-being of all its members and particularly children, should be afforded the necessary protection and assistance so that it can fully assume its responsibilities within the community, recognising that the child, for the full and harmonious development of his or her personality, should grow up in a family environment, in an atmosphere of happiness, love and understanding ...

The Convention promotes the development of the child within the family by setting the child's basic rights in the context of the parent's duties and responsibilities balanced against the equivalent duty of the state to intervene when the best interests of the child so demand. Article 3(2) provides:

> States Parties ... undertake to ensure the child such protection and care as is necessary for his or her well-being, taking into account the rights and duties of his or her parents, legal guardians or other individuals legally responsible for him or her, and, to this end, shall take all appropriate legislative and administrative measures.

Article 5 provides:

> States Parties . . . shall respect the responsibilities, rights and duties of parents or, where applicable, the members of the extended family or community as provided for by local custom, legal guardians or other persons legally responsible for the child, to provide, in a manner consistent with the evolving capacities of the child, appropriate direction and guidance

in the exercise by the child of the rights recognised in the present Convention.

Article 9(1) provides:

> States Parties shall ensure that a child shall not be separated from his or her parents against their will, except when competent authorities subject to judicial review determine, in accordance with applicable law and procedures, that such separation is necessary for the best interests of the child. Such determination may be necessary in a particular case such as one involving abuse or neglect of the child by the parents, or one where the parents are living separately and a decision must be made as to the child's place of residence.

The Convention promotes the principle that a child should in all but the most exceptional of circumstances be cared for within the family. The duties and responsibilities of the parents of the child are to be respected by the state but only to the extent that they are consistent with the child's welfare. Where the exercise of parental duty fails to ensure that the child is properly protected it is expected that the state will intervene and in so doing exercise its own overriding obligation to protect and promote the child's welfare for the good of the child and the good of society generally. In the UK this approach is achieved through the limit on state intervention provided by the Children Act 1989.

As far as the duties of parents are concerned these are expressed by the notion of parental responsibility, a legal concept describing the range of powers encompassed within the function of a parent. Before considering in detail the meaning of parental responsibility it is necessary to define the term parent.

PARENTS AND PARENTHOOD

As with the term 'child' (*Chapter 1*) the term 'parent' has no single definition. It is often used in law to describe those persons with parental responsibility towards a child. The existence of blood ties or a genetic link between a child and a notional parent may assist in the determination of parenthood but such a test can no longer be fully relied upon. The development of assisted reproduction has made the identification of parents far more complicated. The Human Fertilisation and Embryology Act 1990 provides a legal framework for determining the legal consequences of such a scientific procedure.

Position of mother

A person who gives birth to a child is to be treated as the child's mother where the child was conceived naturally or by artificial insemination or *in vitro* fertilisation. Section 27(1) Human Fertilisation and Embryology Act 1990 provides:

The woman who is carrying or has carried a child as a result of the placing in her of an embryo or of sperm and eggs, and no other woman, is to be treated as the mother of the child.

Thus determining who is the child's mother depends on the moment of birth and not on any genetic connection. The Act applies to those children born through assisted reproduction where the assistance took place after 1 August 1991. A procedure exists under the Act to allow for the making of a parental order (below), which leads to a child born through assisted reproduction being treated as the child of a marriage.

Position of the father

Someone whose sperm fertilises an egg and which results in the birth of a child is treated as the father of the child. The existence of a genetic connection is sufficient to establish the legal relationship. This general presumption is subject to two statutory exceptions set out in section 28(6) Human Fertilisation and Embryology Act 1990 which are that a person who has donated sperm for the purposes of licensed treatment for assisted reproduction or where his sperm is used after his death is not to be regarded as the father of any resulting child.

Section 27(1) Family Law Reform Act 1987 provides that a child born to a woman who is a party to a marriage through assisted reproduction is to be treated as a child of both parties to that marriage. Accordingly a father with no genetic connection to the child may become his legal father.

Parental orders

Subject to certain criteria being met as set out in section 30 Human Fertilisation and Embryology Act 1990 a court may make a parental order providing that a child be treated as the child of the parties to a marriage where the child's birth was the result of a process of assisted reproduction. A parental order has the effect of vesting parental responsibility in the applicants. It extinguishes the parental rights of any other person. The procedure clearly applies only where the applicants are the parties to a marriage and are respectively male and female.

Proceedings under section 30 are regarded as family proceedings for the purposes of the Children Act 1989 but the child's welfare is not the paramount consideration in the determination of the application. Section 6 Adoption Act 1976 as applied to proceedings under the Human Fertilisation and Embryology Act 1990 by the Parental Orders (Human Fertilisation and Embryology) Regulations 1994 provides:

6. In reaching any decision relating to an application for a parental order a court shall have regard to all the circumstances, first consideration being given to the need to safeguard and promote the welfare of the child throughout his childhood; and shall so far as practicable ascertain the wishes and feelings of the child regarding the decision and give due consideration to them, having regard to his age and understanding.

Adoptive parents

Parental status may also be acquired via an adoption order in respect of a child. Unlike a residence order available under the Children Act 1989 (see *Chapter 8*) an adoption order brings to an end the legal consequences of parenthood for anyone other than the adopters. Section 12 Adoption Act 1976 provides:[4]

12(1) An adoption order is an order giving parental responsibility for a child to the adopters, made on their application by an authorised court.

(2) The order does not affect parental responsibility so far as it relates to any period before the making of the order

(3) The making of an adoption order operates to extinguish—

(a) the parental responsibility which any person has for the child immediately before the making of the order;

(b) any order under the Children Act 1989; and

(c) any duty arising by virtue of an agreement or the order of a court to make payments, so far as the payments are in respect of the child's maintenance or upbringing for any period after the making of the order.

Parental responsibility

Parental responsibility describes a range of powers and duties which a parent may exercise in relation to a child. Not every natural parent is recognised to have parental responsibility and in certain circumstances it may be shared between people looking after a child or with the state. It is also possible to apply to the court to bring parental responsibility to an end or for it to be brought to an end by operation of law. The following people have parental responsibility:

- both parents if they were married at the time of the child's birth;
- both parents in respect of a legitimate child where they were married at the appropriate time for the purposes of section 2(1) Family Law Reform Act 1987;
- an unmarried mother but *not* an unmarried father;
- both parents by virtue of a parental order under section 30 Human Fertilisation and Embryology Act 1990;
- an unmarried father by virtue of a parental responsibility order under section 4 Children Act 1989;
- an unmarried father by virtue of a parental responsibility agreement;
- both parents by virtue of an adoption order;
- any person to whom a residence order has been granted under section 8 Children Act 1989; and
- the local authority or authorised person by virtue of an interim or full care order under section 31 Children Act 1989.

---

[4] In force at the time of writing. Prospective amendments under the Adoption and Children Bill (2001) were lost with the general election but may be revived during the currency of the Labour administration.

Except where already discussed, the nature and extent of the above orders is discussed in later chapters.

The position of an unmarried father

An unmarried father does not have parental responsibility for his children. On the face of things, this difference in treatment as between a married and an unmarried father appears to amount to discrimination in the enjoyment of family life given the legal consequences for parental responsibility. A father without parental responsibility may be unable to take a full part in making decisions in relation to the upbringing of his child. A challenge to the effect of section 2(2) Children Act 1989 on the basis of Article 8 (right to family life) and Article 14 (the discrimination provisions) of the European Convention On Human Rights failed in the Court of Human Rights where it was held to be legitimate to have a rule of national law which was capable of discriminating between meritorious and unmeritorious fathers. In *B v. UK* ECHR (2000) 1 FLR 1 the Court of Human Rights recognised that the relationship between unmarried fathers and their children varied from ignorance and indifference to a close and stable relationship. This range of relationships provided an objective and reasonable justification for the difference in treatment.

Proposals were made to amend the law in the Adoption and Children Bill (2001) (which ran out of time due to the general election of 2001) to confer automatic parental responsibility upon an unmarried father who became registered as the child's father under the Births and Deaths Registration Act 1953. However the existence of lawful discrimination between married and unmarried fathers reflects Parliamentary choice and provides a useful commentary on the morals and values reflected by legislation within society. The Children Act provides a number of ways in which a father can acquire parental responsibility.

Subsequent acquisition of parental responsibility

A father without parental responsibility may acquire it in a number of ways:

- by marriage to the child's mother;
- by appointment as the child's guardian;
- by entering into a parental responsibility agreement;
- by obtaining a parental responsibility order; or
- by obtaining a residence order.

Where a father marries the mother of his child he brings himself within the ambit of section 2(1) Children Act 1989 and thereby acquires parental responsibility automatically. The father retains parental responsibility even if that marriage should end and the court has no power to bring parental responsibility to an end save by an adoption order or a parental order under the Human Fertilisation and Embryology Act 1990.

A father without parental responsibility may be appointed his own child's guardian but the appointment only takes effect on the mother's death. Where the appointment becomes effective the guardian acquires parental responsibility, however a father without parental responsibility can only acquire it as a consequence of firstly his appointment as the child's guardian and secondly the death of the child's mother.

A parental responsibility agreement is a formal agreement entered into by a child's mother and father and is subject to the Parental Responsibility Agreement Regulations 1991. The agreement has to be in a prescribed form signed by the parties and witnessed by either a justice of the peace, a justice's clerk or an officer authorised by a judge to administer oaths. The completed document must be sent in duplicate to the Principal Registry of the Family Division for registration. A sealed copy will, on registration, be sent to the mother. Until registration has been completed the agreement has no effect. A parental responsibility agreement may be terminated by an order of a court.

Section 4 Children Act 1989 also provides for a father to apply for a parental responsibility order. Unlike many of the orders available under the Children Act 1989 there is no power for a court to make such an order of its own motion. In deciding whether to make an order or not the court is required to treat the child's welfare as paramount and must be satisfied that it is better to make such an order than to make no order at all. The classic test is set out in *Re H (Minors) (Local Authority: Parental Rights) (No. 3)* (1991) Fam. 151 and may be summarised by stating that in deciding whether to make an order the court should take into account:

- the degree of commitment which the father has shown towards the child;
- the degree of attachment which exists between the father and the child; and
- the father's reasons for making the application.

Granting of a parental responsibility order is not automatic although the case law has tended to suggest this. There are a number of examples where the courts have refused to make an order under section 4 above, for example where the father is incapable of embracing the concept due to his mental disposition or where the father was likely to use the order inappropriately. An order may be brought to an end by further court order.

Where a father has been granted a residence order (*Chapter 9*) section 12(1) Children Act 1989 requires the court to make a parental responsibility order at the same time. If the residence order comes to an end that order remains in force until such time as a court makes an order terminating it.

Parental responsibility may be shared between individuals and with the local authority during the currency of public law proceedings or after the making of a care order (see, generally, *Chapter 7*). There is nothing to prevent parents entering into a parental responsibility agreement *after* a care order has been made or indeed in an unmarried father applying for such an order in those circumstances. Parental responsibility agreements and orders cease to be effective when the child reaches the age of majority and becomes legally capable of self-determination.

The concept of parental responsibility

Parental responsibility often appears to be a commodity to be traded between parents. It is certainly the case that the exercise of parental responsibility has the outward appearance of parenthood and where only one party has the right to exercise it there is a diminution of the other's parenthood. However the absence of parental responsibility does not legally detract from the status of someone as a child's parent. The concept embraces a collection of rights: not rights over a child, but rights of determination and—in the case where parental responsibility is shared—rights of co-determination and of unrestricted participation in the decision-making processes which govern a child's upbringing.

Parental responsibility is defined in section 3 Children Act 1989 as follows:

3(1) In this Act 'parental responsibility' means all the rights, duties, powers, responsibilities and authority which by law a parent of a child has in relation to the child and his property.

   (2) It also includes the rights, powers and duties which a guardian of the child's estate would have had in relation to the child and his property.

   (3) The rights referred to in subsection (2) include, in particular, the right of the guardian to receive or recover in his own name, for the benefit of the child, property of whatever description and wherever situated which the child is entitled to receive or recover.

Parental responsibility acquired in any of the ways described above also includes an entitlement or power:

- to apply for a section 8 of the Children Act 1989 order (*Chapter 9*)
- to contact with the child if he or she is in care
- to require his or her consent to be obtained, and the right to withhold such consent in adoption proceedings
- to withdraw the child from voluntary local authority accommodation or to withhold his or her agreement to such accommodation
- to appoint a guardian
- to give consent to medical treatment or to obtain medical details from the child's general practitioner
- to consent to the child's marriage
- to express a preference in the child's education including a right to receive reports from the child's school
- for the child's consent to be given to a removal by the mother of the child from the UK for in excess of a certain period
- to apply for a passport or to oppose the granting of a passport to the child; and
- to be considered to have rights of custody for the purposes of the Hague Convention On International Child Abduction.

The acquisition of parental responsibility does not affect the status of the child. Accordingly a father's citizenship or hereditary title is not capable of passing to the child on his acquisition of parental responsibility.

The capacity for the exercise of parental responsibility to become a source of disharmony in the case of marital and quasi-marital breakdown (see, generally, *Chapter 9*) requires the courts to have careful regard to the motives of a father seeking an order. The aim of parental responsibility is not so much to give the parent rights over the child but to ensure that the limits of responsibility for decision-making are clearly set. It is about defining the environment in which the child's right to a happy, certain and stable childhood is to be enjoyed. The presumption in favour of a marriage-based environment at least in so far as the acquisition of parental responsibility is concerned again illustrates the bias in the Children Act against the non-nuclear, non-traditional family set-up.[5]

State intervention in parenting

In very general terms the state may intervene in the parenting of children only in limited circumstances. The state, through the local authority has an overreaching duty in both international and national law to provide services to children and their parents and to take steps to ensure that children are not at risk in society whether that risk arises from, or is attributable to their parenting or from some other source. Section 17 Children Act 1989 provides:

> 17(1) It shall be the general duty of every local authority –
> (a) to safeguard and promote the welfare of children within their area who are in need; and
> (b) so far as is consistent with that duty, to promote the upbringing of such children by their families,
> by providing a range and level of services appropriate to those children's needs.

Where the provision of a general level of services fails properly to protect children and their welfare, there exists a range of powers permitting the state to intervene directly in the upbringing of children.

---

[5] It can be noted that the Adoption and Children Bill (2001) would have allowed a non-married father to be registered as a father with parental responsibility.

Table 2.1 Emergency powers for the protection of children

Public law			
Police protection order	Section 46 Children Act 1989	Allows the police to remove a child at risk for up to 72 hours	Court order not required
Emergency protection order	Section 44 Children Act 1989	Allows any person to remove a child at risk for up to 8 days	Court order required
Child assessment order	Section 43 Children Act 1989	Requires a person to produce a child for the purposes of an assessment being carried out	Court order required
Interim care order	Section 38 Children Act 1989	Allows a child at risk to be removed to local authority accommodation for up to 8 weeks in the first instance and thereafter for up to 4 weeks per application pending determination of care proceedings. Parental responsibility is shared between the parents and the local authority	Court order required
Care order	Section 31 Children Act 1989	Allows a child at risk to be permanently accommodated by the local authority. Parental responsibility remains shared between the parents and the local authority	Court order required
Supervision order	Section 31 Children Act 1989	Places a child at risk under the supervision of the local authority for up to one year. The child is not removed and the local authority do not acquire parental responsibility	Court order required
Direction to investigate	Section 37 Children Act 1989	Direction to the local authority to investigate the circumstances of a child with a view to the commencement of protection proceedings	Court direction required
Education supervision order	Section 36 Children Act 1989	Places a child under the supervision of an education welfare officer	Court order required
Private law			
Emergency protection order	Section 44 Children Act 1989	Allows a child at risk to be removed to accommodation provided by an individual	Court order required
Non-molestation order	Section 42 Family Law Act 1996	Prohibits the use of harassment or violence against another individual which may include a child in cases of domestic violence	Court order required. May be made with or without notice in an emergency

Occupation order	Part IV Family Law Act 1996	Grants exclusive occupation of a property to one party against another	Court order required. May be made with or without notice in an emergency
Restraining order	Protection from Harassment Act 1997	An order made on conviction in the magistrates' court or the Crown Court for an offence under the Act prohibiting further harassment for a specified period punishable with up to five years imprisonment for more serious offences	Order made in consequence of a conviction under section 2 or 4 of the Act
Restraining order	Protection from Harassment Act 1997	An order made in the county court prohibiting further harassment for a specified period	Court order required
Ancillary intervention			
Parental bind-over	Section 58 Criminal Justice Act 1991	An order binding a parent over to take proper care of and exercise proper control over a minor convicted of a criminal offence	Consequential order on conviction of the juvenile by a youth court
Parenting order	Section 8 Crime and Disorder Act 1998	An order requiring a parent to participate in any form of requirement aimed at preventing the repetition of the conduct which led to the making of the order. Breach of the order is punishable by fine	Court order on conviction of a parent under sections 443 or 444 Education Act 1996, the conviction of a child for any criminal offence or where a child safety order, anti-social behaviour order or sex offender order is in force in respect of the child

By virtue of Article 3 of the European Convention On Human Rights (prohibition on the use of torture, or inhuman or degrading treatment) there is also a positive obligation on the state to take steps to remove children at risk from circumstances which may amount to such treatment. This obligation has been recognised in national law to defeat the local authority's immunity from liability in negligence where it failed to remove children at risk of suffering serious abuse. The duty of the local authority to intervene must however be carefully considered as too early an intervention may result in a disproportionate interference with parental rights and responsibilities. The emergency protection of children in both private and public law is dealt with in *Chapters 7* and *8* respectively. In brief the framework is as shown in *Table 2.1* on pp.37-38.

In addition to formal and direct intervention by the state there are presently a number of other ways in which the state attempts to provide support for children and their parents.

The National Family and Parenting Institute
In 1999 the Home Secretary launched the National Family and Parenting Institute, a charity, to work in partnership with other professional and voluntary family support organizations with the aim of creating a centre of expertise providing accessible and reliable support for families and parents.

The assumption by the state of responsibilities traditionally falling outside the remit of government has led to dire warnings against the emergence of the interventionist state, or the so-called 'nanny state'. The suggestion that the state needs directly to intrude into what many commentators regard as an essentially organic function does raise fundamental questions as to the role of individual responsibility in society. A discussion on whether parenting is a natural and instinctive function of parenthood or whether it is a skill learnt through the process of observation during exposure to an earlier version of it in childhood falls outside the scope of this book. It is perhaps sufficient to say that there is a perception that parenting, relationship and similar life skills require enhancement. The existence of a centrally approved but independent organization promoting family skills allows the state informally to guide and steer without compromising its role in upholding certain values and morals such as those of the traditional family unit.

Formal intervention is also subject to the existing legal framework which is reactive and adversarial rather than preventative. The aims of the National Family and Parenting Institute summarise one of the ways in which the state is able to support the right of parents to bring up their children. While embracing a wide range of opinion, the institute believes that:

- family life should be celebrated in all its diverse forms;
- society has a responsibility to support families by making skills, knowledge and resources available;
- society has a role to play in family life, without interfering in people's freedom and privacy to live their lives as they choose;
- we want parents to be able to raise their children in a society that values what they do and supports them in doing it;
- we want to listen and learn from the experience of parents and children;
- we want to understand the way in which family life is changing, the costs and benefits to families of these changes and how families themselves are adapting;
- we want to ensure that knowledge about relationships, parenting skills and the needs of infants, children and young people are freely and universally available through media and public education;
- we want to make sure the needs of families are fully recognised in economic and social policy;
- we want to find out about and spread knowledge on what works best in supporting families; and
- we want families to be able to ask for and find help when they need it.

The independence of the institute from government has been emphasised by politicians but it is clear that there are at least policy links between the voluntary sector and the 'family friendly' policies arising out of the *Supporting Families* document issued by government in 1998. The construction of a system of support for parents and protection for children beginning with a consistent legislative programme and continuing into services provided at a local or national level outside the ambit of government appears to be an appropriate unified response to the needs of the family.

The challenge for the state
The challenge for the state is to address the needs of parents and children without unlawfully interfering with their right to family life or attaching stigma to those efforts which require some form of compulsion. As far as balancing intervention against freedom is concerned the European Convention On Human Rights provides that the right to respect for family life under Article 8 may be interfered with provided the interference is in accordance with a procedure prescribed by law, pursues a legitimate aim and is necessary in a democratic society. This last condition involves the issue of proportionality. Any restriction imposed by the state on family life has to be at the lowest level to secure the aim of the restriction. A higher and disproportionate level of interference would be in violation of the Convention.

Support, advice and civil intervention
A major strand of government policy is to emphasise the role of support and advice, something not least to be observed in the creation of the Children and Family Court Support and Advice Service (CAFCASS)

(*Chapter 4*). Where a parent fails to meet the standards expected of him or her an element of compulsion enters the armoury of the state. This becomes apparent in the law concerning the emergency protection of children at risk where a child may be removed to local authority accommodation under a care order. The power to so remove a child from his or her family arises where the child is at risk of suffering significant harm and the cause of that harm is attributable to lack of care which it would be reasonable to expect a parent to provide. In other words the state retains a power to intervene where a parent fails to provide an objectively judged standard of care.

Crime, anti-social behaviour and parenting
Where there is a link between the commission of crime or anti-social behaviour and the ability of parents to parent the state can attempt to compel adherence to those same standards by the use of parenting orders. Such orders lead a parent to the advice and support required to meet society's expectation, but stigmatise and coerce the parent into action by the threat of criminal sanctions.[6]

Problems of a twin track approach
The real problem with this twin track approach to the enforcement of parental norms is that it brings parents, almost inevitably, into conflict with the providers of those essential services. Voluntary assistance is effective so long as it is taken up. Where it is not and a child is placed at risk the state is under a duty to intervene - ultimately through the legal system bringing the provider of assistance into direct conflict with the parent in need of assistance. Where the child acts criminally or quasi-criminally the assistance in meeting parental needs is made available through a co-ercive order with the attendant threat of sanctions and stigmatism. Are these the most effective methods of improving parenting skills? A dilemma is faced by both the state and the legal system in balancing the need to protect the child against the interests of parents and their right to freedom of action.

Parents and punishment
An aspect of being a parent is the duty to provide corrective guidance to a child who pursues a course of conduct which is either wrong or dangerous. Correction can take various forms and it is up to the parent to decide the level at which such correction is to be set. Where as a result of correction a child suffers harm or injury the local authority may be required to intervene using one or other of the powers available to it under the Children Act 1989 and already mentioned above to protect children at risk.

---

[6] For a detailed treatment of attempts by local authorities to control perceived anti-social activities through other management strategies and the potentially marginalising effect that this can have (including, of course, on the children of the families concerned), see *Crime and Banishment: Nuisance and Exclusion in Social Housing*, Burney E, Winchester: Waterside Press, 1999.

The law recognises that there may be occasions where the use of moderate physical discipline might be appropriate. A parent using moderate force to punish a child has available to him or her in any subsequent prosecution for assault the defence of 'reasonable chastisement'. Whether physical punishment amounts to reasonable chastisement is a matter of degree and depends on the facts of each case.

The use of physical correction is a subject of controversy. It is the only use of positive physical force sanctioned by the law which otherwise permits the use of reasonable force only in self-defence or in order to save life. Strong arguments exist among commentators as to whether the use of force in any form against a child can ever be justified. Equally there is a public perception that the use of physical correction is sometimes appropriate so long as no mark is left or other lasting injury done.

In January 2000 the government issued a consultation document on the use of physical punishment, *Protecting Children, Supporting Parents*, advocating a change to the law. The need for such a change arose as a result of a decision of the Court of Human Rights, *A v. UK* (1998) 2 FLR 959. The applicant had been beaten with a cane by his stepfather. He received injuries sufficient for the stepfather to be charged with assault occasioning actual bodily harm. At his trial, the stepfather successfully relied on the defence of reasonable chastisement. The Court of Human Rights found firstly that the beating the applicant had received reached the level of severity prohibited by Article 3 of the European Convention On Human Rights and amounted to inhuman or degrading treatment, and secondly that the law in the UK had failed to protect the applicant in allowing for a defence of reasonable chastisement as it was presently phrased.

The question of whether a defence of reasonable chastisement remains appropriate was considered by the Divisional Court in *R v. H* (2001) All ER (D) 193 where it was held that a jury determining the reasonableness or otherwise of the chastisement should consider: (i) the reasonableness or otherwise of the chastisement; (ii) the nature and context of the defendant's behaviour; (iii) its duration; (iv) its physical and mental consequences in relation to the child; (v) the age and personal characteristics of the child; and (vi) the reasons given by the defendant for administering punishment.

Supporting Parents, Protecting Children outlines options for change and it seems likely that a review of the law will be conducted soon. In the introduction to the paper the government identifies the choices which have to be made between freedom and protection. The dilemma for the state in the proper exercise of its powers is that in trying to safeguard children it also faces the charge of 'creeping nannyism':

> Today's children will shape tomorrow's future society. As parents, family members, friends, neighbours and citizens, we all have an interest in making sure that children thrive, and are helped to grow up into healthy and socially responsible adults. We need to achieve a balance between the rights of parents to exercise their parental responsibilities and bring up their children as they think best, without undue interference from government,

the responsibility of parents to bring their children up safely, and the right of children to be protected from harm.

Substitute parents

A person having care of a child but without parental responsibility may exercise some of the powers usually associated with parenthood. Section 3(5) Children Act 1989 provides:

> 3(5) A person who
> (a) does not have parental responsibility for a particular child; but
> (b) has care of the child
> may (subject to the provisions of this Act) do what is reasonable in all the circumstances of the case for the purpose of safeguarding or promoting the child's welfare.

This is a statutory formulation of the commonly recognised notion of *loco parentis*. However the range of powers available to such a carer is limited to the minimum necessary to safeguard the child's welfare. The Children Act 1989 and subsequent legislation provide a detailed system of regulating formal childminding and the powers available to schools and the local authority in terms of the exercise of the powers of parental responsibility. For example, whilst a parent has the right to use physical correction on his or her child no similar right exists in schools, nursery education, children's homes or foster care where such conduct is expressly prohibited by law.

Naming children

One of the key links between a child and his or her heritage lies in his or her own surname. In cases where the mother and father of a child are not married there is no set presumption that the child will travel through life with either his mother's or father's name. The matter can be of considerable importance as the child may have a different surname to the parent who has the care of that child (or have a different surname to other children in his or her family, or suffer a change of surname). Confusion and disagreement may also arise in choosing a first name for a child. However this issue appears to have produced very little, if any, litigation under the Children Act 1989.

Registration

When a child is born there is a duty on the parents to register the child and his or her name in accordance with the Births and Deaths Registration Act 1953. The registration of a name is clearly an important step in establishing the legal identity of the child. It is not however conclusive on the point and it is open for parents who disagree as to whose name the child should use to litigate. In *Dawson v. Wearmouth* (1999) 1 FCR 623 the House of Lords considered the position where a father wished his child to have his own surname and not the mother's name as had been originally registered. In the course of the judgment Lord Jauncey of Tullichettle said:

A surname which is given to a child at birth is not simply a name plucked out of the air. Where the parents are married the child will normally be given the surname or patronymic of the father thereby demonstrating its relationship to him. The surname is thus a biological label which tells the world at large that the blood of the name flows in its veins. To suggest that a surname is unimportant because it may be changed at any time by deed poll when the child has obtained more mature years ignores the importance of initially applying an appropriate label to that child.

Nevertheless the House of Lords concluded the matter by reference to the use of section 1 Children Act 1989. Effectively the welfare of the child is the paramount consideration for a court dealing with litigation relating to the change of a child's surname. The welfare checklist (discussed in *Chapter 7*) applies to such litigation and the presumption in favour of making no order may be overturned only where there is some evidence that making an order changing the child's name would lead to an improvement in his or her welfare.

Parental freedom to name children is accordingly limited in cases where an agreement cannot be reached. The older the children the more important it is for their feelings and wishes to be ascertained. A period of usage may also make it more difficult to persuade a court that a change can be of positive benefit to the child's welfare.

CHAPTER 3

Child Rights in International Law

As a general rule international treaties are entered into by the Executive and have no direct effect on national law until they are ratified by the Legislature. As a source of enforceable rights international treaties also require some form of incorporation into the national legal system before they can be relied upon.

THE EFFECT OF INTERNATIONAL TREATIES IN NATIONAL LAW

In *Maclaine Watson v. Department of Trade* [1989] 3 All ER 523 Lord Templeman set out the position as follows:

> A treaty is a contract between the governments of two or more sovereign states. International law regulates the relations between sovereign states and determines the validity, interpretation and the enforcement of treaties. A treaty to which Her Majesty's government is a party does not alter the laws of the United Kingdom. A treaty may be incorporated into and alter the laws of the United Kingdom by means of legislation. Except to the extent that a treaty becomes incorporated into the laws of the United Kingdom by statute, the courts of the United Kingdom have no power to enforce treaty rights and obligations at the behest of a sovereign government or at the behest of a private individual.

There is however a presumption that the Legislature intends to legislate in accordance with the state's international obligations. Accordingly in *Garland v. British Rail Engineering Ltd* [1989] 2 All ER 402 Lord Diplock said:

> ... it is a principle of construction of United Kingdom statutes ... that the words of a statute passed after [a] treaty has been signed and dealing with the subject matter of the international obligation of the United Kingdom are to be construed, if they are reasonably capable of bearing such a meaning, as intended to carry out the obligation, and not be inconsistent with it.

This principle of interpretation was clarified by the House of Lords in *Brind v. Secretary of State* [1991] 1 All ER 720. Whilst it was correct to say that the courts would presume that Parliament intended to legislate consistently with its international obligations that does not - in the absence of incorporation - empower the courts to review acts or omissions on the basis that they had to be done in conformity with those same international obligations. Only in cases where a statute is properly deemed to be ambiguous might the courts be able to resort to the international treaty to resolve the ambiguity.

The UK is party to a number of international treaties which provide for child-specific and child-related rights and freedoms. Of the following international codes only three have direct effect in national law namely the European Convention On Human Rights, (incorporated into national law by the Human Rights Act 1998), the Hague Convention On the Civil Aspects of International Child Abduction and the European Convention On Recognition and Enforcement of Decisions Concerning Custody of Children and On the Restoration of Custody of Children (these last two measures being incorporated into national law by Parts I and II respectively of the Child Abduction and Custody Act 1985).

The remaining conventions are not legally capable of being the source of enforceable rights and obligations. However the presumption outlined above applies to them and in many cases they have acted as the inspiration behind measures taken in the sphere of child rights, for example changes to the administration of the youth court introduced over recent years reflect the contents of the Beijing Rules.

The following international treaties are of particular importance in the sphere of child rights and are further discussed in this chapter:

- The European Convention On Human Rights
- International Covenant on Civil and Political Rights 1976
- UN Convention On the Rights of the Child 1989
- UN Guidelines for the Prevention of Juvenile Delinquency ('The Riyadh Guidelines') 1990
- UN Standard Minimum Rules for the Administration of Juvenile Justice ('The Beijing Rules') 1985
- UN Declaration of the Rights of the Child 1959
- UN Rules for the Protection of Juveniles Deprived of their Liberty 1990
- Hague Convention On the Civil Aspects of International Child Abduction; and
- European Convention On Recognition and Enforcement of Decisions Concerning Custody of Children and On the Restoration of Custody of Children.

The European Convention On Human Rights
The Convention was drafted in the immediate aftermath of World War II as the first substantive accomplishment of the Council of Europe. It contains a series of basic rights set out in a number of Articles. The Convention is overseen by the Court of Human Rights which sits in Strasbourg. Complaints may be made against a state by another state or by an individual to which the states have granted a right of individual petition. The Court determines both the admissibility of the complaint in a Lower Chamber and the substantive merits of the application in a Grand Chamber. The enforcement of the Court's decision is through the Registrar of the Court and ultimately through the Council of Ministers.

The Court exercises no investigative function and is limited to awarding just satisfaction to an aggrieved party. The most important role of the Court is in the development of human rights law and practice within the member states of the Council of Europe. Although there is no formal connection between the Convention and its institutions with the European Union, membership of the former is a requirement of membership of the latter and the Court of Justice which oversees the European Union has expressed itself—and therefore the Union legal system—to be bound by the fundamental principles of law recognised by the Court of Human Rights (*Cases 60 & 61/84, Cinetheque S. A. and others v. Federation Nationale des Cinemas Francaise* (1985) ECR 2605: Opinion 2/94 Accession by the Community to the European Convention of Human Rights and Fundamental Freedoms (1996) ECR 1-1759 and Article 6(2) of the Consolidated Treaty On European Union).

The Convention itself contains a range of rights from the right to life to the right to elections. There are no specific child or child-related rights. However the rights contained in the Convention have an impact on the position of children within the legal system. It is also the case that the Court of Human Rights in performing its function of interpreting the Convention has developed a jurisprudence on the status of the child and how that inter-relates with the Convention rights.

Prior to 1966 individuals in the UK had no right of individual petition to the Court of Human Rights and the Convention played a relatively marginal role in the nation's legal affairs. After the establishing of such a right many unsuccessful attempts were made to persuade the judiciary that the Convention was a source of enforceable rights and obligations. The UK's judiciary were seldom persuaded by these attempts at back-door incorporation and the defining point - effectively reached in *Brind v. Secretary of State* (above) - showed that the effect of the Convention and its relevance to UK national law and legal processes was limited.

The Human Rights Act 1998

The Human Rights Act 1998 incorporated the Convention into national law from 2 October 2000.[1] The 1998 Act does not fully incorporate the Convention and to a certain extent preserves the power of Parliament to expressly legislate in a manner inconsistent with Convention rights. However, the Act has been described by many commentators as the most significant piece of constitutional legislation enacted in a century in terms of its impact on the national legal system of the UK.

As far as child rights are concerned the Convention does not provide independent rights or freedoms. However all Convention rights apply equally to children and have been so applied by the Court of Human Rights. Where the rights of adults conflict with the rights of children, the child's interests have always taken precedence. Not only is the

---

[1] For an uncomplicated overview of the Human Rights Act 1998 and the Convention see *Human Rights and the Courts*, Ashcroft P *et al*, Winchester: Waterside Press, 1999.

Convention therefore a source of rights which may be asserted by a child against the state and used as a shield against the state, but it has also been the gateway through which other international codes protecting children can be accessed. The Court of Human Rights has expressly referred to a number of other international codes in dealing with applications involving children and through the operation of the Human Rights Act it may be possible to rely more effectively on other treaties as sources, if not of enforceable rights then for clarification and inspiration.

A central purpose of the Human Rights Act is to 'bring home' Convention rights.[2] In summary the Act:

- requires all courts and tribunals to give effect to Convention rights by interpreting all legislation and laws compatibly with them and where they cannot do so to disapply offending provisions unless they are found in primary legislation
- provides for the better protection of rights by placing a duty on public authorities to act compatibly with the Convention and for action to lie in the civil courts where a public authority fails to so act
- provides a Convention right is adversely affected by a provision of primary legislation which the court is unable to interpret compatibly the duty remains to give effect to the will of Parliament, but on appeal the higher courts are given the power to make a declaration of incompatibility which leads to a fast track procedure in Parliament under which a remedial order can me made to cure the apparent incompatibility.

How the 1998 Act achieves its purposes requires a little more detail.

Interpretation of legislation
Section 3(1) Human Rights Act 1998 imposes a duty on all courts and tribunals to give effect to legislation in a way which is compatible with the rights and freedoms in the Convention. This means that every court must strive to find an interpretation of legislation which is consistent with both the rights of the Convention and the way in which they have been applied and explained by the Court of Human Rights.

The duty applies to all forms of legislation whether set out in primary Acts of Parliament or in secondary legislative rules. It goes far beyond the rule which enables courts to take the Convention into account in resolving any ambiguity in a legislative provision. The courts are required to interpret legislation so as to uphold Convention rights unless legislation itself is so clearly incompatible with the convention that it is impossible to do so.

In those rare circumstances where legislation cannot be interpreted so as to uphold Convention rights, the court must follow Parliament's lead. However on appeal it is possible for a higher court to make a

---

[2] This treatment of the effect of the Human Rights Act 1998 appeared also in *Magistrate's Court's Practice*, Vol. 4.4, London: Central Law Training.

declaration of incompatibility. This acts as a judicial signal that the legislative provision in question cannot be interpreted to give effect to Convention rights and triggers the fast track procedure referred to above. At the time of writing only two such declarations have been made, in relation to certain procedures under the Mental Health Act and planning appeals. The latter was subsequently overturned by the House of Lords.

Case law

Although the Human Rights Act is silent upon the issue it appears to be accepted by judges and commentators alike that courts are under a duty to reflect Convention rights in their decisions notwithstanding earlier precedents (i.e. rulings of the higher courts). Again it is likely to be a rare occurrence for a lower court to need to disapply a decision of a higher court in order to give effect to Convention rights.

Public authorities

The Human Rights Act does not rely on the existence of judicial proceedings in order to bring home Convention rights. The Act imposes a duty on all public authorities to act compatibly with Convention rights. Where a public authority does not so act it may be sued under section 7. In deciding how to act a public authority must strive to do so consistently with Convention rights and their interpretation by the Court of Human Rights. However if legislation requires the authority to act in a particular way which is incompatible with the Convention the Act does not render the authority liable. To this extent the sovereignty of Parliament is preserved in the same way as it is for courts dealing with primary incompatible legislation as described above.

A public authority includes any body discharging a function which is recognisably public. In the context of this work that would include the local authority, CAFCASS, the local education authority, the youth offending team and the courts. The susceptibility of these organizations acting on behalf of the state to challenges based on the Convention is likely to entrench child rights further in the legal culture.

Convention rights

The Convention guarantees a number of basic rights and freedoms. These are inalienable and inherent and apply therefore to all individuals—including children—without qualification by age. Article 14 provides specifically that there is a right to enjoy other Convention rights without discrimination and whilst age is not listed as a ground of unlawful discrimination it is reasonably certain to say that a child enjoys the same status in the eyes of the Court of Human Rights as an adult in his or her capacity to benefit from the rights.

Schedule 1 of the Act reproduces those articles of the Convention incorporated into national law and which are shown in brief[3] in *Table 3.1*.

---

[3] The Articles are set out in full in *Human Rights and the Courts*: see footnote 1.

Table 3.1 **European Convention Rights**

Article	Right	Category of right
Article 2	The right to life	Strictly a limited right but effectively absolute
Article 3	The right to be free from torture, or inhuman or degrading treatment	Absolute right
Article 4	The right to be free from slavery or forced labour	Limited right in part absolute in others
Article 5	The right to liberty	Limited right
Article 6	The right to a fair trial	Limited right
Article 7	The right to be free from the retrospective effect of criminal legislation	Absolute right
Article 8	The right to respect for private and family life, home and correspondence	Qualified right
Article 9	Freedom of thought, conscience and religion	Qualified right
Article 10	Freedom of expression	Qualified right
Article 11	Freedom of association and assembly	Qualified right
Article 12	The right to marry and found a family	Qualified right
Article 14	The right to enjoy rights without discrimination	A difference in treatment will not amount to discrimination if it is shown to have a legitimate justification
Article 1 First Protocol	The right to peaceful enjoyment of property and possessions	Qualified right
Article 2 First Protocol	The right to education	Limited right
Article 3 First Protocol	The right to free elections	Limited right

As can be seen from *Table 3.1*, the rights are divided into three categories:

- **absolute rights** which may never lawfully be interfered with by a state;
- **limited rights** where the state may interfere with the right to the extent provided for by the Convention; and
- **qualified rights** where the state may interfere only in so far as the interference is prescribed by law, pursues a legitimate aim and is

necessary in a democratic society. This last element requires the state to show that the measure concerned is proportionate to the aim involved.

In the previous chapter the impact of Article 3 on the right of parents to use physical correction on a child and of Article 8 in so far as the meaning of family life is concerned were considered. In later chapters the Court of Human Rights' interpretation of these and other Articles is considered in relation to the detention of children charged with a criminal offence, the use of secure accommodation, the trial process and the exercise of quasi-parental powers by a local authority under the Children Act 1989.

Welfare and the European Convention
The Convention makes no special provision for children but where issues relating to the upbringing of a child fall to be determined the Court of Human Rights has consistently recognised the need to treat children differently to adults. Case law is littered with references to the importance of the child's best interests.[4] In *Re N* (leave to withdraw care proceedings) (2000) 1 FCR258, Bracewell J was satisfied that the approach of the national courts under the Children Act 1989 was consistent with the Convention's treatment of a child's welfare. Referring to both Convention and national case law she said:

> I have been referred to *Hendriks v. The Netherlands* 1982 5 EHRR 223, where it was held that where there was a serious conflict between the interests of a child and one of its parents which could only be resolved to the disadvantage of one of them the interests of the child had to prevail under Article 8(2).

In *Dawson v. Wearmouth* (1999) 1 FCR 625 Lord Hobhouse stated:

> There is nothing in the European Human Rights Convention which requires the courts of this country to act otherwise than in accordance with the interests of the child.

In reaching a balance between the conflicting interests of children and parents the sum of Convention case law strongly promotes the interests of the child and his or her welfare as the paramount consideration. The welfare principle places the child's welfare as the paramount interest in reaching decisions about its upbringing. The European Court of Human Rights has accorded the child's interests a status best described as 'first among equals' in terms of parental rights. Some commentators have argued that there is a conflict between the national framing of paramountcy and the approach under the Convention. This may, however, be a question of semantics rather than substance.

The duty of courts and tribunals to give effect to Convention rights under the Human Rights Act 1998 requires the decisions of the Court (and formerly the Commission) of Human Rights to be taken into

---

[4] See *Johansen v. Norway* (1996) 23 EHRR 183; Whitear v. UK (1997) EHRLR 291.

account. In a number of cases dealing with rights under the Convention as they relate to children the European institutions have had recourse to other international human rights codes such as the UN Convention On the Rights of the Child, the International Convention On Civil and Political Rights and the Beijing Rules.

Whilst the UK is a party to these treaties their effect is limited and cannot under national law amount to sources of directly enforceable rights and obligations. Reference to them in case law may allow a court to use the rights and freedoms in them as an inspiration in the development of the protection of rights under the Human Rights Act 1998. However national courts will surely be wary of 'backdoor' incorporation of these other international codes. Section 11 Human Rights Act 1998 provides:

> 11. A person's reliance on a Convention right does not restrict—
>   (a) any other right or freedom conferred on him by or under any law having effect in any part of the United Kingdom; or
>   (b) his right to make any claim or bring any proceedings which he could make or bring apart from sections 7 to 9.

This provision complements Article 53 of the European Convention on Human Rights which provides that:

> Nothing in this Convention shall be construed as limiting or derogating from any of the human rights and fundamental freedoms which may be ensured under the laws of any High Contracting Party or under any other agreement to which it is a Party

Accordingly people may rely on other international human rights' codes to the extent that this is permitted under common law in addition to their use by virtue of the Court of Human Rights' having recourse to them.

Other international human rights codes
Table 3.2 lists the international codes to which the Court of Human Rights has had recourse in the course of its judgements.

The remainder of this chapter is concerned with describing the range of child specific rights provided for in a number of these international codes. The rights and obligations in them are not of direct effect – as opposed to potential influence - within the UK legal system as they have not been incorporated into national law.

Table 3.2 **International treaties referred to by the Court of Human Rights**

Treaty	Case reference
International Covenant On Civil and Political Rights	*Pretto v. Italy* (1983) 6 EHRR 183
UN Standard Minimum Rules for the Treatment of Prisoners	*Can v. Austria* (1986) 8 EHRR 121
International Covenant On the Elimination of All Forms of Racial Discrimination	*Koisek v. Germany* (1986) 9 EHRR 328
UN Convention Relating to the Status of Refugees	*Soering v. UK* (1989) 11 EHRR 439
UN Convention Against Torture and Other Cruel, Inhuman or Degrading Treatment or Punishment	*Soering v. UK* (1989) 11 EHRR 439
UN Convention On the Rights of the Child	*Costello-Roberts v. UK* (1995) 19 EHRR 112
International Labour Organization Convention Concerning Forced or Compulsory Labour	*Van der Mussele v. Belgium* (1984) 6 EHRR 163
American Convention On Human Rights	*X v. UK* (1980) 19 DR 244

The UN Declaration On the Rights of the Child 1959

This declaration is a statement of principles, given more effect by the Convention On the Rights of the Child dealt with in *Table 3.3*. The declaration builds on the sound foundations of welfare and family to proclaim the basic entitlements of the child.

Table 3.3 **The UN Convention On the Rights of the Child**

Principle	Right
Principle 1	The right to enjoy rights without discrimination
Principle 2	The right to protection by law The right to development Emphasises the paramountcy of the child's best interests
Principle 3	The right to a name and a nationality
Principle 4	The right to social services such as housing, health and recreation
Principle 5	The right of a disabled child to special treatment
Principle 6	The right to family support
Principle 7	The right to education
Principle 8	The right to paramountcy in receiving protection and relief
Principle 9	The right to protection from neglect, cruelty and exploitation
Principle 10	The right to protection from discrimination

UN Standard Minimum Rules for the Administration of Juvenile Justice ('The Beijing Rules') 1985

The Beijing Rules, listed in *Table 3.4*, provide a detailed scheme for the administration of juvenile justice. A number of the rights and obligations contained in the rules have found their way into government initiatives in the youth court and the youth justice system. Not all of the aspirations of the treaty have perhaps been reached but there are many familiar measures found within the treaty's words. Where the UK system fails to meet the standards set out in the Rules there may be scope for the courts to develop a common law approach which enhances the fulfilment of the state's international obligations.

Table 3.4 **The Beijing Rules**

Rule	Rights and obligations
Rule 1	Duty on the state to take measures to further the well-being of the juvenile and his or her family
Rule 2	Right to enjoyment of the rules without discrimination Duty of the state to introduce and maintain a system of juvenile justice
Rule 4	The establishing of an age of criminal responsibility
Rule 5	Aim of juvenile justice to emphasise the well-being of the juvenile and the principle of proportionality
Rule 6	Duty on the state to provide accountable discretion at all levels of the juvenile justice system
Rule 7	The right to a fair trial
Rule 8	The right to privacy in relation to contact with the juvenile justice system
Rule 9	Provision for the application of other human rights codes
Rule 10	The right on arrest to have parents informed of detention. Right to determination of release by a judge or competent authority without delay
Rule 11	The right to consideration of diversion from formal criminal proceedings
Rule 12	Duty on the state to establish juvenile specialisation in the police
Rule 13	Prohibition of the use of detention pending trial save as a last resort Duty on the state to provide facilities to meet the needs of detained juveniles
Rule 14	The right to an adjudication by a competent authority in accordance with principles of a fair trial and which ensures the effective participation of the juvenile
Rule 15	The right to representation and the right of parents to participate in the proceedings

Rule 16	Duty on the competent authority to obtain social enquiry reports prior to disposal
Rule 17	The principles governing disposition: • proportionality • custody to be imposed only after careful consideration and to be limited in its use to the minimum possible • custody to be limited to serious violence or where there is persistent serious offending • the well-being of the child to be the guiding factor in consideration of disposal
Rule 18	Duty of the state to provide a large variety of disposition measures including financial penalties, community penalties and alternatives to the use of custody
Rule 20	Duty on the state to avoid delay in the juvenile justice system
Rule 21	Duty on the state to ensure confidentiality
Rule 22	Duty of the state to provide training and to establish minimum levels of competence for all people dealing with juveniles
Rule 23	Duty of the state to implement effectively disposals within the juvenile justice system
Rule 24	Duty on the state to provide assistance and support to juveniles in the justice system
Rule 26	Objectives of institutional treatment • care • protection • education The right to fair treatment in institutionalised care or punishment
Rule 28	Promotes the use of conditional release
Rule 29	Duty of the state to provide semi-institutional arrangements to facilitate reintegration into society

UN Convention On the Rights of the Child

Thus far the Convention provides the strongest declaration of the rights of the child in international law. It provides for member states to issue periodic reports of the measures taken to honour its commitments under the Convention. The enthusiasm of the UK to embrace the Convention has been questioned.[5] However the National Standards issued by the Youth Justice Board in April 2000 expressly refer to the Convention as one of its sources.

As with the Beijing Rules certain aspects of the Convention are reflected in the UK legal system. The presumption that Parliament does not intend to legislate contrary to its international obligations may provide the opportunity to develop child rights under the common law. Recourse to the Convention by the Court of Human Rights may also assist in the establishment and development of such rights by virtue of the Human Rights Act 1998 and especially the notion that the European Convention provides a floor but not a ceiling for the protection of rights.

It is almost incontrovertible that there is an emerging raft of child-specific rights in international law.[6] The rights may be derived from express rights belonging to the child or from the implications of obligations and duties imposed on the state to take action or to refrain from taking action. As far as the national position is concerned much depends on the attitude and enthusiasm of the courts and public authorities to have regard for the UN Convention in their practices and procedures relating to the upbringing of children. If there is a wind of change blowing through the legal system as a result of the incorporation of the European Convention it may not be a misplaced hope that the tide will turn in favour of the development of child-specific rights as envisaged by the UN Convention.

The rights and obligations described in *Table 3.5* (although not set out in full) capture the range of duties encompassed by the Convention. Further details of these rights and obligations can be obtained from an examination of the text of the treaty.

UN Guidelines for the Prevention of Juvenile Delinquency 1990 ('The Riyadh Guidelines')

The Riyadh Guidelines set out a series of basic principles to be followed by states in the pursuit of measures to prevent delinquency among juveniles. The purpose of the guidelines is to ensure that states strike a balance between measures which prevent delinquency and measures which protect children. The main objective is the creation of a range of child orientated preventative programmes encompassing socialisation processes, the family, education, the community, mass media, legislation and the administration of juvenile justice.

---

[5] See for example (2000), 30 Fam Law 6.

[6] See for example Powell; 'The Emergence of Child Rights under the Human Rights Act', *The Justices' Clerk* (Journal of the Justices' Clerks' Society), May 2000.

Table 3.5 **Rights and obligations in the UN Convention On the Rights of the Child**

Article	Rights and obligations
Article 1	Definition of a child
Article 2	The right to enjoy rights without discrimination
Article 3	The right of the child's best interests to be accorded paramountcy
Article 4	Duty of the state to give effect to the Convention
Article 5	Duty of the state to respect the rights and duties of parents
Article 6	The right to life and development
Article 7	The right to a name and nationality and to be registered on birth
Article 8	The right to preserve self-identity without interference
Article 9	The right to remain with parents
Article 10	The right to enter or leave the state for the purpose of family reunification
Article 11	Duty of the state to take measures against illicit removal of children
Article 12	The right to express views in accordance with age and maturity
Article 13	Freedom of expression
Article 14	Freedom of thought, conscience and religion
Article 15	Freedom of association and peaceful assembly
Article 16	The right to privacy and family
Article 17	The right of access to information. Duty on the state to encourage the production and dissemination of child-related information
Article 18	Duty of the state to promote the responsibility of parents and to render assistance to them

Article 19	Duty of the state to take measures to protect children from all forms of abuse
Article 20	Duty of the state to provide special assistance to children removed from their family
Article 21	Duty of the state to provide a system of adoption which is procedurally fair and promotes the best interests of the child
Article 22	Duty of the state to provide appropriate protection to children seeking refugee status
Article 23	Duty of the state to promote and facilitate the development of disabled children
Article 24	The right to health and healthcare services
Article 25	Duty of the state to conduct review of children removed from their families
Article 26	The right to the benefit of social security
Article 27	The right to a standard of living adequate for the child's development
Article 28	The right to education and equal opportunity in education
Article 29	The purpose of education
Article 30	The right to manifest minority religion and language
Article 31	The right to rest and leisure and to participate in cultural and artistic life
Article 32	The right to be free from economic exploitation
Article 33	Duty of the state to take measures to protect children from drug trafficking
Article 34	Duty of the state to take measures to protect children from sexual exploitation and abuse
Article 35	Duty of the state to take measures to prevent trafficking in children and abduction
Article 36	Duty of the state to protect children from all other forms of exploitation

Article 37	Prohibition on the use of torture, or inhuman and degrading treatment
Article 38	Restrictions on the use of children in the military
Article 39	Duty of the state to take measures to promote the recovery of children from exploitation and abuse
Article 40	The right to a fair trial and fair process in the juvenile justice system

The guidelines concentrate on principles rather than substantive rights. By providing a philosophical framework the guidelines allow the detail to be completed by the state. However as a fundamental principle Paragraph 5 provides:

The need for and importance of progressive delinquency prevention policies and the systematic study and the elaboration of measures should be recognised. These should avoid criminalising and penalising a child for behaviour that does not cause serious damage to the development of the child or harm to others. Such policies and measures should involve:

(a) the provision of opportunities, in particular educational opportunities, to meet the varying needs of young persons and to serve as a supportive framework for safeguarding the personal development of all young persons, particularly those who are demonstrably endangered or at social risk and are in need of special care and protection;

(b) specialised philosophies and approaches for delinquency prevention, on the basis of laws, processes, institutions, facilities and a service delivery network aimed at reducing the motivation, need and opportunity for, or conditions giving rise to, the commission of infractions;

(c) official intervention to be pursued primarily in the overall interest of the young person and guided by fairness and equity;

(d) safeguarding the well-being, development, rights and interests of all young persons;

(e) consideration that youthful behaviour or conduct that does not conform to overall social norms and values is often part of the maturation and growth process and tends to disappear spontaneously in most individuals with the transition to adulthood;

(f) awareness that, in the predominant opinion of experts, labelling a young person as 'deviant', 'delinquent' or 'pre-delinquent' often contributes to the development of a consistent pattern of undesirable behaviour by young persons.

Measures contained within the Crime and Disorder Act 1998 including child safety orders and anti-social behaviour orders (*Chapter 7*) reflect to a certain degree the aspirations in the guidelines but, in their operation appear to result in the effective criminalisation of children and their families. The obligations under the guidelines require a state to provide a significant level of resource investment in measures falling short of statutory involvement through either the care system or the criminal justice system and a coherent and co-ordinated approach to the problem of delinquency prevention. The continuing rejection by government of a Commissioner for Children with powers equivalent to the various anti-discrimination bodies is a sign of the somewhat inadequate response to the issue of child rights and duties in the UK.

UN rules for the Protection of Juveniles Deprived of their Liberty 1990

These rules were adopted by the United Nations at the same time as the Riyadh Guidelines, above. They build on the Beijing Rules and are intended to establish minimum standards accepted by the United Nations for the protection of juveniles deprived of their liberty in all forms, consistent with human rights and fundamental freedoms, and with a view to counterbalancing the detrimental effects of all types of detention and to fostering integration in society.[7]

The rules apply to all types and forms of detention and include detailed provisions for juveniles under arrest or awaiting trial and the management of juvenile facilities. The basic principles of fairness, development, education, rehabilitation and equal opportunity without discrimination run through the rules. Certain aspects of the rules are contained within the detention and training order (*Chapter 6*). In particular the requirement that an ASSET profile,[8] completed on all potential and actual detainees is consistent with the minimum requirements of rule 27.[9] The rules are summarised in *Table 3.6*.

Table 3.6 **UN Rules for the Protection of Juveniles
Deprived of their Liberty 1990**

Fundamental perspectives	
Rule 1	Imprisonment to be used as a last resort. State duty to protect rights and promote well-being of children
Rule 2	Prohibition on the use of detention otherwise in accordance with the rules and the Beijing Rules
Rule 3	Purpose of the rules
Rule 4	Right to have the rules applied without discrimination

[7] Rule 13.
[8] The ASSETT profile is explained in *Chapter 6*.
[9] The powers of the youth court are considered in more detail in *Chapter 6*.

Rule 5	Aim of the rules
Rule 6	Right of child to access to the rules and an interpreter if so required
Rule 7	Duty of states where appropriate to incorporate rules into national legislation
Rule 8	Duty of state to promote awareness of the rules
Rule 9	Applies other human rights codes to detention
Rule 10	Apportions primacy to Parts of the rules over inconsistent application of other Parts
Rule 11	Defines juveniles and the deprivation of liberty for the purposes of the rules
Rule 12	Requires deprivation of liberty to be in accordance with human rights of juveniles
Rule 13	Prohibition on restricting national and international rights to juveniles in detention
Rule 14	Establishes a requirement that juvenile rights are overseen by an independent competent authority
Rule 15	Defines the scope of the rules
Rule 16	Allows the rules to be implemented in the context of a state's own traditions.

Juveniles under arrest or awaiting trial

Rule 17	Presumption of innocence for pre-trial detainees. Prohibition on the use of pre-trail detention in absence of exceptional circumstances. Requires segregation of untried and convicted juveniles
Rule 18	Provides minimum conditions of detention including the right to legal advice, opportunities for work and education and leisure facilities

The management of juvenile facilities

Rule 19	Confidentiality of administrative records and the right of access to them

Rule 20	Prohibition on receipt into detention without a lawful order of a court or other authority
Rule 21	Minimum standards of records to be kept
Rule 22	Duty to notify parents or guardians without delay
Rule 23	Duty to prepare social reports on the juvenile on admission
Rule 24	Duty to provide regulations of the detention facility to the juvenile with appropriate interpretation
Rule 25	Duty to raise awareness of juveniles of the aims and methods of the institution
Rule 26	Transportation of juveniles to be achieved with dignity and without hardship
Rule 27	Duty to prepare and act on social and psychological interview and reports in terms of placement and programme within facility
Rule 28	Duty to provide placement in accordance with individual characteristics of the child which ensures protection and promotes child's well-being
Rule 29	General prohibition of mixing adults and juveniles in the same facility
Rule 30	Provides for the establishing of local open detention facilities aimed at reintegration
Rule 31	The right to facilities which meet the juvenile's requirements of health and human dignity
Rule 32	Duty to design facilities in keeping with aim of rehabilitative treatment
Rule 33	Provides a standard for sleeping accommodation and the supervision thereof
Rule 34	Provides a standard for sanitary privacy
Rule 35	The right to a basic level of privacy in the possession of personal effects

Rule 36	The right to use own clothing where possible
Rule 37	The right to suitable food and drinking water
Rule 38	The right to education
Rule 39	The right to continue education and access to appropriate educational programmes
Rule 40	Provides that academic awards should not indicate that the juvenile was institutionalised
Rule 41	Duty to provide a library service
Rule 42	The right to receive vocational training
Rule 43	The right to choose work and training
Rule 44	Applies international codes on child labour
Rule 45	The right to perform remunerative work complimentary to vocational training whenever possible
Rule 46	The right to equitable remuneration for work performed. Part of any sum may be retained to provide additional funds on release or be used to compensate victims
Rule 47	Right to a period of free exercise, leisure and recreation
Rule 48	Right to satisfy religious needs and to attend worship
Rule 49	Right to receive preventive and remedial health care
Rule 50	Right to medical examination on admission to detention
Rule 51	Purpose of a medical examination
Rule 52	Reporting duty on a medical officer at a detention facility
Rule 53	Provides for the special and independent treatment of mental disorders
Rule 54	Duty to provide drug treatment and rehabilitation programmes

Rule 55	Provides for the administration of medical drugs subject to prescribed conditions
Rule 56	Right of parents or guardians to be notified of any illness or medical treatment
Rule 57	Provides for procedure on death of juvenile in detention
Rule 58	Provides for procedure on death of immediate family member of a juvenile and includes the right to attend funeral
Rule 59	Right to communication with the outside world
Rule 60	Right to receive regular and frequent visits
Rule 61	Right to communication including letters and telephone calls
Rule 62	Right to be informed of the news through media and of access to non-news related media
Rule 63	Prohibition on the use of physical restraint
Rule 64	Provides limited exceptions to the prohibition on the use of physical restraint
Rule 65	Prohibits the use and carrying of weapons by facility personnel
Rule 66	Disciplinary measures to be used only in accordance with juvenile's human rights
Rule 67	Prohibition on cruel, inhuman or degrading discipline. Prohibition on the use of confinement, dietary control or restrictions on visits and the misuse of educational or work related opportunities
Rule 68	Provides for the legislative regulation of disciplinary proceedings
Rule 70	Disciplinary proceedings to be conducted in accordance with the law and to be properly recorded
Rule 71	Juveniles shall not be empowered to conduct disciplinary proceedings

Rule 72	Duty to undertake inspections of facilities by independent and qualified inspectors
Rule 73	Inspections should include medical and public health inspections
Rule 74	Duty of state to provide facility for the reporting of inspections and to allow for investigation and prosecution of violations of juvenile rights
Rule 75	Right of juveniles to make complaints to the director of the facility
Rule 76	Right of juveniles to make complaints to a judicial or competent independent authority without censorship
Rule 77	Obligation of the state to set up independent office to receive and investigate complaints
Rule 78	Right of juvenile to obtain assistance from family, legal representatives or other bodies to make complaints
Rule 79	Requirement of the state to devise procedures to assist juveniles to return to society
Rule 80	Requires the establishing of a level of services aimed at reintegration
Rule 81	Duty on state to ensure a minimum level of training and competence among personnel
Rule 82	Requires all personnel to be selected on basis of characteristics which accord with philosophy of the rules
Rule 83	Provides principles of employment conditions
Rule 84	Provides for minimum level of operational standards
Rule 85	Provides for minimum standards of training of personnel
Rule 86	Provides professional and personal description of facility director
Rule 87	Establishes the principles to which the facility and personnel should adhere

The Hague Convention On the Civil Aspects of International Child Abduction and the European Convention On Recognition and Enforcement of Decisions concerning Custody of Children and On the Restoration of Custody of Children

The unlawful removal of a child to or from the UK is the subject of the common law. Where the country involved from or to which the child has been abducted is a signatory to either the European Convention or the Hague Convention the law and procedure is governed by those Conventions as incorporated into national law by the Child Abduction and Custody Act 1985. The main purpose of both Conventions is to trace and secure the prompt return of an abducted child. The Hague Convention is primarily concerned with wrongful removals and wrongful retention of a child. The European Convention is primarily concerned with the recognition and enforcement of custody and access orders. The procedure and application of each Convention is broadly similar in purpose but there are a number of important differences (and similarities). These are summarised in *Table 3.7*. All statutory references are to the Child Abduction and Custody Act 1985.

Table 3.7 **Hague Convention and European Convention compared**

The Hague Convention	The European Convention
Creates a Central Authority: in England and Wales, the Lord Chancellor; in Scotland the Secretary of State	Creates a Central Authority: in England and Wales, the Lord Chancellor; in Scotland the Secretary of State
Aims to secure the prompt return of children wrongfully removed or retained in breach of rights of custody in relation to a contracting state	Aims at the recognition and enforcement of decisions relating to custody taken in a contracting state
Not necessary to have a pre-existing court order relating to custody rights	Necessary to have a pre-existing court order in favour of the applicants
Contracting state may require applicant to obtain a declaration from competent authority of the state where the child habitually resides that his or her removal or retention is wrongful	Provided an existing order is in force, no further declaration is required
No procedure for requiring the registration of existing court orders within national law	Procedure in place for the registration of decisions relating to custody to be registered in the national court

Operates from the date of agreement between UK and other state. Cannot operate retrospectively[10]	Operates retrospectively[11]
The Central Authority must order the child's return forthwith unless one of the exceptions in Articles 12 or 13 apply	The child's return is not automatic even where there is a foreign order in force. Grounds for refusal are set out in Articles 9 and 10
The Central Authority is under a duty to promote the peaceful enjoyment of access rights and to take steps in appropriate cases to organize and secure the effective exercise of access rights	Rights of access may also be enforced in the same way as decisions relating to custody.
Central Authority is under a duty to make appropriate arrangements for English solicitors to act on the applicant's behalf under the Children Act 1989 where he or she is seeking contact with a child rather than an order for return	Under the Convention, free legal aid is available to applicants seeking to enforce existing access orders

The Hague Convention and the European Convention remain open for additional states to adopt (and in some cases individual territories within states). A regular list of signatories appears on a quarterly basis in *International Family Law.*[12]

The detailed rules of procedure fall outside the scope of this work. Implicit within the Child Abduction and Custody Act 1985 and the international Conventions themselves is respect for the rights of children

---

[10] *Re H (Minors)(Abduction: Custody Rights)* (1991) 2 AC 476.

[11] *Re L (Child Abduction: European Convention)* (1992) 2 FLR 178.

[12] As of December 1999 the following states, in addition to the UK, had joined the Hague Convention: Argentina, Australia, Austria, The Bahamas, Belgium, Belize, Bosnia and Herzegovina, Burkina, Canada, Chile, China, Columbia, Croatia, Cyprus, Czech Republic, Denmark, Ecuador, Finland, France, Georgia, Germany, Greece, Honduras, Hungary, Iceland, Ireland, Israel, Italy, Luxembourg, Macedonia, Mauritius, Mexico, Monaco, Netherlands, New Zealand, Norway, Panama, Poland, Romania, Slovenia, South Africa, Spain, St Kitts and Nevis, Sweden, Switzerland, Turkmenistan, Yugoslavia, United States, Venezuela and Zimbabwe. The contracting states of the European Convention were: Austria, Belgium, Cyprus, Denmark, Finland, France, Germany, Greece, Ireland, Iceland, Italy, Liechtenstein, Luxembourg, Netherlands, Norway, Poland, Portugal, Spain, Sweden and Switzerland. Proceedings under both Conventions in the same matter are permitted.

and their parents. The views of children (see *Chapter 1*) of appropriate age and maturity are relevant considerations for a court dealing with applications under the Conventions. Practitioners should carefully consider the procedural rules and the large jurisprudence arising in the national legal system on the operation of the 1985 Act.

CHAPTER 4

Working for the Protection of Children

People whose professional practices include the protection of children and the promotion of their rights have an overriding duty to be competently and effectively trained in dealing with children *as children* and not as 'little adults'. Such a sphere of work is a specialist field. Practitioners from across the broad spectrum of agencies involved with children require a high level of knowledge, skill and aptitude. Of these three basic requirements aptitude is the hardest to acquire and is characterised by an awareness and understanding of the principles involved in dealing with children in general and with children at risk in particular. The principles involve the child's welfare, his or her capacity to develop, his or her rights and the role and responsibility of parents and the child's family together with the ability to engage with the child and apply the principles in the light of a child's age, understanding and level of maturity.

The obligation to provide an appropriate level of professionalism within the administrative and legal system rests with the state. In some areas international treaties demand of the state measures which ensure that professional standards are set, maintained and monitored. For example rule 22 of the UN Standard Minimum Rules for the Administration of Juvenile Justice provides:

> Professional education, in-service training, refresher training and other appropriate modes of instruction shall be utilised to establish and maintain the necessary professional competence of all persons dealing with juvenile cases

The extent and depth of the duty to provide education and training is explained in the official commentary to the rules:[1]

> The authorities competent for disposition may be persons with very different backgrounds. For all these authorities, a minimum training in law, sociology, psychology, criminology and behavioural sciences would be required. This is considered as important as the organizational specialisation and independence of the competent authority ... Professional qualifications are an essential element in ensuring the impartial and effective administration of juvenile justice. Accordingly, it is necessary to improve the recruitment, advancement and professional training of personnel and to provide them with the necessary means to enable them to properly fulfil their functions.

In the context of this book there are five areas where a child is likely to engage with professional practitioners, in:

---

[1] The full version is available on the United Nations website: www.unitednations.org\

- the criminal justice system;
- the exercise of public law duties by a local authority;
- the context of private law proceedings within family breakdown;
- the court environment; and
- placements outside the family.

One of the major issues to emerge over the recent past has been the risk of exposure of a child to people with a criminal background and the extent to which the State has a duty to take measures to ensure that information relating to such people is readily available to reduce the risk of harm to the child. This last aspect of working with children forms the final part of this chapter.

THE CRIMINAL JUSTICE SYSTEM

A child arrested and detained on suspicion of committing a criminal offence is likely to pass through the hands of a number of adults before a final decision is made whether to prosecute or not. Generally the detention of a child at a police station is unlikely to provide the level of facilities suitable to his or her age and understanding. Balanced against such issues are the interests of society in seeing that offences are properly investigated.

A detained child suspect, however, has a set of rights additional to those available to an adult suspect. Research has concluded that young suspects can provide information that is unreliable, misleading or self-incriminatory.[2] The additional rights aim to safeguard against these risks. They are also consistent with the international obligations set out in both the UN Convention On the Rights of the Child and the Beijing Rules.[3] A detained child is entitled to prompt access to legal and other appropriate assistance. Article 37 of the UN Convention provides at paragraph (d):

> Every child deprived of his or her liberty shall have the right to prompt access to legal and other appropriate assistance, as well as the right to challenge the legality of the deprivation of his or her liberty before a court or other competent, independent and impartial authority, and to a prompt decision on any such action.

Under the Codes of Practice issued under the Police and Criminal Evidence Act 1984 a child suspect has the right to the services of an appropriate adult. Such a person may or may not be the child's parent or guardian.

The appropriate adult
Code C for the *Detention, Treatment and Questioning of Persons by Police Officers* contains detailed provisions for the treatment of (amongst others juveniles):

---

[2] See 'Appropriate Practice?', Pierpoint, 1999, *ChildRight*, December 8.
[3] *Chapter 3.*

3.7 If the person is a juvenile the custody officer must, if it is practicable, ascertain the identity of a person responsible for his welfare. That person may be his parent or guardian (or, if he is in care, the care authority or voluntary organization) or any other person who has, for the time being, assumed responsibility for his welfare. That person must be informed as soon as practicable that the juvenile has been arrested, why he has been arrested and where he is being detained

3.9 If the person is a juvenile ... then the custody officer must, as soon as practicable, inform the appropriate adult (who in the case of a juvenile may or may not be a person responsible for his welfare, in accordance with paragraph 3.7 above) of the grounds for his detention and his whereabouts and ask the adult to come to the police station to see the person.

The appropriate adult is required to be in attendance at the police station with the juvenile at the time of any of the significant steps in the investigative process including when the juvenile is informed of his or her rights (Code C 3.11), searched (Code C Annex A 5 and 11(c)), charged (Code C 16.3) or takes part in an identification parade.

Section 38(1) and (4) Crime and Disorder Act 1998 further establishes the role of the appropriate adult and places a statutory duty on local authorities to provide a minimum level of service. Since the Crime and Disorder Act central government has issued guidance to local authorities on the role of appropriate adults - as set out primarily in section 38(4) of the Act – which is to 'safeguard the interests of children and young persons detained or questioned by police officers'. This simple statement accords with the role of the appropriate adult at interview described in Code C 11.16 as follows:

Where the appropriate adult is present at an interview, he or she shall be informed that he or she is not expected to act simply as an observer; and that the purposes of his or her presence are, first, to advise the person being questioned and to observe whether or not the interview is being conducted properly and fairly, and, secondly, to facilitate communication with the person being interviewed.

Research has questioned the participative skills of appropriate adults and the extent to which, if at all, the rights and interests of juveniles are protected. Information exists to suggest that parents as appropriate adults often fail to appreciate the rights and wrongs of police interview and detention methods and more often than not parents are either hostile to their child's conduct or towards the police themselves. Sadly, other research has found that 62 per cent of cases where the police used persuasive techniques sufficient to justify (or more properly, require) an intervention by a social worker appropriate adult, a confession was obtained without an intervention on behalf of the juvenile.[4]

---

[4] See *The Conduct of Police Interviews with Young People,* Evans R, 1993, London: HMSO.

Preliminary criminal proceedings

The Crime and Disorder Act 1998 and the Youth Justice and Criminal Evidence Act 1999 establish a coherent and extensive process for dealing with juveniles with regard to the commission of criminal offences. Diversion schemes within criminal proceedings are envisaged under the 1999 Act, whilst the 1998 Act provides for both diversion and criminalisation.[5] *Chapter 6* deals with the powers and procedures of the youth court in more detail.

The Crown Prosecution Service

The Crown Prosecution Service is a public service headed by the Director of Public Prosecutions and answerable to Parliament through the Attorney General. Established under the Prosecution of Offences Act 1985 the CPS is responsible for the prosecution of the vast majority of criminal offences on behalf of the police.[6]

Prosecutions are conducted by Crown prosecutors who must be qualified as solicitors or barristers and employed by the CPS. On occasions agents may be used to conduct proceedings. Within each CPS area (usually co-terminus with police force areas) there are prosecutors with specialisation in dealing with youth offenders and their prosecution. In addition to the power to commence proceedings the CPS also has a power to discontinue cases where the evidence is unlikely to lead to conviction or where prosecution is no longer in the public interest. To assist the decision-making process a Code for Crown Prosecutors is issued pursuant to section 10 of the 1985 Act. Paragraph 6.8 of the Code relates specifically to youth offenders and provides:

> Crown prosecutors must consider the interests of a youth when deciding whether it is in the public interest to prosecute. The stigma of a conviction can cause very serious harm to the prospects of a youth offender or a young adult. Young offenders can sometimes be dealt with without going to court. But Crown prosecutors should not avoid prosecuting simply because of the defendant's age. The seriousness of the offence or the offender's past behaviour may make prosecution necessary.

Reflected within the Code are a number of aspects of international human rights codes, including the Beijing Rules (*Chapter 3*). However the absence of specific reference to the principles of proportionality, the promotion of the well-being of a child and the recognition of the developmental capacity of a child, his age and understanding may lead to decisions which favour the public interest more than the interests of the child's well-being.

---

[5] The Crime and Disorder Act measures were rolled out nationally from 1 June 2000 while from the same date measures under the Youth Justice and Criminal Evidence Act 1999 were being piloted in certain areas.

[6] The range of matters encompassed within the CPS duty to prosecute is set out in section 3 of the Act. Section 6 provides for prosecutions to be conducted otherwise than by the service. Such other agencies are able to bring criminal proceedings against juveniles but it is rare for them to do so.

It is a particularly difficult balance to strike and there is no simple test which may be applied to decide on which side of the line a particular case falls. The decision to prosecute requires the Crown Prosecutor to always take into account the availability of admissible evidence to secure a conviction and the public interest in proceeding. Where a juvenile is involved a Crown Prosecutor can only rely on his or her own aptitude in applying the rather widely drawn guidance in the Code. It is perhaps a failing of the juvenile justice system that a clearer framework does not exist against which a decision to prosecute can be made.

This is especially so given the development of the range of diversion and sentencing options created under the Crime and Disorder Act and the Youth Justice and Criminal Evidence Act. These, despite certain flaws and possible defects more appropriately reflect the range of disposition measures provided for by rule 18 of the Beijing Rules than the previous regime. Whilst UK legislation has taken the youth justice system in a rights-compatible direction it is unfortunate that there seems to have been little reflection of this in the Code for Crown Prosecutors. The failure to provide proper guidance encompassing the principles and perspectives of the Beijing Rules - especially the need for discretion at all stages in criminal proceedings - within the Code is something of an opportunity lost. The absence of a structured framework against which decisions are to be taken does not match the enhanced youth justice system created by the two Acts.

The Youth Justice Board
The Crime and Disorder Act 1998 established a Youth Justice Board for England and Wales. The role of the board is to provide national leadership, raise standards and ensure that consistently high quality youth justice services are available nationwide. The functions of the board are set out in section 41(5) of the 1998 Act:

(a) to monitor the operation of the youth justice system and the provision of youth justice services;
(b) to advise the Secretary of State on the following matters, namely
    (i)   the operation of that system and the provision of such services;
    (ii) how the principal aim of that system[7] might most effectively be pursued;
    (iii) the content of any national standards he may see fit to set with respect to the provision of such services, or the accommodation in which children and young persons are kept in custody; and
    (iv) the steps that might be taken to prevent offending by children and young persons
(c) to monitor the extent to which that aim is being achieved and any such standards met;
(d) for the purposes of paragraphs (a), (b) and (c) above, to obtain information from relevant authorities;
(e) to publish information so obtained;

---

[7] To prevent offending: *Chapter 6.*

(f) to identify, to make known and to promote good practice in the following matters, namely—

    (i) the operation of the youth justice system and the provision of youth justice services;

    (ii) the prevention of offending by children and young persons; and

    (iii) working with children and young persons who are or maybe at risk of becoming offenders;

(g) to make grants, with the approval of the Secretary of State, to local authorities or other bodies for them to develop such practice, or to commission research in connection with such practice; and

(h) themselves to commission research in connection with such practice.

An overall function of the board is to supervise the youth justice system and to do so in a manner which should meet the obligations of the state under the Beijing Rules. The principal aim of the youth justice system is to prevent offending by children and young persons.[8] This aim of preventative action rather than remedial reaction is delivered through a series of local projects called youth offending teams.

Youth offending teams

Section 39 Crime and Disorder Act 1998 provides youth offending teams (YOTs) to be established in local areas. YOTs replace the previous somewhat *ad hoc* regimes of youth justice workers and extend to a much broader church. Each YOT must include at least one probation officer, one social worker, one police officer, one person nominated by the health authority and one person nominated by the chief education officer. Beyond that, the composition of the YOT is largely a matter for the local authority to determine in conjunction with the police, National Probation Service, health and education services. The YOT's statutory duties include:

- co-ordinating the provision of youth justice services for all those who need them;
- carrying out of such functions as are assigned to it in a local youth justice plan;
- providing appropriate adults;
- the assessment and provision of programmes to accompany the administration of a final warning (see *Chapter 6*);
- providing bail support;
- the placement of children and young people remanded to local authority accommodation;
- providing reports to courts;
- providing responsible officers in relation to parenting orders (*Chapter 6*), child safety orders (*Chapter 7*), reparation orders (*Chapter 6*) and action plan orders (*Chapter 6*); and
- supervising children and young people subject to supervision orders, community rehabilitation orders, community punishment

---

[8] Section 37(1) of the Act.

orders, community punishment and rehabilitation orders and detention and training orders.[9]

The youth justice plan is an annual plan devised by the local authority in partnership with other relevant agencies and services setting out how youth justice services are to be provided and funded and how YOTs are to be established, composed and funded.

As already indicated, the principal aim of the youth justice system is to prevent offending and the YOT is the primary vehicle by which this aim is to be delivered. The multi-agency approach has the benefit of ensuring that all services whose work impinges on the lives of young people have a substantial and statutory investment in achieving this aim. The Youth Justice Board has issued a set of National Standards (April 2000) which draw heavily on the UN Standard Minimum Rules for the Administration of Juvenile Justice. The Crime and Disorder Act has moved the focus of the youth justice system away from reacting to offending (although still very relevant at the sentencing stage, especially in relation to reparative measures, and vis-à-vis restorative approaches to offending) to preventing offending.

Referral order panels

From 1 April 2002 all children appearing before a youth court for the first time and pleading guilty will be made the subject of a referral order for up to 12 months unless the offence merits either an absolute discharge or is so serious that only custody can be justified. The referral order places the child within the jurisdiction of the referral order panel. The panel's task is to draw up an intervention plan in respect of the child and to oversee the child's progress during the currency of the order. The panel will meet regularly with the child and thus allows for the direct involvement of an administrative body to supervise the sentence imposed by the youth court. A panel is appointed in each area in which a YOT operates and comprises both professional and lay membership. Further detail is contained in *Chapter 6*.

PUBLIC LAW PROCEEDINGS

Public law proceedings occur where the state in the form of a public authority seeks to intervene in the lives of citizens - as apposed to private law proceedings which take place as between citizens (but where the state may nonetheless have an interest). It should be re-emphasised that all public authorities must be meticulous in complying not just with national statute law and the English common law but also the human rights considerations and other international obligations outlined in *Chapter 3*.

---

[9]   Orders and sentences available in the youth court – and associated procedures, including referral orders - are discussed in more detail in *Chapter 6*

The local authority

Part III of the Children Act 1989 deals with the responsibility of the local authority for children and families. Section 17 of the 1989 Act sets out the authority's general duty as follows:

17(1) It shall be the general duty of every local authority
    (a) to safeguard and promote the welfare of children within their area who are in need; and
    (b) so far as is consistent with that duty, to promote the upbringing of such children by their families.

The 1989 Act was a response to a series of cases where the role played by the local authority had been criticised.[10] It was drafted at the same time as the UN Convention On the Rights of the Child and took into account the European Convention On Human Rights. The Act and a series of regulations issued under it provide the framework for the protection and promotion of children either in private law or public law.[11] Where the state has a duty to intervene in the way children are brought up, the Children Act is the starting point and the obligation to safeguard children at risk rests with the social services provided by the local authority. The *Children Act 1989 Guidance and Regulations (Volume 2): Family Support, Day Care and Educational Provision for Young Children* (1991) state:

Local authorities are not expected to meet every individual need, but they are asked to identify the extent of need and then make decisions on the priorities for service provision in their area in the context of that information and their statutory duties. Local authorities will have to ensure that a range of services is available to meet the extent and nature of need identified within their administrative areas.

The local authority may become involved in public law proceedings (i.e. in seeking the emergency protection of children through a range of orders including emergency protection orders, child assessment orders, care or supervision orders or the use of secure accommodation) in a number of ways:

- through prior or existing involvement with a child or family;
- after a police protection order has been made whereby a child has been removed from his family by the police; or
- after an order under section 37 Children Act where a court requires the local authority to investigate the circumstances of a child with a view to bringing proceedings for either a care or supervision order.

---

[10] For example the *Report of the Inquiry into Child Abuse in Cleveland* (the Butler-Sloss Report), 1987; *A Child in Trust: Report of the Panel of Inquiry Investigating the Circumstances Surrounding the Death of Jasmine Beckford*, 1985; and *A Child in Mind: Protection of Children in a Responsible Society, Report of the Inquiry into the Circumstances Surrounding the Death of Kimberly Carlile*, 1989.

[11] This chapter looks at the professionals engaged in public law and private law proceedings. The procedures and orders available are dealt with in later chapters: see *Chapters 7 and 8*.

Whilst the local authority may engage with the family or child through a variety of personnel including family aides and health visitors the primary involvement will normally be via a social worker. The position of the social worker in a family is crucial. Through him or her the local authority discharges its duty to protect children and to promote care within the family. It is essential that the social worker and the family work together. In the event of a breakdown in that relationship and subsequent proceedings for the removal of the child the social worker has the responsibility to instigate those proceedings, prepare an interim care plan for the child and eventually to prepare a final care plan. In many cases the social worker, once attempting to befriend and assist a family on the verge of trouble becomes the villain in so far as the family is concerned. Simple psychology suggests that a family may feel betrayed by social services, poorly served and most probably hostile and angry. Against this background the efforts of the local authority, again delivered through a beleaguered social worker, must be directed towards rehabilitation.

To assist the social worker (and hopefully the family) there exist a number of sources of guidance including a *Code of Ethics for Social Work* (1975) and *Working Together under the Children Act 1989* (Department of Health, 1989). The latter publication contains guidance on the use of child protection conferences, the use of the child protection register, the investigation of allegations of abuse or neglect and the partnership approach to child protection to be enjoyed between the various agencies[12] involved in the system.

Local authority solicitors

Once proceedings under the Children Act are contemplated it is usual for their conduct to be undertaken by a solicitor for the local authority. The solicitor may well have also been involved in chairing child protection meetings or permanency planning meetings or have otherwise given advice in the course of the case as it develops. The vast majority of local authority solicitors involved in proceedings specialise in that subject and may have been recruited from private practice. As with other solicitors they are also subject to a requirement to undertake continuing professional development each year.

The *Handbook of Best Practice in Children Act Cases* (Children Act Advisory Committee, 1997) provides important guidance to all people involved in the preparation and conduct of Children Act proceedings. Section 1 of the handbook deals with preparation for court in care proceedings and sets out the obligations of local authority solicitors in this regard. At the earliest stage, when first consulted, they must focus on:

- the issues
- the legal framework
- the evidence needed to support the application

---

[12] e.g. education, health and the police.

- the proposed care plan
- the appropriate level of court; and
- the likely timescale for concluding the court case in the light of the complexities involved, and the ages and needs of the children.

Additionally the handbook sets out the ongoing duties of the local authority solicitor with regard to the instruction of experts, the care plan, preparing the evidence and preparing for the final hearing.

National Society for the Prevention of Cruelty to Children

An application for a care or supervision order may be made by either a local authority or an authorised person. Section 31(9) Children Act provides that an 'authorised person' means either the NSPCC or a person authorised by the Secretary of State. At the time of writing no other persons had been duly authorised to bring proceedings for care or supervision orders. To the extent that the NSPCC carries out functions under the Children Act in this regard it is to be considered a public authority for the purposes of section 6 Human Rights Act 1998.[13]

Children's guardian

The Criminal Justice and Court Services Act 2000 came into force in April 2001 and established the Children and Family Court Advisory and Support Service (CAFCASS). This national organization combines the roles previously allotted to guardians ad litem in public law proceedings and to children and family reporters in private law proceedings. Under the Act the term 'guardian ad litem' is replaced with the term 'children's guardian', a phrase better describing the work of the officer.

Under certain enactments the appointment of a children's guardian is either required or expected. The role of the guardian is to conduct an independent investigation into the circumstances of a particular child and to represent to the court what order would objectively best protect or promote the child's welfare. A guardian is appointed for a child either in specified proceedings under the Children Act or under the Human Fertilisation and Embryology Act 1990. Specified proceedings are defined in the Children Act to include:

- applications for a care or supervision order, or its variation or discharge
- where a direction is made to the local authority under section 37 of the Act to investigate the circumstances of a child in contemplation of making such an application
- where the court is considering an application for a residence order where the child is subject to a care order
- applications relating to contact with a child in care
- applications for the making or discharge of an emergency protection order, or for the making of a child assessment order

---

[13] Consequently the NSPCC has the same duty to act compatibly with the rights and freedoms set out in the European Convention On Human Rights as the local authority. The significance of this is discussed in *Chapter 3*.

- applications for the use of secure accommodation in family proceedings under section 25 of the Act
- applications for a change of surname or to remove a child from the UK under section 33(7) of the Act
- proceedings to approve a child in care living abroad
- applications to extend a supervision order; and
- any appeal arising from these applications or proceedings.

Under the previous regime the guardian was appointed by the court from a panel established and funded by the local authority. In *R v. Cornwall County Council, ex parte G* (1992), Fam. Law 110 the Divisional Court made it plain that no action should be taken by a local authority which might compromise the independence of the guardian. In this case certain financial and time constraints were imposed on the investigation of cases by guardians. The transfer of the guardian's role to CAFCASS has removed the last connection between the local authority and the guardian and the national service is now designed as a truly independent welfare service.

Guardians are professionally qualified; often and usually with extensive experience in social work, probation work or other forensically-based child-centred disciplines. The regulations prevented someone from being appointed to the former panel as a guardian if he or she was employed by the local authority in any capacity other than as a full-time guardian. He or she cannot be appointed in a particular case if they have been employed in any capacity by any of the agencies directly concerned in any aspect of services which have been enjoyed by the child during the five years prior to the commencement of the proceedings in question. A guardian should not be appointed in proceedings where there is also a children and family reporter since such an appointment would result in duplication of effort. Subject to these important qualifications a guardian should always be appointed in specified proceedings unless such an appointment is not necessary to safeguard the interests of the child concerned.[14]

The guardian is a party to the proceedings and may be represented by a solicitor. Indeed it is one of the guardian's duties to appoint a solicitor for the child. It is usual for the solicitor representing the children to also act for the guardian unless a conflict arises between his or her instructions and the views of the guardian or it appears that the child is capable of conducting the proceedings directly through the solicitor. In such situations the solicitor generally continues to act for the child and the guardian must, with the leave of the court, seek representation of his or her own. There is, however nothing to prevent a competent guardian from continuing to act in the proceedings without legal advice or representation. Where the child's solicitor also represents the guardian such representation is usually covered by way of state funded representation for the child. Where the guardian instructs his or her own

---

[14] Rule 4.10(7) Family Proceedings Rules 1991.

solicitor state funded representation is not available and the funding of this falls on CAFCASS.

The powers and duties of the guardian are set out in Rule 4.11 of the Family Proceedings Rules 1991 and include the following. The guardian shall advise the court concerning:

- whether the child is of sufficient understanding for any purpose including the child's refusal to submit to a medical or psychiatric examination or other assessment that the court has power to require, direct or order
- the wishes of the child in respect of any matter relevant to the proceedings, including his or her attendance at court;
- the appropriate forum for the proceedings
- the appropriate timing of the proceedings or any part of them;
- the options available in respect of the child and the suitability of each such option including what order should be made in determining the application
- any other matter concerning which the court seeks his or her advice or concerning which he or she considers that the court should be informed; and
- the existence of any other person whose joinder in the proceedings would be likely to safeguard the interests of the child and the extent to which he or she has been able to notify such people of their right to apply to be so joined.

The guardian must also serve and accept service of documents on behalf of the child and advise the child of the contents of any documents and shall also:

- make such investigations as may be necessary to carry out his or her duties
- contact or seek to interview such people as he or she thinks appropriate or as the court directs
- inspect such records as are available to him or her to inspect and bring to the attention of the court and the parties as the court may direct all such documents and records which assist in the proper determination of the proceedings
- obtain such professional assistance as is available to him or her which he or she thinks appropriate or which the court directs him or her to obtain; and
- otherwise provide to the court such assistance as it may require.

There is additionally a general expectation that the guardian will undertake to co-ordinate the investigation of expert witnesses and in many cases he or she will also facilitate the appointment of experts and supervise or assist in letters of instruction to them. The guardian is not however to be regarded as an expert, other than in those particular matters which fall within his or her field of competence.[15]

At least seven days before the final hearing of any case in which a guardian has been appointed he or she must file and serve a report setting out the findings of his or her investigations and make a recommendation representing the disposal of the case which is in the best interests of the child. The guardian may be examined on the contents of and recommendation contained in the, report and - whilst the court is in no way bound to follow the guardian's recommendation - there is strong case law whereby a court deviating from that view will need to provide cogent reasons for so doing.[16]

The Children and Family Court Advisory and Support Service

CAFCASS (above) unifies the work previously undertaken by locally provided and funded guardians ad litem, children and family reporters and the Official Solicitor. The agency was established under Part I of the Criminal Justice and Court Services Act 2000 and came into effect in April 2001 following recommendations in a consultation paper *Support Services in Family Proceedings—Future Organization of Court Welfare Services* (1998). CAFCASS serves the High Court, county courts and the family proceedings courts and is subject to independent inspection in order to monitor and report on its activities. CAFCASS is empowered to set and disseminate national standards in relation to the investigative and reporting function. The creation of a national service under the Lord Chancellor's Department integrates child-focused services into an independent agency with a stated purpose of improving the assistance given to courts in making decisions about the upbringing of children by way of investigation and reports. The work of officers of CAFCASS is dealt with in later chapters by reference to the proceedings in which they are involved.

The introduction of CAFCASS has led inevitably to the wholesale amendment of many rules of court but broadly the changes reflect structural rather than substantive changes to the former work of guardians ad litem and welfare officers. The formation of a national service is likely to lead to the development of a more a consistent approach to the function, duties and powers of professional services relating to children.

Solicitor for the child

In public law proceedings under the Children Act a child must be represented. The primary duty to arrange the appointment of a solicitor for the child falls on the children's guardian. Under Law Society rules no solicitor may act for a child in public law proceedings unless he or she is a member of the Children's Panel. Membership of the panel is obtained

---

[15] *The Manual of Practice for Guardians Ad Litem and Reporting Officers,* HMSO, 1992. This is being replaced by national standards under CAFCASS which adopt the same key principles.

[16] For example *Re S (A Minor)* (1992) (unreported).

through an application by a solicitor having appropriate experience in dealing with family and child-related issues. Legal representation of a child requires a degree of knowledge and aptitude not always necessary to represent the interests of an adult client and a flavour of the required characteristics may be gleaned from his or her duties, which include:

- to act in accordance with the instruction of the children's guardian
- to act in accordance with the child's instructions where the solicitor is satisfied that the child has sufficient understanding to give instructions on his or her own behalf and having taken into account the views of the guardian and any directions of the court
- to act in accordance with the child's instructions where there is no children's guardian and the child is of sufficient understanding to provide instructions
- where the child is incapable of providing instructions, to act in furtherance of the child's best interests
- to represent the child's instructions to oppose the local authority plan; and
- to consider making an appeal against any order made or not made at the conclusion of the case.

The child's solicitor is able to serve and accept service of documents and has a similar role to the children's guardian in co-ordinating the appointment of experts. He or she will attend any child protection meetings or permanency planning meetings and has a number of responsibilities appropriate to his or her role and similar to those of the solicitor for the local authority pursuant to the *Handbook of Best Practice in Children Act Cases*. The solicitor must be especially vigilant when taking full instructions from a disturbed but otherwise articulate and intelligent child. The nature and form of disturbance may adversely affect the child's understanding and capacity to give proper instructions. Where this may be the case the proper way forward is to seek expert opinion and advice.[17]

Available to all solicitors are the *Guide to Professional Conduct* and *Guidance on the Attendance of Solicitors at Child Protection Conferences* published by the Law Society. The role of the child's solicitor is also discussed in the various guides issued under the Children Act including *Working Together Under the Children Act 1989* (above) and nine volumes of Children Act 1989 guidance issued by the Department of Health.

Expert witnesses

A court dealing with an application for a care or supervision order under the Children Act (*Chapter 7*) has two decisions to make. The first stage in the proceedings is for the local authority to show that the threshold criteria have been met. The second stage, only reached if the court is satisfied that the grounds for making an order set out in section 31(2) of the Act have been met according to the evidence, is for the court to decide what order, *if any* is necessary to secure the best interests of the

---

[17] *Re M (Minors) (Care Proceedings: Child's Wishes)* (1994) 1 FCR 866.

child. This stage is sometimes described as the 'welfare stage' or 'disposal stage.' In order to meet the requirements of either the first or second stage the court may often have to rely on opinion evidence. It is a rule of evidence that opinion evidence may only be given by a person of sufficient qualification and experience to be regarded as an expert in the relevant field. However evidence given by an expert witness is not determinative of the issue addressed. It remains the case that whoever makes an allegation must prove it.[18] Nevertheless the expert brings an expertise on which the court is dependent.[19] There is no property in an expert witness (or any witness for that matter); that is to say an expert instructed by one party does not act on behalf of that party but should adopt an independent and impartial stance in the conduct of his or her investigations, conclusions and in giving of his or her evidence.

There is a duty on legal advisers to assist experts in the preparation of their reports. This duty extends to preparing joint letters of instruction where it is appropriate to do so or approving or commenting on the letter of instruction where the expert is instructed by one party. To facilitate the trial process it is expected by the court that as many factual issues as possible will have been resolved in advance of the hearing. This extends to the evidence and opinions of experts and it is good practice for experts to meet or confer in order to reach agreed conclusions or to narrow the issues.[20]

Practice has developed in recent times to limit the number of experts and to avoid their proliferation in proceedings. The court[21] is ultimately responsible for controlling the appointment of experts as leave is required for a party to file an expert's statement and often leave is also required either for case papers to be released to him or her, or for him or her to be allowed to assess or examine the child. The purpose of limiting the number of experts is to reduce delay and unnecessary litigation. It also prevents 'witness shopping'; the unwelcome practice of instructing a range of experts until an opinion favourable to the instructing party is obtained.[22]

It would appear that reports from experts obtained in contemplation of their use in family proceedings must be disclosed to the court and other parties. The appellate courts have struggled for a consistent approach to the issue of confidentiality and privilege in this area. In *Re B (Minors) (Disclosure of Medical Reports)* (1993) 2 FCR 241 the Divisional Court took the view that parties were required to disclose only those reports on which they intended to rely. In *Oxfordshire County Council v. M* [1994] 2 All ER 269 the Court of Appeal that in the determination of matters relating to children, legal representatives had a positive duty to disclose any report obtained even where it was against their own client's

---

[18] *Re M (Sexual Abuse Allegations: Interviewing Techniques)* (1999) 2 FLR 92.
[19] Section 60 of the *Handbook of Best Practice in Children Act Cases* emphasises the crucial distinction between the respective functions of the expert and the judge.
[20] See 15 above.
[21] See *Re CS (Expert Witnesses* (1996) 2 FLR 115.
[22] See *H v. Cambridgeshire County Council* (1997) 1 FCR 569.

interests. The House of Lords followed this line in the leading authority on the disclosure of adverse expert reports.[23]

This decision was taken up by the aggrieved party in a petition to the Court of Human Rights alleging a violation of the right to a fair trial under Article 6 of the European Convention On Human Rights. His complaint was declared to be inadmissible by the Commission because it failed to disclose a breach of the Convention. The two main grounds relied upon by the Commission were, firstly, that there was no inequality of arms between the parties. The requirement to provide disclosure applied to both parties in the proceedings and each was under the same potential dilemma. Secondly, there existed a practical solution to resolve the consequences of the disclosure of an unfavourable report and that was to seek leave to instruct a further expert so as to demonstrate that the conclusions of the first were unreliable.[24]

To this extent the decision of the House of Lords remains the the law. Where an unfavourable report is received from an expert there is a duty to disclose it in children related proceedings but a power to seek to instruct another expert. Clearly this option stands against the trend towards limiting the appointment of experts not only in children proceedings but throughout civil litigation.[25]

Where an expert is instructed in proceedings the *Handbook of Best Practice in Children Act Cases* provides, at sections 74 to 79, as follows:

Duties of experts

74. The role of the expert is to provide independent assistance to the court by way of objective, unbiased opinion, in relation to matters within his expertise. Expert evidence presented to the court must be, and be seen to be, the independent product of the expert, uninfluenced by the instructing party.

75. Acceptance of instructions imposes an obligation to:
    (a) comply with the court's timetable; and
    (b) notify the instructing solicitors promptly if there is any risk that the timetable cannot be adhered to.

76. Experts should not hesitate to seek further information and documentation when this is required. Such requests should form part of the court bundle.

77. In his report, the expert should:
    (a) state the facts or assumptions on which his opinion is based, and not omit to consider material facts which detract from his concluded opinion;
    (b) make it clear when a particular aspect of the case is outside his expertise;
    (c) indicate, if appropriate, that his opinion is not properly researched because of insufficient data, and is therefore provisional; and
    (d) inform the other parties, and, where appropriate the court, if at any time he changes his opinion on a material matter.

---

[23] *Re L (a Minor) (Police Investigation: Privilege)* (1996) 2 All ER 78.

[24] *L v. UK* (2000) EHRLR 39.

[25] See the Civil Procedure Rules (The Woolf Reforms).

78. If an opinion is based, wholly or in part, on research conducted by others, the expert must:
    (a) set this out clearly in the report;
    (b) identify the research relied on;
    (c) state its relevance to the points at issue; and
    (d) be prepared to justify the opinions expressed.
79. It is unacceptable for any expert in a child case, whose evidence is relevant to the outcome, to give evidence without having read, in advance, the report of the Children's guardian.

The Expert Witness Group has developed an 'Expert Witness Pack' to assist the standardisation of processes and procedures. Additionally the various guidance and guides mentioned earlier in this chapter also also with the role and responsibilities of experts. By their very nature the majority of expert witnesses will also be professionally qualified and members of the relevant professional agency. It is common to find professional guidance or standards issued by that professional body.

The Official Solicitor
The office of Official Solicitor dates back to 1875. An independent solicitor of at least ten years call, funded by the Lord Chancellor, he or she has a number of roles in the legal system including the representation of people suffering from mental disorder, claims made in civil law for or against a child, in wardship proceedings and in proceedings where the child's welfare is the subject of the dispute itself. The duties and powers of the Official Solicitor are set out in a *Practice Note: The Official Solicitor: Appointment in Family Proceedings* (1999) 1 FCR 1.

The Official Solicitor may be appointed, subject to his or her consent either on application by a party to proceedings or by the judge of his or her own motion. There is no power for a family proceedings court to appoint the Official Solicitor. Where a matter arises in the family proceedings court requiring consideration of the appointment of the Official Solicitor the court has power to transfer the case to the county court (and that court has power to transfer it onwards to the High Court, if deemed appropriate).

In discharging his or her functions the Official Solicitor has an unlimited discretion to take whatever steps are required to present to the court the evidence which he or she considers to be material on the child's behalf.

The position post-CAFCASS
The position of the Official Solicitor has been incorporated within the remit of CAFCASS and his or her children's casework will in future be conducted by specialists and in-house lawyers. Accordingly the term 'Official Solicitor' seems likely to disappear but the functions carried out will continue, but under the auspices of this new national agency. Accordingly references to the appointment and duties of the Official Solicitor need now to be considered in the light of CAFCASS and the withdrawal of the actual Official Solicitor from children work. However

the principles governing the circumstances in which the Official Solicitor was appointed and operated remain unaffected by the establishing of CAFCASS. The *Practice Note* provides insofar as the Official Solicitor is involved in child-related family proceedings:

2. In specified (public law) proceedings under the Children Act 1989, the Official Solicitor may only be appointed in the High Court, in accordance with a direction of the Lord Chancellor where the court considers that the circumstances are that:

    (1) the child does not have a children's guardian in the proceedings; and
    (2) there are exceptional circumstances which make it desirable in the interests of the welfare of the child concerned that the Official Solicitor, rather than a panel guardian, should be appointed, having regard to—
        (a) any foreign element in the case which is likely to require inquiries, or other action, to be pursued outside England and Wales;
        (b) the burden of having to represent several children;
        (c) other High Court proceedings in which the Official Solicitor is representing the child;
        (d) any other circumstances which the court considers relevant.

The Official Solicitor, in accordance with the direction, may also give advice and other assistance as he considers appropriate to any children's guardian in specified proceedings in the High Court

3 In non-specified (private law) proceedings under the Children Act 1989, and in proceedings under the inherent jurisdiction of the High Court, the Official Solicitor may act either in the High Court or in a county court (but not in a family proceedings court) under rule 9(5) of the Family Proceedings Rules. In most cases a child's interests will be sufficiently safeguarded by a children and family reporter's report. It is only where this is not so that the question of the appointment of the Official Solicitor may arise and, even then, the Official Solicitor's involvement should be exceptional rather than automatic.

4 He will accept appointment in those exceptional cases in which it has been established that a child's interests may not be adequately protected by a children and family reporter's report, and that it is desirable that the child should be separately represented. Such exceptional cases will include those where:

    (1) there is a substantial foreign element;
    (2) there appears to be exceptional or difficult points of law;
    (3) there are unusual or complicating features, such as where one parent has killed the other, or is a transsexual;
    (4) there is conflicting or controversial medical evidence
    (5) the child is ignorant of the truth as to its parentage or is refusing contact with a parent in circumstances which point to the need for psychiatric assessment; and

(6) he is acting for the child in other proceedings.

5 He will almost invariably accept appointments in a case which falls into the classes of cases upon which judicial guidance has been given about his appointment, that is to say:

(1) where a child has sought separate representation by solicitor but the court does not consider he is competent;

(2) if a child is separately represented but the court needs the assistance of the Official Solicitor as amicus curiae;

(3) if difficult issues of medical confidentiality arise;

(4) 'special category cases' such as sterilisation and abortion, where application should be made under the inherent jurisdiction of the High Court

PRIVATE LAW PROCEEDINGS

As already indicated, private law proceedings are those involving disputes between citizens, in the present context parents, guardians, children and other interested parties. The state may have an interest in the outcome, but intervention by the state is not the basis for the proceedings (see *Public Law Proceedings*, above).[26] Private law proceedings under the Children Act 1989 include those concerning residence, contact, specific issues, prohibited steps, parental responsibility, and proceedings under the Family Law Act 1996 (FLA) for non-molestation orders or occupation orders, and financial orders, including ancillary relief.[27]

The parties

The scheme set out in the Children Act (*Chapters 8* and *9*) allows anyone to make an application to a court about a child's upbringing. Some people are able to make an application as of right, or are entitled to become a party to an application. Other classes of persons require the leave of the court to bring proceedings. Under the FLA a limited class of people may bring proceedings for a non-molestation order or an occupation order.[28] Whether and when a court will grant leave to a particular individual to bring proceedings was considered in *Re M (Care: Contact—Grandmother's Application for Leave)* (1995) 2 FLR 98 as follows:

(1) If the application is frivolous or vexatious or otherwise an abuse of the process of the court, of course it will fail;

(2) If the application for leave fails to disclose that there is any eventual prospect of success, if those prospects are remote so that the application is obviously unsustainable, then it must also be dismissed;

---

[26] Except to the extent to which a local authority may become involved in such proceedings via a family assistance order or the completion of reports under section 37 Children Act, private law proceedings are characterised by the absence of any parties other than the applicant and respondent or respondents.

[27] *Chapter 8, 9 and 10.*

[28] These provisions are discussed in more detail in *Chapter 8.*

(3) The applicant must satisfy the court that there is a serious issue to try and must present a good arguable case.

Although the subject of the dispute is generally the child it is unusual to find the child as a party to the proceedings. His or her wishes and feelings must be taken into account by the court in reaching its decision as to whether an order is in the best interests of the child's welfare and this information is usually brought to the attention of the court through the children and family reporter's report. Where a child is making the application in person there is a requirement to transfer the matter to the High Court for determination of both the issue of leave and the substantive application in accordance with *Practice Direction (Applications by Children: for Leave)* (1993) 1 FCR 573.

The court has power under section 91(14) of the 1989 Act to prevent subsequent applications by any person, including those otherwise entitled to apply under the Children Act without the leave of the court but exercise of this power should only occur where the welfare of the child requires it.[29]

The requirement for leave is intended to act as a filter to protect children from inappropriate applications and unnecessary litigation. However this restriction on the right of access to a court in respect of extended family members such as grandparents may also amount to interference with their right to family life under Article 8 of the European Convention On Human Rights. If the restriction has a legitimate purpose there may be nothing incompatible about it as far as the Human Rights Act 1998 is concerned but the 'arguable case' test may overstate the lawful extent to which the state can interfere with the exercise of family life.

Representation
Parties to private law proceedings may be represented by a solicitor of their choice. In practice representation is likely to be obtained from suitably qualified and experienced solicitors. Changes to the way solicitors are paid by the state makes it probable that only solicitors in practices holding state franchises to conduct business in family law will be able to represent state funded clients. It is also usual for such solicitors to be members of the Solicitor's Family Law Association and often of the Children's Panel. In any event all solicitors are required to undertake a period of continuing professional development each year to maintain their name on the roll of practicing solicitors.

The children and family reporter
Section 7 Children Act empowers the court to seek reports on the welfare of the child when considering any question relating to the child's upbringing. Where the report is to be obtained from a reporter other than an officer of the local authority - and it is more usual not to involve the local authority unless there is a specific public law issues in the

---

[29] *B v. B (Residence Order: Restricting Applications)* (1997) 1 FLR 749.

background—the report will be obtained from a children and family reporter. This officer replaces the court welfare officer who was ordinarily from the Probation Service until CAFCASS was established (above) and the transfer of children functions from local Probation Services to CAFCASS. The duties that were previously the function of court welfare officers are essentially transferred to CAFCASS and references to the court welfare officer can now be construed to refer to the children and family reporter.

New national standards under CAFCASS provide guidance. At the time of writing these standards were as yet unavailable, but it is understood that they will reflect traditional practices and approaches to report writing under the former regime, except that there is a greater emphasis on the nationwide nature of CAFCASS and its responsibilities. The original national standards[30] provide the following key statement:

> The primary objective of all family court welfare work . . . is to help the courts in their task of serving the needs of children whose parents are involved in separation or divorce, or whose families are involved in disputes in private law.

Principal private law tasks of the family court welfare service have been integrated into CAFCASS and remain, at the request of the court, to:

- meet the parties before or during a directions appointment to make a preliminary assessment of the case and to identify any areas of agreement
- meet the parties at the direction of the court in order to assist them to make agreed decisions about their children
- carry out enquiries and prepare a welfare report to assist the court to make decisions in the best interests of the children; and
- provide advice and assistance to people named in a family assistance order.

The aim of the children and family reporter's report is to assist the court to reach its decision of what order, if any, is in the best interests of the child's welfare. Accordingly the welfare officer must approach his or her task independently and impartially. The existing national standards further provide that a report should:

- generally be in writing
- be as short and as focused as possible
- balance description and background with evaluation, summary and assessment
- differentiate fact from opinion
- verify significant facts and justify opinions;
- present the information with sensitivity and in a way which does not exacerbate the relations between the parties;
- be fair to the parties; and

---

[30] The original standards are were contained in *National Standards for Probation Service Family Court Welfare Work* (HMSO, 1994).

- avoid unnecessary repetition of material which is available in other documents before the court.

In addition to national standards, the *Handbook of Best Practice in Children Act Cases* (1997) issued by the Children Act Advisory Committee sets out a note of best practice for the judiciary and family proceedings courts when ordering a children and family reporter's report. The recommendation provided in that report is never determinative of the issue addressed by it. It remains for the court to apply the welfare checklist (*Chapter 7*) and decide what order, if any, is best for the welfare of the child. However, where the court is minded to depart from the reporter's view, full and cogent reasons must be provided.[31]

Mediation and mediators

In order to save unnecessary litigation, to avoid delay and to reduce the mounting costs state funded legal representation certain measures were introduced in 2000 to facilitate compulsory mediation between parties in dispute. The FLA - when fully in force - will require all parties to a marriage seeking divorce to attend an information meeting with a professional which aims to promote mediation and reconciliation. At present after what can only be described as a disastrous piloting of the reforms to divorce law, the relevant provisions have been postponed indefinitely. Not so however reforms to the provision of state financial assistance. The Legal Services Commission (which replaced the Legal Aid Board) is responsible for the grant of legal assistance in private law proceedings. An applicant for such assistance must, subject to certain statutory exceptions first attend a mediation appointment to discuss the arrangements in place to resolve any dispute without resort to the courts. Only if that mediation fails can an application be made for state funding. The application must be accompanied by a certificate from the mediator indicating its failure. Clearly if state funded representation is not an issue there is no requirement for a party to proceed through this alternative dispute resolution scheme.

However recognition that the court may not be the best medium through which to resolve disputes between parents over their children is welcome and it is often the practice of courts to seek to persuade parties to step back from their own inter-relationship difficulties and to attempt to facilitate some kind of agreement between them at least in so far as their children are concerned.

---

[31] *Re L (Residence: Justices Reasons)* (1995), 2 FLR 445.

COURTS DEALING WITH CHILDREN

As already emphasised, the totality of measures to protect children fall within separate jurisdictions according to the nature of the case:

Criminal proceedings

Criminal proceedings against children take place mainly in the youth court (*Chapter 6*), a specialist court operating under the auspices of the local magistrates' court. The youth court is composed of magistrates appointed to the youth panel for a given petty sessions area (PSA). This is followed by a period of additional, specialist training and competence led preparation for dealing with young offenders. The responsibility to train magistrates is a local matter for the magistrates' courts' committee (MCC), and often undertaken by the justice's clerk for the PSA.

The youth court usually comprises three magistrates, one of whom must be a woman if her colleagues are male and vice versa, or a District Judge (Magistrates).[32] Youth court justices are assisted and advised by a a justices' clerk or other professionally qualified court legal adviser on such matters as law, practice, procedure and the sentencing. The powers and procedures of the youth court are outlined in *Chapter 6*.

Where certain juveniles are charged with what are called 'grave crimes' such as homicide, rape, robbery and blackmail they either can or in some instances must be dealt with in the Crown Court before a judge and, if there is to be a trial of a not guilty plea, a jury. Where a juvenile is jointly charged with an adult he or she may be tried in a magistrates' court with the adult or even in the Crown Court depending on the seriousness of the offence. However, wherever possible and the interests of justice and a fair trial allow this, the practice is to separate juveniles from adults by remitting the juvenile to the youth court for either trial or sentence.[33]

Family matters

Proceedings under the Children Act 1989, the Human Fertilisation and Embryology Act 1990, the Child Support Act 1991 and the Family Law Act 1996 may be commenced in either the family proceedings court, the county court or the High Court. Powers exist to transfer proceedings between the three levels of court. Certain specific applications may only be started in one level of court and in respect of some applications a particular court may lack jurisdiction to make a final order.[34] The allocation of proceedings is governed by the Children (Allocation of Proceedings) Order 1991. A further practical restriction on the choice of

---

[32] District judges used to be called stipendiary magistrates. Essentially they are paid professional judges (normally full-time), as opposed to lay (or unqualified) magistrates.

[33] See further in *Chapter 6*.

[34] For example the family proceedings court is unable to make a property adjustment order; the county court is unable to make an emergency protection order except within proceedings currently before the county court; care proceedings may only be dealt with in a county court which is also designated as a care centre.

court may be set by a condition on the grant of state funded representation. Under the order there are four classes of county court:

- divorce county courts: competent to deal with divorce cases;
- family hearing centres: competent to deal with applications under Part I and II of the Children Act and adoption;
- care centres: competent to deal with care and related proceedings; and
- non-designated county courts: competent to deal with domestic violence proceedings involving children.

Many of the county court centres combine these functions and are able to offer and provide a 'one-stop shop' to litigants.

As far as allocation of the judiciary (outside the family proceedings court) to cases is concerned the scheme is overseen by the President of the Family Division of the High Court. Below appellate level there exist the arrangements illustrated in *Table 4.1.*[35] The responsibility for professional judicial training rests with the Judicial Studies Board and the judiciary itself. Magistrates are trained locally, usually by their justices' clerk.

Other possibilities

Other civil proceedings not falling within the ambit of the family jurisdiction can involve children such as an application for a injunction or proceedings involving the administration of property usually by way of a trust. These are highly specialised matters beyond the scope of this work.

---

[35] By virtue of the *Family Proceedings (Allocation to Judiciary) Directions* (1999) 2 FLR 799.

Table 4.1 **Allocation of judiciary below High Court level**

Type of judicial office	Specific nomination	Type of proceedings
Circuit Judge	Public family proceedings	All applications
Circuit Judge	Private family proceedings	Any private law application
Deputy Circuit Judge Recorder Assistant Recorder District Judge of the Principal Registry	Private family proceedings	Any application for parental responsibility, under section 10 for section 8 orders, for the change of a child's surname or his or her removal from the jurisdiction or to vary a section 8 order when a family assistance order is in force
District Judge	Public family proceedings	All applications under section 10 for section 8 orders
District Judge	Private family proceedings	Interlocutory proceedings and unopposed trials in respect of all applications under section 10 for section 8 orders. May deal with opposed trials but only where the application is for contact and the principle is unopposed or is in respect of an interim period pending a hearing by a judge with full jurisdiction
District Judge of the Principal Registry District Judge	Public family law	Public law proceedings but limited in the case of a District Judge to

		interlocutory matters, unopposed hearings or where the application is for contact and the principle is unopposed

CHAPTER 5

The Protection of Children as Victims

A child may be a victim in a number of ways, i.e. he or she:

- may be the subject of criminal conduct directed against him or her by adults or other children;
- may be the victim of abuse, exploitation or neglect which does not amount to a crime but is a civil wrong;
- may be the innocent party affected by marital or quasi-marital breakdown;
- may be at risk from adults with a criminal background and require preventative protection by the state against such individuals;
- may be the perpetrator of crime or civil wrong and require protection in the way he or she is treated within the justice system;
- may be a witness to criminal acts against him or her or others; or
- may be a child in legal proceedings seeking be heard by the court.

In whatever form a child engages the legal system there is an obligation on the state to provide him or her with a voice, to respect his or her rights as a child and not simply as a 'little adult' - and to protect his or her interests. The obligation is created by virtue of the state's fundamental responsibility to all its citizens; that is to say it is a general function of the state to protect its citizens and to take steps to ensure their safety. International treaties also provide a basis for the state's duties towards children as victims.

THE UN CONVENTION ON THE RIGHTS OF THE CHILD

The Convention sets out a number of child-specific rights. In some cases the rights are expressed as belonging to the child; in others the rights are expressed in terms of state duties to take action or to avoid omission.

General protection
Article 19 provides:

> (1) State Parties shall take all appropriate legislative, administrative, social and educational measures to protect the child from all forms of physical or mental violence, injury or abuse, neglect or negligent treatment, maltreatment or exploitation, including sexual abuse, while in the care of parent(s), legal guardian(s) or any other person who has the care of the child.

(2) Such protective measures should, as appropriate, include effective procedures for the establishment of social programmes to provide necessary support for the child and for those who have care of the child, as well as for other forms of prevention and for identification, reporting, referral, investigation, treatment and follow-up of instances of child maltreatment described heretofore and, as appropriate, for judicial involvement.

The criminal law provides the primary measure under which the state protects children and other people, by imposing criminal sanctions. Any crime which may be committed against an adult may be committed against a child and in addition there are a range of child specific crimes ranging from serious forms of abuse to employment matters. It is also an established principle of sentencing law that, other things being equal, an offence against a child is more serious than the same offence against an adult.

Reponsibilities of parents

From a different perspective, the Crime and Disorder Act 1998 introduced measures reflecting the duty of the state to provide support for a child and his or her parents. These are dealt with further in *Chapter 6*, but it is important that such an order should not just be seen as an adjunct to punishment, but rather as protection. A parenting order made under section 8 of the 1998 Act requires a parent to comply with certain requirements including compulsory counselling and guidance aimed at improving parental skills so as to avoid further offending or further anti-social behaviour by his or her child. Such an order may only be made where:

- another social programme order has been imposed in respect of the child such as a child safety order or anti-social behaviour order (*Chapter 7*) under the same Act;
- the child has been convicted of an offence (*Chapter 6*); or
- the parent has been convicted of an offence under the Education Act 1996 of failing to ensure the attendance of the child at school, or failure to comply with a school attendance order.

Employment and economic exploitation

Article 32 of the UN Convention provides:

(1) State Parties recognise the right of the child to be protected from economic exploitation and from performing any work that is likely to be hazardous or to interfere with the child's education, or to be harmful to the child's health or physical, mental, spiritual, moral or social development.

(2) State Parties shall take legislative, administrative, social and educational measures to ensure the implementation of the present article. To this end, and having regard to the relevant provisions of other international instruments, State Parties shall in particular:

(a) provide for a minimum age for admission to employment;
(b) provide for appropriate regulation of the hours and conditions of employment;
(c) provide for appropriate penalties or other sanctions to ensure the effective enforcement of the present article.

The extent to which the UK legal system reflects these provisions is considered in *Chapter 11.*

Drugs education
Article 33 of the UN Convention provides:

> State Parties shall take all appropriate measures, including legislative, administrative, social and educational measures, to protect children from the illicit use of narcotic drugs and psychotropic substances as defined in the relevant international treaties, and to prevent the use of children in the illicit production and trafficking of such substances.

This specific emphasis on the misuse of drugs reflects the globalisation of drug abuse. In the UK it is often said that the majority of crime, especially property crime is drug-related. The state's response has included the development of specific drug treatment and testing orders as a sentence, or part of a sentence, for people convicted of offences involving drugs, and a range of social and educational programmes and events to raise awareness with children and their families of the consequences of drug misuse.

Sexual exploitation and abuse
Article 34 of the Convention provides:

> State Parties undertake to protect the child from all forms of sexual exploitation and sexual abuse. For these purposes, State Parties shall in particular take all appropriate national, bilateral and multilateral measures to prevent:
>
> (a) the inducement or coercion of a child to engage in any unlawful sexual activity;
> (b) the exploitative use of children in prostitution or other unlawful sexual practices;
> (c) the exploitative use of children in pornographic performances or materials.

Thus, as with misuse etc. of drugs, measures to prevent sexual abuse and exploitation are a specific requirement of the Convention. The UK has taken a series of measures aimed at addressing this issue including establishing a Sex Offender Register (see later in this chapter) and enabling the courts to impose sentences longer than is commensurate with the seriousness of the offence in the case of sex offences.[1] Other measures include a response to the development of 'sex tourism' a practice whereby offenders journey to certain parts of the world where child sexual exploitation is dealt with less severely.[2] One of the major challenges facing all states is the regulation of the Internet which has become a major source of accessible child pornography. The nature of the World Wide Web is such that its control is technologically and legally very difficult. The passive role played by many users of child pornography taken from the Web often distances the offender from the exploitation and abuse of the child concerned. The position is very similar to the abuse of drugs. Without a user of the product there would be no supplier; a passive user has the capacity to become active either in terms of actual physical abuse or in the supply of the product. The detection of passive use is difficult and the prosecution of suppliers more so given that the trail to them from the end user usually exceeds the jurisdiction of a particular state.

Other forms of exploitation
Article 36 of the UN Convention provides:

> State Parties shall protect the child against all other forms of exploitation prejudicial to any aspects of the child's welfare

In addition to protecting against exploitation and abuse the state has an international duty to provide services to assist children who have not been protected. Article 39 of the Convention provides:

> State Parties shall take all appropriate measures to promote physical and psychological recovery and social reintegration of a child victim of: any form of neglect, exploitation, or abuse, torture or any other form of cruel, inhuman or degrading treatment or punishment; or armed conflicts. Such recovery and reintegration shall take place in an environment which fosters the health, self-respect and dignity of the child.

The extent to which the UK satisfies these requirements falls outside the scope of this work as such measures as there may be to facilitate recovery and reintegration take place beyond the legal system. However certain features of the way children as victims are dealt with - such as in relation to recording of and giving evidence and reintegration processes on release from custody - clearly impact upon recovery and relief.

Children as offenders
Article 40 of the Convention provides a detailed set of rights and principles governing the minimum standards to be attained in dealing with children as offenders. It is a fault of the legal system that people are

---

[1] Section 2 Criminal Justice Act 1991; section 58 Crime and Disorder Act 1998.
[2] See the Sex Offences (Conspiracy and Incitement) Act 1996 which criminalises in the UK sex crimes against children committed abroad.

categorised by reference to their role in legal proceedings. There is a strong argument for considering children who are offenders to be victims as well. Article 40 is supplemented by the more detailed provisions of the UN Standard Minimum Rules for the Administration of Juvenile Justice (the Beijing Rules) and is of course also reinforced through the rights and freedoms set out in the European Convention On Human Rights Article 40 provides:

(1) State Parties recognise the right of every child alleged as, accused of, or recognised as having infringed the penal law to be treated in a manner consistent with the promotion of the child's sense of dignity and worth, which reinforces the child's respect for the human rights and fundamental freedoms of others and which takes into account the child's age and desirability of promoting the child's reintegration and the child's assuming a constructive role in society.

(2) To this end, and having regard to the relevant provisions of international instruments, State Parties shall, in particular, ensure that:

(a) no child shall be alleged as, be accused of, or recognised as having infringed the penal law by reason of acts or omissions which were not prohibited by national or international law at the time they were committed;

(b) every child alleged as or accused of having infringed the penal law has at least the following guarantees:

   (i) to be presumed innocent until proven guilty according to law;

   (ii) to be informed promptly and directly of the charges against him or her, and, if appropriate, through his or her parents or legal guardians, and to have legal or other appropriate assistance in the preparation and presentation of his or her defence;

   (iii) to have the matter determined without delay by a competent, independent and impartial authority or judicial body in a fair hearing according to law, in the presence of legal or other appropriate assistance and, unless it is considered not to be in the best interest of the child, in particular, taking into account his or her age or situation, his or her parents or legal guardians;

   (iv) not to be compelled to give testimony or to confess guilt; to examine or have examined adverse witnesses and to obtain the participation and examination of witnesses on his or her behalf under conditions of equality;

   (v) if considered to have infringed the penal law, to have this decision and any measures imposed in consequence thereof reviewed by a higher, competent, independent and impartial authority or judicial body according to law;

   (vi) to have the free assistance of an interpreter if the child cannot understand or speak the language used;

   (vii) to have his or her privacy fully respected at all stages of the proceedings.

(3) State Parties shall seek to promote the establishment of laws, procedures, authorities and institutions specifically applicable to

children alleged as, accused of, or recognised as having infringed the penal law, and, in particular:

(a) the establishment of a minimum age below which children shall be presumed not to have the capacity to infringe the penal law;

(b) whenever appropriate and desirable, measures for dealing with such children without resorting to judicial proceedings, providing that human rights and legal safeguards are fully respected.

(4) A variety of dispositions, such as care, guidance and supervision orders; counselling; probation; foster care; education and vocational training programmes and other alternatives to institutional care shall be available to ensure that children are dealt with in a manner appropriate to their well-being and proportionate both to their circumstances and the offence.

The extent to which the youth justice system reflects these ideals is considered in *Chapter 6* which deals with the youth court. The Beijing Rules also require that the administration of juvenile justice contains a degree of discretion. The enforcement of community penalties in accordance with national standards and the prescription of certain disposals in the event of previous convictions under the Crime (Sentences) Act 1997 or in the event of a previous final warning under the Crime and Disorder Act 1998 appear to remove or fetter the exercise of discretion. Whether the restriction on the use of sentencing discretion enacted by this legislation is unwarranted or not may be the subject of debate and possibly of litigation.

CRIMES AGAINST CHILDREN

Crimes may be committed by adults or children subject only to the minimum age of criminal responsibility. Any crime which can be committed against an adult may also be committed against a child. The criminal law also recognises a range of offences which can only be committed against or in respect of a child. In relation to this latter category, child-specific crime reflects measures designed to regulate, to prohibit and to protect the child from neglect, exploitation and abuse. The following illustrations of categorisation are not intended to be exhaustive.

Regulatory crime

Certain conduct such as the sale of tobacco is regulated by legislation which imposes criminal penalties on individuals or organizations for failing to protect children or others. The majority of crimes of this type concern safety issues. In relation to children, examples of regulatory crime include:

- failing to provide for the safety of children at entertainments under the Children and Young Persons Act 1933;
- failing to display notices in relation to the sale of tobacco under the Children and Young Persons (Protection from Tobacco) Act 1991;

- failing to supply prescription drugs in child-proof containers under the Medicines (Child Safety) Regulations 1975; and
- the regulation of the capacity to drive under road traffic legislation.

Regulatory crime also encompasses the offences in relation to services provided to and for children, e.g. the regulation of adoption under the Adoption Act 1976, surrogacy under the Human Fertilisation and Embryology Act 1996 and child care under the Children Act 1989.

Prohibitive crime

There are some things which it is lawful for an adult to enjoy but not for a child. The criminal law provides for the enforcement of such choices made by society through the criminalisation of otherwise lawful behaviour. Examples of prohibitive crime include:

- the sale of tobacco to children: Children and Young Persons Act 1933;
- the sale and supply of alcohol to children: Licensing Act 1964;
- betting by children: Betting, Gaming and Lotteries Act 1963;
- gaming by children: Gaming Act 1968;
- access by children to sex establishments: Local Government (Miscellaneous Provisions) Act 1982;
- tattooing children: Tattooing of Minors Act 1969; and
- possession and ownership by children of firearms, crossbows and knives: Firearms Act 1968, Crossbows Act 1987 and Criminal Justice Act 1988.

In addition, the Confiscation of Alcohol (Young Persons) Act 1997 prohibits the possession of alcohol outside licensed premises and allows a police officer to confiscate it from children.

Protective crime

It can be surmised that the ultimate aim of the criminal law is to protect either the individual or society and the community. The degree of protection is related to the degree of vulnerability of potential victims. In the case of children examples of protective crimes include:

- cruelty, ill-treatment, abandonment etc. of a child: Children and Young Persons Act 1933;
- exposing a child to risk or burning or keeping a child in a brothel: Children and Young Persons Act 1933;
- exposing a child to harmful or obscene publications: Children and Young Persons (Harmful Publications) Act 1955;
- violence against a child: Offences Against the Persons Act 1861, Infant Life (Preservation) Act 1929 and Infanticide Act 1938.

Crimes of exploitation

A distinction must be drawn between exploitation and abuse although the boundaries of the distinction are blurred at the edges. Exploitation covers the misuse of children in conduct which is otherwise lawful. Abuse covers the misuse of children in conduct which whilst possibly lawful in the case of an adult is unlawful in the case of children. Examples of exploitive crime include:

- using a child to beg: Children and Young Persons Act 1933;
- exceeding the regulations concerning employment (economic exploitation): Children and Young Persons Act 1933;
- using a child in a hypnotism display: Hypnotism Act 1952.

Examples of abusive crime include sexual offences under any of the following enactments:

- Sexual Offences Act 1956
- Indecency with Children Act 1960
- Criminal Law Act 1977
- Criminal Justice Act 1988
- Sex Offences Act 1993
- Sex Offenders (Conspiracy and Incitement) Act 1996; and
- Sex Offenders Act 1997.

Lawful and unlawful chastisement

It is a defence to a charge of assault that a parent, or person *in loco parentis* has used only reasonable chastisement to correct a child. In *A v. UK*[3] the Court of Human Rights found that the UK was in breach of its obligation to take measures to prevent the infliction of inhuman or degrading treatment on an individual under Article 3 of the European Convention On Human Rights. Child A's stepfather used a cane on his charge inflicting actual bodily harm. At the stepfather's trial he successfully raised the defence of reasonable chastisement and was acquitted by a jury. On application by child A to the Court of Human Rights it was held that the infliction of corporal punishment in the case amounted to inhuman or degrading treatment under Article 3 of the Convention. By allowing for the defence of reasonable chastisement the state had failed to safeguard child A's rights to be protected from inhuman or degrading treatment.

The decision led to the publication by the government of a document entitled *Protecting Children, Supporting Parents*. The consultation paper seeks to gather representations from those people with an interest in the subject, with a view to changing the law relating to the use of physical correction and bringing it in line with the decision in *A v. UK*.

The criminal background of people with access to children

The criminal justice system caters for the punishment of offenders. The aim of punishment includes elements of retribution, reparation, rehabilitation and deterrence. By its nature the criminal law is reactive and the only measure of prevention afforded by it is reflected in the last

---

[3] (1998) 2 FLR 959.

of these elements. The state is responsible for enforcing the criminal law but the existence of international treaties may impose a positive duty to take measures, including under the criminal law to protect basic rights and freedoms. *A v. UK* is an example of this positive obligation.

In addition to punishing adequately individuals who commit crimes against children there is a general duty on the state to prevent crimes from being committed – including crimes against children. Individuals with a criminal background with access to children present an obvious risk to those children and others. However the state also has a duty to offenders to facilitate their reintegration into society and to have respect for their privacy. There is a clear tension between protecting children from risk and ensuring that a particular class of people is not discriminated against in an unjustifiable way. There are a number of a devices designed to balance these competing interests.

Rehabilitation of Offenders Act 1974

The Rehabilitation of Offenders Act 1974 makes provision for people to be treated, as a matter of law, as persons of good character after certain periods of time have elapsed since they were convicted of certain offences. The conviction becomes spent and can only be referred to in limited circumstances. Section 7 of the 1974 Act places limitations on rehabilitation including that the requirement as to spent convictions (i.e. those in relation to which the time bar has come into effect) shall not affect the determination of any issue, nor prevent the admission of any evidence relating to someone's previous conviction in any proceedings:

- under the inherent jurisdiction of the High Court
- under the Children Act 1989
- relating to the discharge or variation of a supervision order; or
- for the making of a sex offenders order, below.

Vetting

It is a risk, inherent in all direct services to children, that there may be a danger of exposing a child to harm caused through the actions or omissions of a particular individual engaged in providing those services. In particular, the Sex Offender Register, sex offender order and reforms to the protection of children in Part II of the Criminal Justice and Court Services Act 2000 were designed to make it easier to prevent unsuitable people from working with children. They reflect the international duty on the state to take measures to protect children from exploitation and abuse and are supplemented by measures to facilitate recovery and reintegration of children who have so suffered as victims.

Sex Offender Register

A person of any age cautioned or convicted of a specified offence[4] is required to register with the police in accordance with section 1 Sex

---

[4] Under section 7 Sex Offenders Act 1997 this may include offences committed outside the United Kingdom.

Offenders Act 1997. The period during which the requirement to register remains in force depends upon the sentence received for the offence giving rise to the requirement to register and ranges from five years to an indefinite period. Whilst subject to the requirement to register the person concerned must notify the police of:

- his or her name and any name he or she uses;
- his or her home address; and
- any address where he or she is staying for a period of 14 days or more.

Failure to register is an offence punishable on conviction by up to five years imprisonment, a fine or both. Schedule 1 to the 1997 Act details the offences to which the requirements to register apply and in so far as England and Wales is concerned this includes:

- rape;
- intercourse with a girl under 13;
- intercourse with a girl between 13 and 16;
- incest by a man;
- buggery;
- indecency between men;
- indecent assault on a woman;
- indecent assault on a man;
- assault with intent to commit buggery;
- causing or encouraging prostitution of, intercourse with or indecent assault on, a girl under 16;
- indecent conduct towards a young child;
- inciting a girl under 16 to have incestuous sexual intercourse;
- certain offences relating to the fraudulent importation of certain material; and
- possession of indecent photographs of children.

However the requirements to register as a sex offender do not apply where the offences of intercourse with a girl between 13 and 16, buggery and indecency between men were committed by an offender aged under 20 or where the victim was 18 or over except in the cases of rape or unlawful sexual intercourse.[5]

Sex offender order
Under section 2 Crime and Disorder Act 1998 the chief officer of police may apply to the magistrates' court sitting in its civil jurisdiction for a sex offender order. The application may only be made where:

---

[5] By way of lacuna in the law an adult who receives a caution from the police in respect of a relevant offence is required to sign the Sex Offender Register whereas a person convicted by a court but receiving a conditional discharge is not.

- the person is a sex offender; [6] and
- that person has acted in such a way as to give reasonable cause to believe that an order is necessary to protect the public from serious harm from him or her.

A sex offender order may be until further order and in any event cannot be for less than five years. Whilst it is in force the person subject to it is subject to the requirements of registration which apply under section 1 Sex Offences Act 1997. The order may contain any condition which appears to the court to be necessary to protect the public from serious harm from the individual concerned. Failure to comply with the terms of a sex offender order is punishable by imprisonment of up to five years, a fine or both.

THE CRIMINAL JUSTICE AND COURT SERVICES ACT 2000

Part II of the Criminal Justice and Court Services Act 2000 introduced measures which aim to establish an integrated system for the protection of children. Explanatory notes available from the House of Commons website explain the provisions and the advice goes on to say that:

> Under this system those 'who come to notice', either when working with children or by commission of a serious criminal offence against a child, as posing a risk to children may, after a proper process, be made subject to a statutory ban on 'working with children'. This builds on the provisions of the Education Reform Act 1988, the Education Act 1996 and the Protection of Children Act 1999.
>
> Part V of the Police Act 1997 provided for a new criminal record system to be established which would provide three different levels of certification according to the authority of the individual requesting the information and purpose of the requirement. This will be managed by a new Criminal Records Bureau. The Protection of Children Act 1999 provides for the Criminal Records Bureau to include information from the lists of those banned by the Secretary of State in the two higher level certificates. It also provides for the further positions prescribed by the Secretary of State to be added to those areas where information on those banned by the Secretary of State may be requested. This will permit the full scope of the new definition of working with children . . . to be covered.
>
> This part sets out that, where an individual is identified as being unsuitable to work with children, that individual should, after due process, be banned from such work. The Education Reform Act 1988, the Education Act 1996 and the Protection of Children Act 1999 provide for lists to be kept by the Secretary of State or National Assembly for Wales of individuals banned from working with children in organizations in the area of

---

[6] A person is a sex offender if he or she has been convicted of an offence to which Part I of the Sex Offences Act 1997 applies: section 3 Crime and Disorder Act 1998.

healthcare, social services and education. The new measures will provide a further way to ban unsuitable people from working with children. They provide that those who commit a serious offence against a child can be banned by a disqualification order by a judge from all such work as part of their sentence or the disposal of their case. The measures also provide a . . . review process for those subject to a ban, whether imposed by the Secretary of State or a judge

This part . . . further provides that those identified as unsuitable to work with children and banned from working with children under any of the specified methods, should be subject to criminal sanctions if they breach the ban. It will also be an offence for someone to offer the opportunity to work with children to an individual whom they know is subject to disqualification from such work.

The provisions include a new and comprehensive definition of 'working with children' to enable all such areas of work to be covered by the ban. This will apply to work with children in all services, including voluntary work and irrespective of whether the work is paid or unpaid. Those banned by the Secretary of State will also be banned from all areas covered by the new definition.

Under the Police Act 1997, as amended by the Protection of Children Act 1999, access to information about those banned by whatever means will be available as part of criminal and enhanced criminal records certificates when certificates are sought in respect of working with children, once the Criminal Records Bureau is in operation

CHILDREN PROCEEDINGS AND CHILD RELATED SERVICES

As far as the provision of services to children under the Children Act 1989 and other family proceedings legislation is concerned the following guidance deals with the issue of access to children by those with a criminal background:

- Home Office Circular 9 (HOC) 88/1982, 'Disclosure of Convictions to Probation Officers and Social Workers Preparing Welfare Reports for the Courts Determining Care and Custody of Children'
- HOC 105/1982, 'Disclosure of Convictions to Local Authorities in Respect of Prospective Childminders'
- HOC 47/1993, 'Protection of Children: Disclosure of Criminal Background of those with Access to Children'
- HOC 42/1994, 'Protection of Children: Disclosure of Criminal Background to Voluntary Sector Organizations'; and
- HOC 43/1997, 'Police Checks on Staff Working in Registered Private Children's Homes and Small Unregistrable Children's Homes'.

In HOC 47/1993 the general principles of disclosure were summarised as follows:

Recent cases of abuse of children by staff entrusted with their care have focused attention on the need for careful selection and recruitment. There has been a growing awareness of the need to establish identity, take up references, interview carefully and supervise staff effectively after appointment. Our knowledge of the value of criminal record checks has been enhanced by the evaluation of three experimental schemes testing disclosure of criminal records to voluntary organizations. This indicated that criminal record checks were of most importance where the children being cared for were most vulnerable or where supervision was difficult or impossible, but generally of less importance where adults were working together or with larger groups of less vulnerable children (although the need to maintain effective management and supervision of staff in such circumstances is no less important).

SEXUAL ABUSE

One of the major influences on the development of the Children Act 1989 was the *Report of the Inquiry into Child Abuse in Cleveland* (1987) (the Butler-Sloss report). This report was shortly followed by the inquiry into ritual sex abuse in the Orkneys and as recently as February 2000 the inquiry into the abuse of children in residential care in North Wales (the Waterhouse report) was published. Other similar inquiries continue across the UK.[7]

There is clearly a duty on the state through the local authority to investigate the circumstances of a child where it is believed that he or she may have been the subject of sexual abuse, or is at risk of the same. The duty extends to removing the child from those circumstances where the abuse has or may take place. In terms of the powers available to a local authority the Children Act 1989 provides short, medium and long-term solutions.[8]

The investigation of allegations of the sexual abuse of children by a member of the family can raise sensitive issues. The investigation by the local authority may also overlap with a concurrent criminal investigation. HOC 52/1988 on the 'Investigation of Child Sexual Abuse' provides the starting point for any investigation. *Working Together Under the Children Act 1989* also provides guidance to assist in the proper investigation of allegations of sexual abuse.

One of the major difficulties in gathering evidence in cases of sexual abuse is the ability of the child to provide the primary evidence of abuse. Where there is any prospect of criminal proceedings arising out of the investigation it would be usual to have the child interviewed in accordance with the *Memorandum of Good Practice on Video Recorded*

---

[7] e.g. Forde Parke, Devon covering over 20 years of alleged institutional abuse.
[8] See *Chapter 7.*

Interviews with Child Witnesses for Criminal Proceedings.[9] It would also be usual to seek leave for a full medical examination of the child to be carried out at the earliest possible stage in the investigations. The pitfalls for a hasty or over-enthusiastic investigation are many and not all techniques are appropriate to gather the evidence needed. Appellate courts have expressed concern in a number of cases, for example about the misuse of anatomical dolls.[10] Similarly difficulties may arise in the function of the clinician involved with a child in such circumstances. In *Re M (a Minor) (Child Abuse: Evidence)*[11] Mr Justice Latey considered the implications of interviewing techniques originally developed for the therapy of sexually abused children to detect cases of sexual abuse.

The balance to be struck within the legal system is basically one of fairness. The duty on the state to protect a child from sexual abuse cannot properly outweigh the need to ensure that any investigation of it or criminal or civil proceedings arising from it are fair; fair to the victim and to the alleged perpetrator. Where a child has been interviewed and it is proposed to adduce the evidence of that interview the following matters bear on the issue of fairness:[12]

- whether the child should have been called to give evidence personally;
- whether informed consent was given to the interview by the child or his or her parent;
- whether the interview was video-recorded or audio-recorded and whether there is a transcript of this;
- whether appropriate leave has been granted by the court;
- the purpose of the interview (i.e. diagnostic, therapeutic or forensic);
- the experience of the persons conducting the interview;
- the venue and timing of the interview;
- the danger of pressuring a child by lengthy or repeated interviewing against the likely reluctance of a child to tell his or her whole story in one sitting;
- the existence or otherwise of a spontaneous statement by the child;
- the child's age, maturity and understanding especially in terms of his or her sexual awareness and comprehension;
- the use of leading questions;
- whether the child was given the opportunity to deny that any abuse had taken place;
- any apparent presumption by the interviewer that the abuse had taken place; and
- the use of dolls, drawings or other aids to communication.

---

[9] HMSO, 1992. This provides detailed guidance on the circumstances in which children should be interviewed, how the interview should be conducted and describes the kind of questions which nest elicit accurate testimony from children.

[10] See *Re Z (Minors) (Child Abuse: Evidence)* (1998) FCR 440.

[11] (1988) FCR 47.

[12] After Clarke, Hall and Morrison, 1/990.

The burden of proof under the Children Act re sexual abuse
The burden of showing that a child has suffered abuse or neglect lies with the local authority and the standard is the standard of proof applicable to all forms of civil proceedings, that is to say upon a balance of probabilities. In the case of sexual abuse there is no different standard of proof, however the more serious the allegation the more cogent is the evidence required to overcome the unlikelihood of what is alleged and thus to prove it.[13]

The burden of proof in criminal proceedings involving sexual abuse
There is no distinct offence of sexually abusing a child. However the sexual abuse of children is generally covered by the range of offences set out in the Sexual Offences Act 1956 (and see above). In criminal proceedings, the burden of proof lies with the prosecutor and is always to the same high standard, that is to say the he or she must prove their case beyond reasonable doubt. The rules of evidence governing a criminal trial are generally more exacting than those regulating civil proceedings under the Children Act 1989.[14] Research in 1999[15] identified a number of flaws in the present arrangements for the use of evidence from children in criminal proceedings. Where someone has been acquitted in criminal proceedings of offences arising out of child abuse it remains open to the family proceedings court to make its own findings on the underlying facts which gave rise to the allegation and the court is not prevented from making adverse findings which are apparently in contradiction of the jury's decision.[16] There is no requirement that family proceedings be delayed to await the outcome of a related criminal trial, although there may be circumstances where it is in the best interests of the child to do so.[17]

CHILDREN GIVING EVIDENCE

A child may wish to give evidence in the course of proceedings either as a party to them or as a witness to the issues at trial. In family proceedings and in criminal proceedings a child witness is both competent and compellable. However the legal system has recognised the need to treat children differently from adults and accordingly a number of special rules apply regulating the conditions in which a child's evidence is presented.[18] The aim of the rules is to balance the right of the child to

---

[13] *In Re H (Minors) (Sexual Abuse: Standard of Proof)* (1996) 1 FCR 509.
[14] For example, hearsay evidence is admissible in family proceedings but generally inadmissable in criminal proceedings, subject to certain exceptions.
[15] Davis *et al.*, *An Assessment of the Admissibility and Sufficiency of Evidence in Child Abuse Prosecutions*, Home Office, 1999.
[16] See *Re G (A Minor) (Care Proceedings)* (1994) 2 FCR 216.
[17] See *Re TB (Care Proceedings: Criminal Trial)* (1996) 1 FCR 101.
[18] Consistent with this has been the development of a Child Witness Support Schemes on a local level and the national monitoring of child witnesses across the UK.

testify and the right of a party to proceedings to be able to call a child witness against any risk to the child's welfare.

Fairness
The starting point for all trials is the right to a fair trial guaranteed by Article 6 of the European Convention On Human Rights. The right to a fair trial includes a number of specific guarantees in relation to both criminal and civil proceedings. These include the rights to:

- a public hearing
- call witnesses in one's own behalf
- test witnesses giving evidence against oneself
- defend oneself either in person or through legal representation; and
- equality of arms: implying that no one party to proceedings should be at a procedural or substantive disadvantage in the conditions in which he or she presents his or her case—including his or her evidence—vis-à-vis an opponent.[19]

The right to a fair trial is a limited right (see *Chapter 3*) and one of the limitations relates to the interests of juveniles. It is clear from the words of the Article itself that the right to a public hearing may be limited where it is in the interests of juveniles for the press to be excluded from part or all of the trial. In searching for the extent of the limits to the right to a fair trial the Court of Human Rights has carefully to weigh the rights of the accused against the interests of child parties and witnesses.

Children as witnesses
As already indicated, in criminal proceedings a child is competent and compellable as a witness, he or she may give evidence in a trial and if he or she is under 14 years of age this will be given unsworn.[20] The requirement that unsworn evidence must be corroborated was abolished by section 34 Criminal Justice Act 1988. It is no longer necessary or appropriate for a court to hear expert evidence[21] on the ability of a child to give evidence: so long as his or her evidence is capable of being understood it is admissible. The weight attaching to the evidence of younger children may however not be great.

A witness summons may be issued against a child in criminal proceedings but it is for the trial judge to decide whether the harm to the party seeking to call the child is outweighed by the interests of the child. In such a case the judge seemingly has power to prevent the child from giving evidence.[22]

---

[19] *Dombo Beheer BV v. Netherlands* (1994) 18 EHRR 213.
[20] Section 33A Criminal Justice Act 1988.
[21] *G v. DPP* [1997] 2 All ER 755 .
[22] *R v. Highbury Corner Magistrates' Court, ex parte D* (1997) 2 FCR 568.

The use of screens

In order to protect a child witness in certain proceedings, section 37 Children and Young Persons Act 1933 allows the court to be cleared while a child or young person gives evidence. Similarly, to protect a child witness from intimidation it is appropriate in the right case to use screens to conceal him or her from the defendant during a trial. However the use of screens is not a practice to be generally followed and - as part of a defendant's right to a fair trial - a hearing should usually be conducted without such concessions. It is important that the judge, jury (or magistrates), and prosecuting and defence counsel are able to see the child and to assess the manner in which his or her evidence is given.[23]

TV links and video-recordings

An alternative method of protecting child witnesses from the rigours of an appearance in the courtroom is provided by section 32 Criminal Justice Act 1988 which provides for the use of television links. The court's leave to use a television link is required and the procedure only applies to a limited range of offences generally involving assault, cruelty or sexual offences against a child. The procedure may apply to any witness and not only the victim of such an offence. The purpose in using a television link is to minimise the trauma to the child who would otherwise need to give evidence from the witness box in court and confront the accused in person. Rules of court provide govern a detailed procedure for the use of television links in both the magistrates' court and the Crown Court.[24]

In certain criminal proceedings the testimony of a child witness may have been video recorded during the course of the investigation. Section 32A Criminal Justice Act 1988 provides for the admission of such video evidence in a trial. The use of such testimony arises in relation to the trial of the same offences covered in section 32 of the Act and again Rules of Court have been made to detail the finer points of procedure.[25] The conduct of interviews with children in contemplation of criminal proceedings requires a degree of experience and considerable sensitivity on behalf of the interviewer.

The power to permit video evidence to be given was inserted into the Criminal Justice Act 1988 by the Criminal Justice Act 1991 as a result of recommendations made by the Pigot Committee in 1989. The statutory procedure does not match the recommendations and has been disparagingly called 'Half Pigot'. In a report conducted on behalf of the Home Office by Bristol University, amendments to current practice were proposed.[26] Similarly a report from the Home Office Policing and Reducing Crime Unit focused further attention on the flaws in present

---

[23] *R v. DIX, SCY, GCZ* (1989) 91 Cr App Rep 36.

[24] For example the *Magistrates' Courts (Children and Young Persons) Rules* 1992 Rule 23.

[25] *Ibid*, Rule 24. As far as the Crown Court is concerned see *Practice Note* [1992] 3 All ER 909.

[26] See note 14 above.

practice and may foreshadow additional reforms as part of the government's policy of speeding up justice.[27]

Other considerations

Where the attendance of a child before a court would involve serious danger to his or her life or health,[28] section 42 Children and Young Persons Act 1933 confers power on a justice of the peace to take a sworn deposition from him or her. Section 43 of the same Act makes provision for the admission of such a deposition in a trial. This procedure is rarely used. The Criminal Justice Act 1998 and the Criminal Justice and Youth Evidence Act 1999 make provision for the use of evidence admitted by way of video testimony or forensic testimony by video link or conferencing. A juvenile can therefore be allowed to give evidence in court from a protective environment free from the intimidation of the courtroom without adversely interfering with a defendant's right to test evidence or confront witnesses against him.

Family proceedings

In family proceedings a child is competent and compellable. In public law proceedings his or her voice is usually heard through the children's guardian and in private law proceedings through the children and family reporter. It is incumbent upon the court to take into account the feelings and wishes of the child in discharging its function under the welfare checklist (*Chapter 7*). Again there are no specific age requirements and provided his or her evidence can be understood it is admissible.[29] A witness summons may be sought against a child in family proceedings but it may be refused if it would be oppressive or not conducive to the child's welfare.[30]

Where a child is a party to proceedings the minimum rights of effective participation guaranteed by Article 6 of the European Convention will have to be carefully considered by a judge tempted to prevent a *Gillick* competent child (*Chapter 1*) from giving evidence himself or herself rather than relying upon the voice given to him or her by the children and family reporter and the children's guardian.

Where the child is a ward of court

In both family and criminal proceedings the leave of the court appears to be required to interview a child as a prospective witness who is a ward of court. Where criminal proceedings are conducted by the Crown Prosecution Service this requirement may be relaxed.[31]

---

[27] Davies and Westcott, *Interviewing Child Witnesses under the Memorandum of Good Practice: A Research Review*, Paper 115 in the Police Research Series. 1999.

[28] The proposition must be established by the evidence of a qualified medical practitioner.

[29] Section 96 Children Act 1989.

[30] *R v. B County Council, ex parte P* [1991] 2 All ER 65.

[31] *Re K (Minors) (Wardship: Criminal Proceedings)* [1988] 1 All ER 214.

PUBLICITY IN PROCEEDINGS INVOLVING CHILDREN

As a general rule reporting proceedings involving children is unlawful. The purpose behind this rule is to protect the interests of the child concerned and it extends to both criminal and family proceedings. The rule is also an exception to the general requirement that trials take place in public. Article 6 of the European Convention On Human Rights guarantees the right to a public hearing as a crucial aspect of a fair trial. In the Court of Human Right's view, publicity is conducive to fairness and provides one of the means by which public confidence in the courts and the legal system may be maintained.[32] However the right to a public hearing is a limited right (*Chapter 3*):

> Article 6(1) The press and public may be excluded from all or part of the trial in the interest of morals, public order or national security in a democratic society, where the interests of juveniles or the protection of the private life of the parties so require, or to the extent strictly necessary in the opinion of the court in special circumstances where publicity would prejudice the interests of justice.

The reporting of criminal proceedings in a youth court (or appeal arising therefrom) is governed by section 49 Children and Young Persons Act 1933 which allows publicity only where the court permits it. The court may only do so:

- where it is satisfied that it is in the public interest to do so in relation to a child who has been convicted of an offence (the 'naming and shaming' provision);
- where it is satisfied that it is appropriate to do so in order to avoid an injustice to the child; or
- on application on notice by the DPP where a child is unlawfully at large having been charged or convicted of an offence punishable by imprisonment of 14 years or more and the court is satisfied that it is necessary to do so for the purpose of apprehending him or her to bring him or her before a court or to return him or her to the place where he or she was in custody.

Where a child is involved in any other proceedings before any court other than a youth court, section 39 Children and Young Persons Act 1933 empowers the court to prohibit the publication of anything likely to lead to the identification of the child. The prohibition extends to the publication of any picture of the child. The court has a discretion to make such an order and may grant leave for its terms to be varied. As a rule of natural justice it is good practice for a court considering whether to make

---

[32] *Axen v. Germany* (1984) 6 EHRR 195.

an order under this section to allow the press to make representations on the issue and on the terms of any order so made.

The right of the press to publish details of cases where children are involved arises from Article 6 of the European Convention, where public scrutiny is regarded as a crucial element of a fair trial and from Article 10 of the Convention which provides for freedom of expression and freedom of access to information. The latter right is a qualified right and may be restricted (in this context by an order under section 39, above) only where it is necessary in a democratic society to do so. Accordingly the poor practice of making prohibition orders whenever a child is involved in proceedings may require revisiting in order to balance the risk of harm to the child against the public interest in the proper and full reporting of proceedings.

In family proceedings the rules governing publicity are contained in section 97 Children Act 1989 which prohibits the publication of any material which is intended or likely to identify any child as being involved in any proceedings in the High Court, a county court or a magistrates' court, or the address or school of any such child. Section 71 Magistrates' Courts Act 1980 makes similar but more detailed provision prohibiting the newspaper reporting of family proceedings. In any event members of the press are not permitted under section 69 of the same Act to be present in family proceedings courts.

The Broadcasting Act 1990 makes identical provision to prohibit the reporting of any proceedings covered by either the Children and Young Persons Act 1933, the Magistrates' Courts Act 1980 or the Children Act 1989. The reporting of proceedings through the Internet may be a violation of these provisions. A more practical problem is one of control and at the time of writing significant concern had been expressed in the media concerning the likelihood that the identity of the killers of Jamie Bulger would be revealed by internet disclosure by individuals operating outside the jurisdiction of the English courts within which such disclosure is currently prohibited.[33]

The protection of children as victims in private law and public law family proceedings

In public law proceedings under the Children Act 1989 (*Chapter 9*) children are most likely to appear as the victims of abuse or neglect or as a result of being beyond parental control. The powers available to protect such children at risk are considered in *Chapter 7*.

In private law proceedings children are again most likely to appear as the subject of parental dispute. Whether it is appropriate to describe children of families experiencing breakdown as victims is at best a moot point. However in order to protect a child's right to have his or her upbringing regulated and to fulfil his or her legitimate expectation of contact and maintaining the bond between his or her blood family the courts are often required to intervene and to make decisions according to their perception of the child's welfare. To this extent the position of a

---

[33] However the nature of the Internet is such that regulation may prove very difficult.

child may be best described as equivalent to that of a victim for the purposes of this treatment of the subject. In a very real sense a child in marital or quasi-marital breakdown may be a victim where there are elements of domestic violence or intimidation present in the family's background[34]. The powers available to the courts to protect children in private law are considered in detail in *Chapter 7*.

---

[34] See for example the Advisory Board on Family Law: Children Act Sub-Committee, *A Report to the Lord Chancellor on the Question of Parental Contact in Cases where there is Domestic Violence*, 1999.

CHAPTER 6

Safeguards for Children as Offenders

Any discussion of children as offenders can now only be fully understood in the light of the responsibility and authority of the Youth Justice Board for England and Wales and local youth offending teams (YOTs) as established by the Crime and Disorder Act 1998. As indicated in *Chapter 4* these agencies play a pivotal role nationally and locally in delivering youth justice – as does the now statutory principal purpose of youth justice – preventing offending.

Principles into action
Under the auspices of the Youth Justice Board the principles and aims of youth justice translate into six key objectives which all contributors to the youth justice system are asked to reflect in the way they plan, carry out and monitor their work, as appropriate to their individual roles and responsibilities:

- the swift administration of justice so that every young person accused of breaking the law has the matter resolved without delay[1]
- confronting young offenders with the consequences of their offending, for themselves and their family, their victims and the community and helping them to develop a sense of personal responsibility
- intervention which tackles the particular factors (personal, family, social, educational or health) that put the juvenile at risk of offending and which strengthens protective factors
- punishment proportionate to the seriousness and persistence of the offending
- encouraging reparation to victims by young offenders; and
- reinforcing the responsibilities of parents.

These clear aims and objectives provide the philosophical framework against which the procedural aspects of the youth court operate. In addition the procedure in the youth court is designed to reflect the age, maturity and comprehension of those appearing before it. One of the major complaints against the UK in *T v. UK* and *V v. UK*[2] was the lack of effective participation engendered by the procedure and practices adopted in the Crown Court. The conduct of proceedings should be such as to promote the child's ability to understand and participate in the case taking into account his or her intellectual and emotional capacities.

---

[1] Especially in the case of persistent young offenders or 'spree' offenders.
[2] See under the heading 'The Crown Court in relation to the youth court' later in this chapter.

INTERNATIONAL OBLIGATIONS

The concept of a child offender as a victim (as in other situations described in *Chapter 5*) may be controversial, but it is beyond argument that a child accused of an offence requires protection. Procedural safeguards exist under Article 6 of the European Convention to ensure that a child receives a fair trial and recourse may be had to other international codes which both emphasise and inspire additional safeguards to be developed. For example the introduction of the referral panel order (see later in this chapter) under the Youth Justice and Criminal Evidence Act 1999 mirrors a number of international obligations to divert children from the criminal courts rather than to prosecute and sentence them.

This apart, there is a difficult balance to be struck between punishment and rehabilitation in the case of a child who offends. Society has an expectation that measures will be taken to protect it from offenders and the state itself has a duty to divert children away from crime - and where this is unsuccessful to provide a system in which the child may be appropriately punished as well as rehabilitated, the victim adequately compensated and the community protected from his or her conduct. An overarching principle is the welfare principle (*Chapter 7*), reflecting the balance to be struck between these competing interests.

Measures available to deal with child offending must be sufficiently flexible to take into account the age, maturity and understanding of the offender and the risk he or she presents to himself or herself and to the community at large. The importance of developing systems that adequately meet such obligations and provide for child offenders is recognised in a number of international codes including the:

- UN Convention On the Rights of the Child;
- UN Guidelines for the Prevention of Juvenile Delinquency (The Riyadh Guidelines);
- UN Standard Minimum Rules for the Administration of Juvenile Justice ('The Beijing Rules');
- UN Rules For the Protection of Juveniles Deprived of their Liberty; and
- European Convention On Human Rights.

Chapter 3 of this book provides a general overview of these international treaties and their broad contents. The UN Convention On the Rights of the Child lays down the minimum standards expected of national juvenile justice regimes. The Beijing Rules describe in more detail the minimum standards of procedure for the administration of such regimes. Together these treaties establish the practical arrangements for child offenders and accordingly are mentioned in more detail below.

The Riyadh Guidelines set out the state's obligations to take measures to prevent juvenile delinquency. The principles emerging from the guidelines cover social policies, family policies and education policies aimed at creating a child orientated environment in which government measures secure the stable and safe upbringing of children free from delinquency. The UN Rules For the Protection of Juveniles Deprived of their Liberty set out in international law the minimum standards required in the use of the secure estate to accommodate child offenders. Together, the rights and freedoms established by these international treaties provide a framework for the special protection of children within a state's criminal legal system. The treaties provide a series of principles which, whilst not directly enforceable in the UK provide a standard against which a proper assessment of national arrangements can be made.

The European Convention On Human Rights - whilst containing no specific child rights - applies as much to children as it does to adults (*Chapter 3*). Accordingly, children may engage certain rights and freedoms as their rights are dealt with by the various public authorities involved in the delivery of youth justice.

UN Convention On the Rights of the Child
The UN Convention contains specific guarantees in respect of the state's international obligation as regards the child's rights as they arise in criminal proceedings. Article 40 is set out in *Chapter 5*. The Convention does not attempt to describe a model system of youth justice and nation states are left individually to translate the minimum standards into practice in accordance with their own legal and social traditions.

The Beijing Rules
The Beijing Rules provide a more detailed approach to the subject but again are not prescriptive, but rather identify internationally accepted principles. They provide a common starting point for the administration of youth justices. The full contents of the Beijing Rules are set out in *Chapter 3* and the most important principles explored in more detail in this chapter.[3]

Article 5 of the Beijing Rules sets out the aims of juvenile justice, a principle of heightened relevance in the UK following section 37 Crime and Disorder Act 1998, which, for the first time, identifies a principal national aim for youth justice. Article 5 provides:

> 5.1 The juvenile justice system shall emphasise the well-being of the juvenile and shall ensure that any reaction to juvenile offenders shall always be in proportion to the circumstances of both the offender and the offence.

By contrast section 37 of the 1998 Act provides:

> 37(1) It shall be the principal aim of the youth justice system to prevent offending by children and young persons.

---

[3] The UN Web-site (www.unitednations.org\) provides access to both the text of, and a commentary on, the Beijing Rules.

(2) In addition to any other duty to which they are subject, it shall be the duty of all persons and bodies carrying out functions in relation to the youth justice system to have regard to this aim.

The two principles recognised in the Beijing Rules are however reflected in the national youth justice system. The well-being of the child translates into the welfare principle set out in the Children Act 1989 and in section 44(1) Children and Young Persons Act 1933 which provides:

Every court in dealing with a child or young person who is brought before it, either as an offender or otherwise, shall have regard to the welfare of the child or young person, and shall in a proper case take steps for removing him from undesirable surroundings, and for securing that proper provision is made for his education and training.

Proportionality
The principle of proportionality is described in the UN's commentary as follows:

This principle is well-known as an instrument for curbing punitive sanctions, mostly expressed in terms of just deserts in relation to the gravity of the offence. The response to young offenders should be based on the consideration not only of the gravity of the offence but also of personal circumstances. The individual circumstances of the offender (for example social status, family situation, the harm caused by the offence or other factors affecting personal circumstances) should influence the proportionality of the reactions (for example by having regard to the offender's endeavour to indemnify the victim or his or her willingness to turn to wholesome and useful life).

Proportionality is reflected in the sentencing framework established under the Criminal Justice Act 1991.[4] Thus a community penalty may only be imposed on an offender where the offence is *serious enough* for such a sentence. Detention may only be imposed where the offence is *so serious that only a custodial sentence can be justified.* In assessing the seriousness of an offence the court is required to take into account aggravating factors and mitigating factors based on the circumstances of the offence and the offender.[5] Remorse and credit for a timely acceptance of responsibility are matters which, other things being equal, entitle an offender to a reduction in sentence, whilst the introduction of aspects of restorative justice under the Crime and Disorder Act 1998 goes some way towards the principle of indemnity.

---

[4] Now consolidated in the Powers of Criminal Courts (Sentencing) Act 2000 but also currently under review: see *Making Punishments Work: Report of a Review of the Sentencing Framework for England and Wales* (London: Home Office, 2001).
[5] Often described as 'offence mitigation' and 'offender mitigation'.

Discretion

The Beijing Rules make provision for the exercise of discretion at all stages of the criminal justice process, the basic rights of children in the investigative process, prosecution, detention pending trial, trial, adjudication and disposition, non-institutional treatment and treatment within the secure estate. The rights of a child to a fair and just hearing are similar in extent to the rights established by Article 6 of the European Convention and enforceable through the Human Rights Act 1998. Article 17 of the Beijing Rules sets out the guiding principles in adjudication and disposition. It provides:

> 17.1 The disposition of the competent authority shall be guided by the following principles:
>
> (a) The reaction taken shall always be in proportion not only to the circumstances and gravity of the offence but also to the circumstances and the needs of the juvenile as well as to the needs of the society;
> (b) Restrictions on the personal liberty of the juvenile shall be imposed only after careful consideration and shall be limited to the possible minimum;
> (c) Deprivation of personal liberty shall not be imposed unless the juvenile is adjudicated of a serious act involving violence against another person or of persistence in committing other serious offences and unless there is no other appropriate response;
> (d) The well-being of the juvenile shall be the guiding factor in the consideration of his or her case.

The UN commentary remarks:

> The main difficulty in formulating guidance for the adjudication of young persons stems from the fact that there are unresolved conflicts of a philosophical nature, such as the following:
>
> • Rehabilitation versus just desert;
> • Assistance versus repression and punishment;
> • Reaction according to the singular merits of an individual case versus reaction according to the protection of society in general;
> • General deterrence versus individual incapacitation.
> • The conflict between these approaches is more pronounced in juvenile cases than in adult cases. With the variety of causes and reactions characterising juvenile cases, these alternatives become intricately interwoven.

Sentences

As far as the range of sentence dispositions is concerned the Beijing Rules merely enumerate some of the important responses and sanctions which have proved successful in different legal systems. Again the list is neither exhaustive nor prescriptive but provides an inventory of sentencing disposals which should be available to deal with criminal behaviour. These include:

- care, guidance and supervision
- probation
- community service orders
- financial penalties, compensation and restitution
- intermediate treatment and other treatment orders
- orders to participate in group counselling and similar activities
- orders concerning foster care, living communities or other educational settings; and
- other relevant orders.

The power of a UK criminal court to make care orders was removed by the Children Act 1989 as was the power to make a care order solely on the grounds of facilitating a child's education. However a child beyond parental control and at risk of suffering significant harm may be removed into public care or placed in secure accommodation through proceedings under the Children Act 1989.[6]

Delay
Article 20 provides:

> 20.1 Each case shall from the outset be handled expeditiously, without any unnecessary delay.

The issue of delay in youth court proceedings has troubled the government in recent times. Youth courts are presently under scrutiny to ensure that cases are dealt with swiftly but fairly. The target time set by the government for the completion of proceedings in the case of persistent offenders - from the date of arrest to sentence - is 71 days. Many courts endeavouring to meet this target have set themselves a shorter period of time.[7]

The European Convention On Human Rights
A child involved with the youth justice system may engage the rights guaranteed by the European Convention. As already indicated, Article 6 provides for his or her right to a fair trial (a right enjoyed by all people concerned as defendant or as a party to civil proceedings). The particular minimum standards recognised by the Court of Human Rights as ensuring a fair trial largely meet the common approach set out in both the UN Convention On the Rights of the Child and the Beijing Rules. The trial of a youth before the Crown Court was the subject of a challenge in *T v. UK* and *V v. UK* (1999) 30 EHRR 121. The Court of Human Rights held that such a trial did not amount to inhuman or degrading treatment

---

[6] See *Chapter 7*.
[7] For example in Central Devon, the Youth Court User's Group has set a preferred target of 42 days monitored on a quarterly basis.

under Article 3 of the Convention but that overall the trial procedure was unfair and in breach of Article 6. At the same time the Court found that the tariff setting powers of the Home Secretary were incompatible with both Article 6 and Article 5(4) of the Convention see *Chapter 3*). Juveniles can still be tried in the Crown Court in certain circumstances (see later) but as a consequence of those rulings a *Practice Direction* has been issued to Crown Court judges detailing Convention compatible practices to be adopted in trials involving child defendants.[8] This provides, for example, that the Crown Court should be set out in an informal way allowing children direct access to their counsel, that security officers should be dressed as civilians and that the officers of the court should refrain from wearing gowns and wigs. The aim of the direction is to model Crown Court proceedings on the successful and less intimidating surroundings of most modern youth courts.

Article 7 of the Convention prohibits punishment without law. It also prohibits the imposition of a heavier sentence than was available at the time the offence was committed. This article may have a surprising impact on the sentencing powers of the court in the case of a young offender who was aged 17 at the time of the offence but has turned 18 either by the time of his or her appearance or conviction. In an adult court such an offender may be detained for a minimum of 21 days in respect of imprisonable offences. In a youth court the minimum period of a detention and training order is four months and accordingly an offender may not be sentenced to a period of detention where the maximum sentence is less than four months. It would seem to follow that a 17-year-old committing an offence punishable with less than four months imprisonment[9] but dealt with in an adult court - by virtue of the passage of time so that they are no longer a juvenile - may be able to rely on Article 7 to pre-empt any purported a custodial sentence of less than four months being passed. An alternative approach is that the punishment has always been at large and that all that has changed is the defendant's age. This argument rejects the relevance of Article 7. Although this is but one example of an awaiting challenge pursuant to the Human Rights Act 1998, the English youth justice system does seem largely to accord with the Convention and other obligations detailed in international codes. The protection of children may be affected by observance of minimum standards of fairness, welfare and proportionality promoted by international obligations balanced against two principles in conflict: rehabilitation and just deserts.

ARREST, DETENTION AND INVESTIGATION

Young people suspected of committing criminal offences require special consideration. The Police and Criminal Evidence Act 1984 (PACE) and the Codes of Practice made under that Act make specific provision for the treatment of juvenile offenders. The general safeguards guaranteed

---

[8]   16 February 2000.

[9]   e.g. criminal damage of a value less than £5,000, obstructing a police officer etc.

by the Act and Codes in the case of an adult apply equally to juveniles. But there are extra safeguards.

For the purposes of the PACE Codes anyone appearing to be under 17 years of age must be treated as a juvenile in the absence of clear evidence to the contrary.[10] An offender aged 17 is treated as an adult for the purposes of PACE save to the extent that once charged he or she will appear in the youth court (assuming that he or she is still under 18) or is jointly charged to the adult court with an adult offender.

The specific safeguards in respect of a juvenile under the Act and Code C[11] are as follows:

- where a juvenile has been arrested, the arresting officer is under a duty to try to notify his or her parent[12]
- the interviewing of a juvenile should take place in the presence of an appropriate adult[13]
- a juvenile should not generally be detained in a police cell and should be frequently visited
- once charged with a criminal offence a juvenile should be transferred to local authority accommodation unless it is impracticable to do so, or no secure accommodation is available and without such accommodation the public may not be adequately protected from serious harm from the offender[14]
- a juvenile offender in police detention should be separated from adult offenders.

Interviewing a juvenile suspect

An interview of a juvenile suspected of committing a crime must take place under the further conditions prescribed in PACE and Code C. In addition to the general rights contained therein a juvenile should not be interviewed otherwise than in the presence of an appropriate adult. The role of the appropriate adult is more fully described in *Chapter 4* but this implies something more than the mere presence of an adult with responsibility towards the juvenile. The juvenile's general right to fair treatment may not be as well protected by the provision of a duty social worker by the local authority who may not be known to the child. Criticism of the way the appropriate adult scheme acts in the interests of a child's rights has been made.[15]

Juveniles may only be interviewed at their place of education in exceptional circumstances and with the leave of the school principal.

---

[10] Section 37(15) of PACE.

[11] Code of Practice for the Detention, Treatment and Questioning of Persons by Police Officers.

[12] Or the person responsible for his or her welfare or the local authority if he is accommodated by the local authority.

[13] See *Chapter 4*.

[14] See further NACRO Briefing Sheet, *Police Refusal of Bail and Transfer to Local Authority Accommodation*, March 2001.

[15] See, e.g. Pierpoint, H., *ChildRight*, December 1999.

Otherwise, interviews should be conducted at the police station in accordance with PACE.

The rights set out in PACE and the Codes accord in general terms with those aspects of fairness recognised by the Court of Human Rights under the fair trials provisions of Article 6 of the European Convention. Indeed, the statutory scheme provides for a raft of additional rights which in combination seek to guarantee the interests of the child. A substantial breach of the procedural rules relating to detention and questioning may result in the court exercising its discretion under section 78 of the Act to exclude evidence obtained thereby in a trial.[16] Where a child has made an admission of guilt in an interview it is for the prosecutor to show that it was not obtained as a result of anything said or done by the investigating officers.[17]

THE FINAL WARNING SYSTEM

On 1 June 2000 the Crime and Disorder Act 1998 introduced a new scheme for the diversion of juvenile offenders from court by way of a final warning system.[18] The scheme allows the police to impose either a reprimand or a final warning on a juvenile as an alternative to court proceedings where the offender has accepted responsibility for his or her actions. The objectives are to:

- end the discredited former practice of repeat cautioning and to provide a progressive response to offending behaviour
- ensure appropriate and effective action when a juvenile starts to offend so as to prevent re-offending; and
- ensure that juveniles who do re-offend after a final warning are dealt with quickly and effectively by the courts.

The responsibility for the decision-making process rests entirely with the police. An officer retains a very limited discretion to take informal action outside of the regime and only in exceptional circumstances. Where an officer decides that formal action is appropriate his or her options are to either reprimand, issue a warning or to charge the juvenile to appear in court.

Criteria
Before either a reprimand or a final warning may be considered four criteria must be met:

- there must be evidence against the young person sufficient to give a realistic prospect of conviction if he or she were to be prosecuted

---

[16] *R v. Sang* [1980] AC 402.

[17] Section 76 Police and Criminal Evidence Act 1984.

[18] Sections 65 and 66 Crime and Disorder Act 1998. This system replaced the former scheme of cautioning set out in HOC 18/1994.

- the young person must admit the offence
- the young person must not have been previously convicted of an offence; and
- it must not be in the public interest for the young person to be prosecuted.

In addition the statutory scheme and guidance provides for the following factors to be taken into consideration:

- first-time offenders should normally receive a reprimand for a less serious offence;
- second-time offenders who have been previously reprimanded cannot be given a further reprimand and should normally receive a final warning;
- second-time offenders who have already been finally warned should normally be charged to appear in court except where the new offence has been committed more than two years after the warning was administered and is not so serious that prosecution is required;
- third-time offenders who have received a reprimand and a final warning cannot be given a further reprimand and should not generally receive a further final warning. They should usually be charged to appear in court; and
- fourth-time offenders cannot be either reprimanded or warned. They must be charged to appear in court.

The key issues in deciding whether to charge, reprimand or warn other than the statutory considerations are the seriousness of the offence in question and the young person's offending history. Each case must be considered on its merits by the police officer responsible for making the decision and he or she must take into account the offender's circumstances, his or her age and maturity and any aggravating or mitigating factors. The decision is essentially one of quality in the first instance and provides for the degree of flexibility commensurate with the state's obligations in international law. It allows the officer to introduce a concept of proportionality between the offender, his or her offence and society's response to it. At the same time the community's right to be protected from criminality is respected by requiring the officer to exercise his or her discretion only to the extent that the final warning scheme allows.

A reprimand or final warning is not the appropriate response to the most serious indictable offences such as murder or rape and generally indictable offences are likely to be met by the juvenile being charged rather than diversion. The impact of the offence on the victim is also a matter to which the responsible officer must have regard in making his or her decision. The nature and extent of any harm or loss and, where it is possible to gauge them, the views of the victim about the offence are of equal importance. The Crime and Disorder Act 1998 affirms the government's commitment to making the role of the victim more central to the criminal justice system in general and the youth justice system in particular. Restorative justice - victim focused justice - is a common feature of many other legal systems in the world[19] but has been generally neglected in the UK. The requirement for the court to take into account the impact of crime on a victim when sentencing an offender, the introduction of measures such as reparation orders (see below) and the shift in underlying policy from offender to victim reflect a new approach and purpose for the criminal justice system.

Effect of a reprimand or final warning

A reprimand and a final warning may be cited in court in the same way a conviction can be. Once a final warning has been imposed the offender will be referred to his or her local youth offending team (YOT) as soon as practicable. Under this referral the juvenile will be assessed and arrangements made for him or her to participate in a rehabilitation programme. Failure to take part in the programme may also be cited in court.

The programme is designed to rehabilitate juveniles involved in crime and prevent them from re-offending. An assessment of the juvenile will be carried out by the YOT with a view to drawing up a suitable programme in discussion with him or her and his or her parents and others, as appropriate. A main aim of the rehabilitation plan is to address the offending behaviour and to prevent re-offending. The content of the plan will vary according to the circumstances of the offence and the offender and its intensity should be proportionate to the gravity of the criminal conduct. An element of reparation may be included within the plan under a final warning but only where the victim has given his or her consent both to the possibility and the particular reparation concerned.

THE REFERRAL SCHEME

The Youth Justice and Criminal Evidence Act 1999 introduced the referral panel order[20] as a disposal available to the youth court in the case of a child appearing before it for the first time - and pleading guilty to an offence or offences. The scheme requires the court to make a referral order in every such case unless – at either extreme – the offence merits an absolute discharge or is so serious that only a custodial sentence can be justified. The referral order may be made for three, six, nine, or 12 months and places the child under the jurisdiction of the panel.

The referral panel and its functions

The referral panel comprises both professional and lay members[21] and is established under the auspices of the YOT. It is tasked with devising an

---

[19] See, generally, *Restoring Respect for Justice,* Wright M, Winchester: Waterside Press, 1999.

[20] The term 'referral order' is commonplace and is used in what follows.

[21] The involvement of lay members invites the comment that the system appears to erode the traditional role of the lay magistracy, and imposes quite significant training demands on yet another level of voluntary part-time personnel.

intervention plan for the child subject to the order. The plan becomes the regime to which the child is then subject for the period specified in the youth court's order. The plan may include elements of reparation and behavioural work and make provision for welfare issues such as accommodation, benefit concerns and education to be addressed. The child and the panel meet on a regular basis to monitor and supervise the sentence. If the child fails to comply with the terms of the plan there are powers permitting breach action to be taken before the panel which may, in accordance with national standards, return the child to the youth court for sentence.

The referral order shares characteristics with other methods of diversion. It is likely to follow either a reprimand or final warning and the involvement of the YOT at that earlier stage – and it partly fills the gulf between diversion and court proceedings. The juvenile loses his or her good name due to the conviction being recorded but the contract (a term used by YOTs) to which he or she is then made subject provides for intensive supervision by a quasi-judicial body than a sentence of a court. Hopefully, the principal aim of the youth justice system – preventing offending – is also more likely to be achieved by this high level of tutelage and supervision in that the intervention plan is inevitably going to address the issue of offending behaviour. The contents of that plan are therefore crucial to the success or otherwise of the post-conviction diversion scheme and require skill and care in their drafting.

The referral order process is consistent with the international obligations discussed earlier in this text in that states are required to have available a range of options to deal with children who offend, short of traditional punitive and therefore exclusionary disposals. Moving the focus of the operation of a sentence from the court to a panel has the appearance of creating just such an inclusionary option.

THE YOUTH COURT

As already indicated, the youth court before which a first-time offender appears has no discretion in the matter and must make a referral order unless punishment is inexpedient to the extent of an absolute discharge or where the case is only suitable for a detention and training order and, accordingly, the range of other sentences otherwise available cannot be passed at the outset. Similarly, where the offence involved is extremely serious the court retains the power to determine that the Crown Court should deal with the offence as a grave crime. The referral order procedure does not affect such decisions save that where a court requires a pre-sentence report (PSR) before imposing a detention and training order and as a result of the report decides that a lesser sentence is appropriate it must then make a referral order. These matters are all discussed further below. Where a reprimand or final warning is either unavailable or inappropriate an offender may be charged or summoned to appear in court. For the purposes of detention and bail a juvenile aged 17 is treated as an adult and may accordingly be refused bail and held in police cells pending his or her appearance before the court. A juvenile under 17 years should generally be granted bail to appear. Where his or her detention is authorised by a custody sergeant in accordance with PACE it is normal for the juvenile to be transferred to local authority accommodation unless it is impracticable to do this or in the officer's opinion the child should be placed in secure accommodation and none is available. Where the young person is released on bail the custody sergeant has power to impose conditions on his or her release.[22] Someone below the age of 18 will usually appear before a youth court. However in certain circumstances proceedings must be commenced in the adult court if or where:

- the juvenile is jointly charged with an adult
- the juvenile is charged with an offence arising out of the same circumstances from which an adult is charged
- an adult is charged with aiding, abetting, counselling or procuring, allowing or permitting the juvenile to commit the offence
- similarly, the juvenile is charged with assisting etc. an offence by an adult
- proceedings have been commenced in an adult court and it only becomes apparent later that the child is under 18; or
- the court is conducting remand proceedings.

The Crown Court in relation to the youth court
A juvenile (i.e. *any* defendant aged between ten and 17) charged with offences which in the case of an adult must or may (depending on the offence) be tried in the Crown Court will normally be dealt with in the youth court.[23] However, a juvenile must be tried in the Crown Court:

- where he or she is charged with homicide
- where the youth court is of the opinion that the crime is grave and that the Crown Court may impose a custodial sentence in excess of two years; or
- where the youth is jointly charged with an adult and the court considers it necessary in the interests of justice to commit them both for trial.

Detention is also available under the grave crimes provisions as a result of section 91(2) Powers of Criminal Courts (Sentencing) Act 2000 in respect of:

---

[22] Section 3A Bail Act 1976.
[23] The system whereby indictable only matters in the adult court now progress straight to the Crown Court on first appearance before a magistrates' court does not apply to juveniles charged on their own (i.e. in the youth court), and there is a presumption that the case will be remitted to the youth court if a juvenile is jointly charged with an adult in the magistrates' court with such an offence (unless, that is, it is in the interests of justice that they be dealt with together, i.e. in the Crown Court).

- any offence punishable with imprisonment for 14 years or more
- indecent assault on a man or woman; or
- causing death by dangerous driving or by careless driving while under the influence of drink or drugs.

The youth court must first determine where the case should be tried before proceeding either to committal proceedings or to take the offender's plea. In the case of a juvenile under the age of 15 the court should have regard to any previous findings of guilt or warnings from the police in order to ascertain the sentence of detention is available as this is dependent on whether he or she is a persistent offender.

The youth court in practice

The youth court operates under the general auspices of the local magistrates' court. Proceedings are less formal in the youth court than in the adult court. Defendants are addressed by their first names, less formal or archaic language is used by the officers of the court, the oath is more simply worded and, in general, support is allowed for the juvenile from his or her parents or guardians. The layout of the court should facilitate the participation of the juvenile and reflect the protective aspects of the court's function rather than emphasise its punitive features.[24] Justices appointed to the youth court receive special training to assist them in dealing with children. The YOT (above) is also comprised of experts in their own fields having usually a background in the care of offenders and children.[25]

Procedure

The prosecution of juveniles in the youth court is influenced by the same principles described earlier in this chapter. The Code for Crown Prosecutors provides guidance as to the circumstances where it is appropriate to bring proceedings and notwithstanding the final warning system the Crown Prosecution Service retains its overall power to discontinue proceedings in accordance with section 23(3) Prosecution of Offences Act 1985 where it is either not in the public interest to proceed or there is insufficient evidence to sustain a reasonable prospect of conviction. The public interest ground for discontinuing proceedings is most likely to be engaged and informed by the welfare principle and the principal aim of the youth justice system – to prevent offending.

Rules of evidence and procedure are similar to those governing proceedings in the adult court and, of course, the court has a duty to ensure that a juvenile receives a fair trial. He or she is perhaps more likely to obtain state funded legal representation than in the case of an

---

[24] I.e. security staff and prisoner escort officers should usually not be in uniform, the accused should not be isolated from his or her advocates or parents and the justices should generally sit on the same level as the other participants.

[25] It is perhaps worth commenting that solicitors are not required to undertake specialist training to act in the youth court, unlike those representing children in public law proceedings (*Chapter 4*).

adult, and the interests of justice test in the Access to Justice Act 1999 may be more easily met where the offender is a juvenile. State funded representation is only available where it is in the interests of justice for the state to fund it. The test is usually applied by the proper officer of the magistrates' court having regard, e.g. to the likelihood of a custodial sentence, the complexity of the case and the ability of the defendant to present his or her case without assistance. Generally, a juvenile is less likely to be able to deal with his or her case without assistance than an adult defendant. Similarly, the need to expedite the process and link directly the offender with his or her offence by confronting delay is both attractive and sensible, although courts also have a duty to ensure that an offender has adequate time and facilities to prepare a defence. In the case of a child some allowance should also be made for his or her age, maturity and comprehension in deciding what is an appropriate period of delay.

Adjournments, remands, bail and secure accommodation
Where proceedings are adjourned the court may – and in some cases must - remand the accused. Where the court decides to remand it may do so on bail, or, if bail is refused, into local authority accommodation or - subject to what is said below - into custody at an establishment operated by HM Prison Service. Bail must be granted unless one of the exceptions to the right to bail exists as set out in the Bail Act 1976 and the court is satisfied to the requisite degree concerning a particular ground for refusing bail and must give its reasons for such a conclusion.

By way of an anomaly, where a juvenile aged 17 is refused bail he or she will be treated as an adult for the purposes of the Bail Act 1976 and may be remanded into prison custody in the same way as an adult.

A juvenile aged 16 years or less who is refused bail will be remanded to accommodation provided by the local authority.[26] In consultation with the local authority the court may impose any condition that it could have imposed if the offender had been granted bail. Such post-remand conditions may not specify an address where the child is to live but may be so worded as to prevent the local authority from placing the child with a specific person. A child breaching a condition may be arrested by a police officer and detained pending his or her appearance before a competent court.

A juvenile may not be placed by the local authority in secure accommodation without the express permission of the court. Section 25 Children Act 1989 applies in the criminal jurisdiction.[27] Where the court has found any of the criteria in the Children Act or the regulations to be satisfied it is bound to make a secure accommodation order.[28]

Under section 23(4) Children and Young Persons Act 1969 the court may remand a child aged 15 or 16 years to accommodation provided by

---

[26] Section 23 Children and Young Persons Act 1969.
[27] Supplemented by the Secure Accommodation Regulations 1991 and Secure Accommodation (No 2) Regulations 1991.
[28] *Re (M) (Secure Accommodation Order)* (1995) 3 All ER 407.

the local authority and require him or her to be placed and kept in secure accommodation. The power may only be exercised where the juvenile:

- is charged with or has been convicted of a violent or sexual offence or an offence punishable in the case of an adult with imprisonment for a term of 14 years or more; or
- has a recent history of absconding while remanded to local authority accommodation and is charged with or has been convicted of an imprisonable offence alleged or found to have been committed while so remanded

if (in either case) the court is of the opinion that only remanding him or her to a remand centre, or to local authority accommodation with a requirement that he or she be placed and kept in secure accommodation, would be adequate to protect the public from serious harm from him or her.

Unless the juvenile has been declared by the court to be vulnerable in accordance with section 23(5A) of the Act by reason of his or her physical or emotional immaturity or a propensity to self-harm so that it would be undesirable to remand to a remand centre, it would be usual to expect the juvenile meeting these criteria to be remanded into prison.

In the case of a juvenile aged 12 years or more a court may remand to accommodation provided by the local authority and impose a security requirement requiring him or her to be placed and kept in secure accommodation but only if the child:

- is charged with or has been convicted of a violent or sexual offence or an offence punishable in the case of an adult with imprisonment for a term of 14 years or more; or
- has a recent history of absconding while remanded to local authority accommodation and is charged with or has been convicted of an imprisonable offence alleged or found to have been committed while he or she was so remanded,
- if (in either case) the court is of the opinion that only such a requirement would be adequate to protect the public from serious harm from him or her.

The court may not remand a boy of under 15 or a girl aged 15 or 16 years to a remand centre but may if they meet the statutory criteria require them to be placed in secure accommodation for the period of the remand. In the case of a 15 or 16-year-old boy meeting the amended criteria unless the court has declared him vulnerable, he shall be remanded to a remand centre. The apparent difference in treatment between the sexes may be justified on the basis that the number of females meeting the criteria for such a remand is so few that it is unreasonable and impracticable to provide remand accommodation. At the time of writing the compatibility of this state of affairs with the right to liberty in the European Convention was still exercising some commentators. However a distinction could be drawn between the issue of how bail is determined (in which procedure there is no discrimination) and the determination of the accommodation available after that decision has been made (which would not engage Article 5 or the Convention at all).[29]

The sentence of the youth court

Where a juvenile has been found guilty of an offence the youth court has range of sentencing options. Some of these dispositions may only be imposed after the court has received a report from the YOT about the offender by way either of a written specific sentence report (SSR) or pre-sentence report (PSR). In any event the court should inform the child, his or her parent and legal representative of the manner in which it proposes to deal with the case and allow representations to be made.[30] The sentence imposed by the court should reflect the welfare principle, the need for a proportionate response and be principally aimed at preventing re-offending. Under the ethos of the Crime and Disorder Act 1998 the court should also address the issue of restorative justice and include, in appropriate cases, an element of either victim-based or community-based reparation.

The sentencing framework

The current sentencing framework for both adults and youths was introduced by the Criminal Justice Act 1991 (now consolidated by the Powers of Criminal Courts (Sentencing) Act 2000) and reflects what is known as the 'just deserts' principle. They key to the framework is the seriousness of the offence. A custodial sentence can be imposed only where the offence is 'so serious' that no other sentence can be justified. A community penalty can be imposed where the offence is 'serious enough' for such a penalty. If neither of these thresholds are crossed the court cannot impose a community penalty or, as the case may be, a custodial sentence. The court is entitled to have regard to a single offence or a combination of offences and previous convictions may aggravate the seriousness of the offending behaviour. Within this framework the sentences available in the youth court – which are also set out in the chart on pages 136 to 137 together with their seriousness thresholds - are:

- **Referral panel order**[31]
  As outlined above, a court dealing with a child for his or her first offence must, after conviction, make a referral order. The order falls somewhere between a diversionary disposal and a sentence in that it has procedural and substantive characteristics of both. As described, the juvenile can later find his or her way back to court and face other sentences in this list.

---

[29] See *Chapter 7* for secure accommodation orders in the context of family proceedings.
[30] Rule 11 of the Magistrates' Courts (Children and Young Persons) Rules 1992.
[31] From 1 April 2002.

- **Deferred sentence**

Sentence on a juvenile may be deferred for up to six months subject to terms or goals being set that must be achieved by the offender by the date of sentence. Compliance with the terms of a deferred sentence will usually lead to a lesser sentence than might have been imposed. Deferred sentences are useful measures where the court may otherwise be unable to avoid imposing a sentence of detention. However a deferment distances the offender from his or her offending behaviour and may impose too great a burden due to his or her maturity and comprehension. The order also conflicts with the general premise that cases should be dealt with swiftly and that delay is usually against the welfare interests of the juvenile.

- **Absolute and conditional discharge**

Where the court is of the opinion that it would be inexpedient to punish the offender for the offence having regard to its nature and his or her character the court may impose either an absolute discharge or a conditional discharge for a period of not more than three years. If a further offence is committed during the period of the conditional discharge the court has power to impose an alternative penalty for the original offence. A conditional discharge is not available in respect of a juvenile who has been subject to a final warning (see earlier in the chapter) save in exceptional circumstances.

- **Fine and compensation**

The maximum fine that may be imposed on a child (aged ten to 13 years inclusive) is £250 and on a young person (14 to 17 inclusive) the maximum is £1,000 (subject also to any ceiling in relation to a particular offence). Compensation may be ordered in the youth court, i.e. an amount to be paid by an offender to the victim of his or her offence, either as a penalty in its own right or ancillary to some other sentence. The upper limit for compensation is £5,000[32] per offence. The court is obliged to make the parent or guardian responsible for any such financial order where the child is under 16 unless it is satisfied that they cannot be found or that it would be unreasonable to do so having regard to the circumstances of the case - and it may do so where the child is 16 or 17 years old. Where the child is accommodated by the local authority the court may require the local authority to pay unless it would be unreasonable to do so having regard to the circumstances of the case. In the case of a compensation order the local authority should only be made responsible where there is a causative link between the fault of the local authority and the offence.[33]

---

[32] Any offences with which the juvenile asks the court to take into consideration (TICs) can be considered in arriving at the appropriate amount and recompense.

[33] *R v. Sheffield Crown Court, ex parte Clarkson* (1986) 8 Cr App Rep (S) 454.

▪ Reparation order

A reparation order is an order requiring the offender to make reparation specified in the order to the victim of his or her crime or to the community at large. The order sets out the nature of the work concerned which may be for no more than 24 hours duration to be completed within three months of the order. A responsible officer appointed usually from the YOT oversees the order. Victim-based reparation may only be required with the express consent of the victim and may include a letter of apology and a face-to-face meeting between the youth and the victim. The government's faith in restorative justice as a means of preventing crime in the future is reinforced by the court being required to indicate why it has not made a reparation order where it has power to do so but does not make such an order.[34]

▪ Action plan order

An action plan order requires an offender to comply with the terms and requirements of the order for a period of three months. It places the juvenile under the supervision of a responsible officer of the YOT. The order may contain provision for the child to:

- participate in certain specified activities
- present himself or herself to a person specified at specified times and places
- attend at an attendance centre (below) for a number of specified hours
- stay away from a specified place or places
- comply with specified educational arrangements
- make reparation as specified; and
- attend any review hearing set by the court.

The court may review the order and set a date on which to do so, not more than 21 days after making the order to consider its effectiveness and to either insert or cancel any of the specified requirements. If someone fails to comply with the terms of an action plan order the court can, on application by the YOT, revoke the order and re-sentence the youth.[35]

---

[34] Section 67 and 68 Crime and Disorder Act 1998.

[35] Some YOT practitioners have expressed concern that action plan orders are being effectively abandoned due to the fact that offenders appearing before the youth court for the first-time must normally be made the subject of a referral order (see earlier in the text). The work usually associated with action plan orders is likely to form a significant part of any earlier such referral order intervention plan and accordingly doubt has been raised whether an action plan order can be viable at any later stage, i.e. whether the two orders and systems can really stand together or make sense in terms of proportionality.

Youth Court Sentencing Grid

Sentence and Relevant Statute	Age Range	Representation Order Essential?	Reports?
Fine, ss 135–138*	Any	No	No
Absolute Discharge	Any	No	No
Conditional Discharge	Any	No	No
Reparation Order, ss 73–75	Any	No	Yes – not PSR
"Serious Enough Threshold"			
Attendance Centre, ss 60–62	Any	No	No
Action Plan Order, ss 69–72	Any	No	Yes – not PSR
Supervision Order, ss 63–68	Any	No	PSR if add. req., medical if treatment imposed
Community Rehabilitation Order, ss 41–45	16–17	No	PSR if conditions imposed, medical if treatment imposed
Community Punishment Order, ss 46–50	16–17	No	PSR
Community Punishment and Rehabilitation Order, s 51	16–17	No	PSR and medical as for CRO
Curfew Order, ss 37–40	Any	No	Yes – re premises (and family if D under 16)
Drug Treatment and Testing Order, ss 52–58	16–17	No	PSR
"So Serious Threshold"			
Detention and Training Order, ss 100–107	12–17	Yes	PSR

* Statutory references are to the Powers of Criminal Courts (Sentencing) Act 2000.

Range	Not With Other Sentences?	Statutory Criteria?	Procedural Points
Up to £1,000 for 14–17 Up to £250 for 10–13	N/A	Means or means of parent/guardian	Parent/guardian may be made liable for payment
N/A	N/A	No	
Up to three years	N/A	No	Not available within 2 years of final warning
24 hrs work within three months	DTO, CPO, CPRO, SO with Sched 6 requirements, APO	No	
"Serious Enough Threshold"			
12 hrs min unless D is under 14 and 12 hrs excessive. 24 max (10–15) 36 max (16–17)	N/A	No	Centre must be available within reasonable distance of D's home. Imprisonable only.
Three mths – standard	DTO, CRO, CPO, CPRO, Attendance Centre, SO	Order must be desirable to ensure D's rehab or prevent further offending	Cannot be made if APO already in force. Imprisonable only if attendance centre included.
Up to three years	RO, APO	No	Requirements can be attached under Sched 6.
Six months to three years	APO	Order must be desirable to secure D's rehab or protect the public from harm from him or prevent further offending	
40–240 hours all within twelve months	RO, APO	No	Imprisonable only
As for CRO and CPO above – but max 100 hours	RO, APO	Order must be desirable to secure D's rehab or protecting public from harm from him or prevent further offending	Imprisonable only
2–12 hours in any day. Max duration six mths (three if under 16)	N/A	No	May be electronically monitored by contractors.
Six months to three years	N/A	D is drug dependant or misuser and susceptible to treatment.	Offence must have been committed after 29 September 1998.
"So Serious Threshold"			
Fixed term – 4, 6, 8, 10, 12, 18, 24 months	RO, APO	D aged 12–14 must be persistent offender	Imprisonable only. Half served in secure accom, half in community.

Youth Court Sentencing Grid

▪ Attendance centre order

Where a youth has been convicted of an imprisonable offence the youth court may make an attendance centre order requiring him or her (assuming that there is provision for females locally) to attend an attendance centre. The centre must be reasonably accessible to the offender having regard to his or her age, the means of access available and any other circumstances. The order does not require the juvenile to participate in any specific activities. The aggregate number of hours - as fixed by the court - is not be less than 12 except where the offender is under 14 years of age and the court is of the opinion, having regard to his or her age, or any other circumstances, that 12 hours would be excessive; and the hours must not exceed 12 except where the court is of the opinion, having regard to all the circumstances, that 12 hours would be inadequate, and in that case shall not exceed 24 hours if the offender is under 16 years. Otherwise it must not exceed 36 hours.[36]

▪ Supervision order

A supervision order may be made in respect of any offence. This places the offender under the supervision of a responsible officer of the YOT. It is the duty of the supervisor to advise, assist and befriend the supervised person. A supervision order in criminal proceedings should not be confused with that available in the family proceedings court under the Children Act 1989 (*Chapter 7*). It may include a number of specific requirements directed towards what is sometimes called 'intensive supervision and surveillance' or generally dealing with:

- residence
- intermediate treatment
- night restrictions
- specified activities
- supplementary requirements
- treatment for a mental condition
- educational requirements; and
- reparation.

On non-compliance with a supervision order, the court may, on application, revoke the order and re-sentence the juvenile. Alternatively, the court has the option of allowing the order to continue and imposing a penalty[37] for failure to comply with its terms.

▪ Community rehabilitation order

A juvenile aged 16 years or over may be placed on what historically is known as probation - and under the supervision of a probation officer. Non-compliance with such an order empowers the court, on application, to revoke the order and re-sentence the juvenile.

---

[36] Section 17 Criminal Justice Act 1982.

[37] A fine, community punishment order, curfew order or an attendance centre order.

Alternatively, the court has the option of allowing the order to continue and imposing a penalty[38] for failure to comply with its terms.

▪ Community punishment order

A juvenile aged 16 years or over may be made the subject of what was formerly called a community service order requiring him or her to perform unpaid work in the community for up to 240 hours. The sentence is only available in respect of imprisonable offences.[39] Non-compliance with such an order empowers the court, on the application to revoke the order and to re-sentence the juvenile. Alternatively, the court has the option of allowing the order to continue and imposing a penalty[40] for failure to comply with its terms.

▪ Community punishment and rehabilitation order

A juvenile aged 16 years or over may be made the subject of a what used to be known as a combination order requiring him or her to be under the supervision of a probation officer for up to three years and to perform community service for up to 100 hours. Non-compliance with such an order empowers the court, on application to revoke the order and to re-sentence the juvenile. Alternatively, the court has the option of allowing the order to continue and imposing a penalty[41] for failure to comply with its terms.

▪ Curfew order

A curfew order may be made in respect of any offence and may also require an offender to wear an electronic tag to monitor the curfew. The curfew order requires the offender to remain indoors at a specified address (or addresses) during specified hours for a specified period. The order may be for no more than 12 hours a day for up to six months. The order thus allows a court to impose a curfew order of up to 2,160 hours in a six month period. Very little guidance as to the appropriate length of curfew orders exists to assist sentencers so that courts must make judgements based on their own assessment of what is a proportionate response. In the case of an offender aged under 16 years the court is under a duty to obtain and consider information about his or her family circumstances and the likely effect of the order upon them.

▪ Drug treatment and testing order

In the youth court such orders are available in the case of a juvenile aged 16 years or over. The order contains provision requiring the

---

[38] A fine, community punishment order, curfew order or an attendance centre order.
[39] Meaning that the offence must be carry imprisonment (not that imprisonment is to be used in the present case) in the case of an adult.
[40] A fine, community punishment order, curfew order or an attendance centre order.
[41] A fine, community punishment order , curfew order or an attendance centre order.

offender to submit to treatment with a view to the reduction and elimination of the offender's dependency or propensity to misuse drugs. The order may require such treatment to be either residential or non-residential. It seems likely that such an order will be at its most effective where it is used in conjunction with a community rehabilitation order or supervision order.

The order deals directly with the link between crime and drug abuse. Once a culture of abuse is established a pattern of crime often develops characterised by property crime to fund the dependency, violent crime as a function of that dependency and substance abuse crime as a manifestation of that dependency. The traditional approach of expecting an habitual user of illicit substances to demonstrate their ability and willingness to come off the substance of their own volition has not, overall, reduced the volume of crime attributable to dependency. The order seeks to redress this by introducing an intense and compulsory programme of testing and treatment.

▪Detention and training order

The detention and training order is now the only custodial sentence available in the youth court. The order subjects the offender to a period of detention and a period of supervised release in the community. The order may be made in respect of any imprisonable offence[42] where a child aged 12 years or more has been convicted in the youth court. The order may only be imposed where the justices are satisfied that the offence is so serious that only a custodial sentence can be justified or where the offence is an offence of violence or a sexual offence and the public need to be protected from serious harm from the offender.[43]

In the case of a child aged under 15 years the court may only make a detention and training order where it is of the opinion that the child is a persistent offender. This term is not defined in the statute but clearly implies a history of offending behaviour, although not necessarily a pattern of previous criminal convictions.[44]

Under the order half the sentence is served within the secure estate and half in the community under supervision. The type of secure accommodation to which an offender is committed and detained is a decision for the Secretary of State and not for the court. Accordingly a child may be placed and kept in a young offender

---

[42] Subject to the minimum period of the order which may, in certain cases be longer than the maximum sentence for the offence. In such cases the court will be unable to impose a custodial sentence.

[43] Section 1 Criminal Justice Act 1991; section 73 Crime and Disorder Act 1998.

[44] In the case of a child under 12 years of age (when in force in relation to such children) additionally the order may only be made if the court is satisfied that only a custodial sentence would be adequate to protect the public from further offending by him or her. See also the comments in relation to 'grave crimes' committed by this age group earlier in the chapter.

institution (YOI) or in other forms of secure accommodation such as regional secure units at the discretion of the Home Office. Such discretion allows a decision to be made on the suitability of accommodation according to the needs of the juvenile and his or her circumstances. For this reason, YOTs have a responsibility to provide a detailed profile of the child concerned before an order is made (i.e. when preparing a PSR). A similarly detailed report is also required after sentence describing a programme of activities, education and treatment, if appropriate, to be followed in detention and providing a risk assessment of the youth.[45]

A detention and training order may only be made for four, six, eight, ten, 12, 18 or 24 months. The court is under a duty to take into account any time spent on remand and to give credit for the timeliness of a guilty plea. In practice these obligations may give rise to problems. In particular a child spending time on remand and pleading guilty may, according to a literal interpretation of the legislation face an effective maximum sentence of 12 months.[46] Whether such a restriction of the youth court's powers was intentional is difficult to discern from the Parliamentary debates during the passage of the Crime and Disorder Act.

Once a juvenile has served half the period of the order in the secure estate he or she will be released subject to the remaining part of the order being served in the community under supervision. If the requirements of his or her release are not complied with the youth court may, on application, either fine the offender or return him or her to the secure estate for up to three months or the remainder of the period of the detention and training order.

In a letter addressed to magistrates. Lord Warner, Chairman of the Youth Justice Board, sought to reduce the use of DTTOs as a sentencing option. The basis of his comments was that the secure estate for juveniles was 96 per cent full and that there was little benefit in making orders were offenders were incarcerated for two to six months as no education or training could be provided in that

---

[45] The ASSET profile.

[46] i.e. if the maximum sentence is 24 months and a child pleads guilty his or her sentence should generally be reduced by up to one third. This means an effective maximum period of detention of 16 months which is not available, as a detention and training order may not be made for such a period. The court would appear to be required to consider instead 12 months. If the child has also been on remand for some time this period should again be reduced to reflect that time. Effectively the period now available to a court would be ten months or less. Interestingly the Divisional Court has held that credit for a guilty plea may be given without reducing the period of detention and that the requirement to take into account periods spent on remand may be met without reducing the overall sentence, at least in so far as short periods of remand are concerned. This attempt by the judiciary to make sense of what could be described as inconsistent legislative provisions does not provide the lower courts with much actual assistance. As far as the rights of the child are concerned this arrangement is simply unsatisfactory. See *R v FWW* (2001) 165 JP 77; *R v B* (2000) Crim LR 870; and compare *R v Kelly* (2001) Crim LR 583.

time. It was noted that in the year ending March 2001, some 6,600 DTTOs had been made.[47]

Parents and parenting orders

Parents have a crucial role to play in protecting their children in criminal proceedings. Where a juvenile is not cared for by his or her parents many of their duties fall on the person with parental responsibility for the child. The processes by which parents become involved in criminal proceedings apply equally to people with parental responsibility. The government has repeatedly stated its view that parents must exercise responsibility for their children. Measures in the youth justice arena exist to place this principle on a statutory footing:

- on arrest by a constable it is the duty of the officer to inform the juvenile's parents of his or her arrest and the place of detention
- at interview a juvenile should have the assistance of an appropriate adult. While there is no requirement for that person to be a parent it would be usual for that to be the case wherever possible
- parents are required to accompany their children to court
- before sentence a court is under a duty to explain to the juvenile's parents the proposed method of dealing with the child and to invite representations from them
- parents will generally be made responsible for the payment of their children's fines, costs or compensation (above) - and may be pursued through the adult court in order to enforce such orders
- where a juvenile is under 16 years of age the court has a duty, on conviction, to consider making a parental bind-over. This order requires a parent to take proper care of and exercise proper control over his or her child to prevent the child from re-offending. If the child does offend again the parent may be required to forfeit the amount of the bind-over (to a maximum of £1000)[48]
- where a child is convicted of an offence in the youth court the court is required to make a parenting order (see below).[49]

Parenting orders

In any court proceedings where:

- a child safety order (*Chapter 7*) is made in respect of a child
- an anti-social behaviour order (*Chapter 7*) or sex offender order (*Chapter 5*) is made in respect of a child or young person
- a child or young person is convicted of an offence; or

---

[47] *The Times*, 23 August 2001.

[48] Parental bind-overs have had a poor record of success. Generally the Crown Prosecution Service is reluctant to bring proceedings for the estreatment of the recognisance and the court has no power of its own motion to take action against a parent whose child has committed a further offence.

[49] Section 8 Crime and Disorder Act 1998.

- an adult is convicted of an offence under either section 443 or 444 of the Education Act 1996 (of failing to secure the attendance of their child at school)

the court may make a parenting order.

The order may only be made where the court is satisfied that it would be desirable to do so in order to prevent the repetition of the conduct giving rise to either the child safety order, the anti-social behaviour order or the sex offenders order or to prevent the commission of further offending as the case may be. A parenting order requires the parent to comply with such requirements specified in the order and to attend for a period not exceeding three months such counselling or guidance sessions as may be specified in directions given by the responsible officer of the YOT. The requirements that may be specified in the order are those which the court considers desirable in the interests of preventing any such repetition or - as the case may be - the commission of further offences. The order is for a specified period of 12 months and its terms may be varied or discharged. Failure to comply with a parenting order is punishable on conviction by the court with a fine on Level 3 of the standard scale.[50]

---

[50] i.e. up to £1,000.

CHAPTER 7

Emergency Protection of Children: *Public Law* Safeguards

The local authority has a general duty under the Children Act 1989 towards children in need. Where a child is at risk it is charged with a intervening in the interests of the child to remove him or her from harmful surroundings. This positive obligation is a reflection of the child's right to be protected from abuse and neglect and to a safe upbringing. Also, apart from employing a range of professionals whose task is to deal with aspects of child care and development, each local authority has multi-agency child protection strategies which lead to action in individual cases, including an 'At-risk Register' in which reports of suspicions of abuse from, e.g. doctors, teachers, neighbours and others are recorded plus the action taken. Where a child is in need of emergency or more long-term protection the Children Act 1989 provides a range of measures which the authority can pursue. The situation is reinforced in Wales by a Children's Commissioner (see end of chapter).

Others engaged in child protection
Many other individuals and agencies, both statutory and non-statutory are involved in providing services to and for children. Some are regulated through the local authority such as foster carers, child minders and accommodation providers. Others such as teachers, education welfare officers, health visitors, doctors are regulated in the first place through their employment by the relevant administrative agency and then through their own professional regulatory body.

The non-statutory sector generally comprises voluntary or non-profit organizations – often with charitable status. This sector also performs a key task in promoting child rights and protecting them. Of these non-government organizations the NSPCC has received statutory recognition but there are many others. The regulation of such service providers depends on their own codes of practice and their maintaining standards of ethics in relation to the treatment of children.

International obligations
The European Convention On Human Rights contains no specific requirements for the intervention of the state to assist children at risk. However such a positive obligation may be deduced from Articles 2 and 3 of the Convention. The right to life and the prohibition on the use of torture and inhuman and degrading treatment require the state to take measures to ensure that an individual is protected from the kind of conduct that could amount to such treatment.

In *A v. UK*[1] the Court of Human Rights found the UK to be in violation of Article 3 (prohibition of torture, or inhuman or degrading treatment) where the defence of reasonable chastisement was available to a step-father charged with assaulting his step-child by the use of a cane. Where a child is suffering or is at risk of suffering physical, mental or sexual abuse the same obligation may arise on the local authority to take steps to safeguard the child.

Intervention by the state in such circumstances however also engages the right to the respect for family and private life enjoyed under Article 8 of the Convention, which permits the state to interfere with a person's rights so long as the interference is prescribed by law, and is legitimate and necessary in a democratic society. The Court of Human Rights has accorded national authorities a wide margin of appreciation in how care systems and the protection of children are regulated.[2] Accordingly under the human rights law the decision to intervene to protect children through the powers available to a local authority under the Children Act need to be reviewed in the light of the Convention. So long as a proper balance is struck between the duty of the state to intervene, the rights of the parents to enjoy family life and the interests of the child the procedure for the protection of children at risk is likely to prove compatible with Convention rights.

Where the rights and interests of parents and children are in conflict and the conflict can only be resolved to the detriment of one of the parties the interests of the child should generally prevail.[3]

Article 9 of the UN Convention On the Rights of the Child affirms the principle that children should be brought up by their parents. It also reflects the same principle of family life recognised by Article 8 of the European Convention On Human Rights above. However there may be circumstances where the child's right to a family upbringing may be restricted in his or her best interests. Article 9(1) provides:

States Parties shall ensure that a child shall not be separated from his or her parents against their will, except when competent authorities subject to judicial review determine, in accordance with applicable law and procedures, that such separation is necessary for the best interests of the child. Such determination may be necessary in a particular case such as one involving abuse or neglect of the child by the parents, or one where the parents are living separately and a decision must be made as to the child's place of residence.

Article 19 of that Convention deals with the general state duty to prevent abuse:

(1) States Parties shall take all appropriate legislative, administrative, social and educational measures to protect the child from all forms of physical or

---

[1] (1998), 2 FLR 959.
[2] *Scott v. UK* (2000) 2 FCR 560.
[3] Johansen v. Norway 1996 23 EHRR 33.

mental violence, injury or abuse, neglect or negligent treatment, maltreatment or exploitation, including sexual abuse, while in the care of parents, legal guardians or any other person who has the care of the child.

(2) Such protective measures should, as appropriate, include effective procedures for the establishment of social programmes to provide necessary support for the child and for those who have the care of the child, as well as for other forms of prevention and for identification, reporting, referral, investigation, treatment and follow-up of instances of child maltreatment described heretofore, and, as appropriate, for judicial involvement

Accordingly a child has the right to be protected and, in appropriate cases, to be removed from harmful surroundings where the risk to which he or she has been exposed is attributable to his or her parents or other people with care of that child, both in international and national law. The extent to which national law provides for such protection is described below

Directions under section 37 Children Act 1989

Where a court is dealing with any form of family proceedings and it appears to the court that it may be appropriate for a care order or a supervision order to be made in respect of the child which is the subject of the proceedings, or any other child, it may direct the local authority to investigate the child's circumstances.[4] The local authority is required to conduct the investigation and to report back to the court with its decision whether to make an application for either a care order or a supervision order within eight weeks.[5] The power to order such investigations does not give the court power to make either a care order or supervision order of its own motion. Such orders may only be made *on application* and as the application may only be made by either the local authority conducting the investigation or the NSPCC the decision of the local authority whether or not to bring proceedings – as opposed to the outcome of any such proceedings – is conclusive.

This power is particularly useful in cases where a child may be perceived to be at risk of suffering harm by a court dealing with, for example, private law proceedings under the Children Act (*Chapter 8*). However the direction itself provides no protection for the child concerned in the short-term unless it triggers action from the local authority. There is also a danger that the power may be misused or misapplied by the court on application by one of the parties to a private law dispute.

CHILD ASSESSMENT ORDERS

A child assessment order is again an order that may be used to assess the needs of a child as a prelude to an application being made by the local

---

[4] *See Re H (Child's Circumstances: Direction to Investigate)* (1993) 2 FCR 277.
[5] Section 37(4) Children Act 1989.

authority for a care order or supervision order. The order was not designed to be used in an emergency and accordingly provides little in the way of immediate protection for a child at risk. A child assessment order is an *inter partes* application and should not be made without notice being given to all concerned parties. The order is appropriate where other methods of investigative intervention by the local authority have failed or been frustrated rather than in an emergency. The court may make a child assessment order on application by a local authority or the NSPCC if it is satisfied that:

(a) The applicant has reasonable cause to suspect that the child is suffering, or is likely to suffer, significant harm;

(b) An assessment of the state of the child's health or development, or of the way in which he or she has been treated, is required to enable the applicant to determine whether or not the child is suffering, or is likely to suffer, significant harm; and

(c) It is unlikely that such an assessment will be made, or be satisfactory, in the absence of an order under this section.[6]

An application for a child assessment order may be treated by the court as an application for an emergency protection order (below) and if it is satisfied that the grounds for making such an order it may do so.[7] Guidance from the Department of Health concerning child assessment orders states as follows:

> The child assessment order should be used sparingly. Although a lesser order than others in Parts IV and V of the Act, it still represents substantial intervention in the upbringing of the child and could lead to yet further intervention. It should be contemplated only where there is reason for serious concern for the child. It should not be used for a child whose parents are reluctant to use normal child health services.

POLICE PROTECTION ORDERS

Section 46(1) Children Act 1989 permits a constable to take a child into police protection for up to 72 hours if he or she has reasonable cause to believe that the child would be likely to suffer significant harm if not removed to suitable accommodation. There are no powers of search associated with this power.

The police do not acquire parental responsibility for the child and must make appropriate provisions for contact between the child and his or her parents as appear to the designated police officer to be reasonable and in the child's best interests. The power is insufficient to allow a medical examination or a full and detailed interview or assessment.

---

[6] Section 43(1) Children Act 1989.
[7] Section 43(4) Children Act 1989.

However the designated officer has the duty to do what is reasonable in all the circumstances of the case for the purposes of safeguarding or promoting the welfare of the child having regard to the period during which the child will remain in police protection. This duty may include the power to authorise certain medical examination or treatment depending on the urgency and gravity of what is required.

When a child is removed from surroundings under a police protection order the designated officer is under a duty to inform the local authority.[8] Often the police and local authority will work together in cases where a child's removal is urgent. The 72 hours allowed by the legislation can be put to good use by the local authority[9] in working with parents and in making the arrangements for other emergency orders such as an emergency protection order (below). The designated officer also has power to apply for an emergency protection order. Police protection is also a useful device for securing the child's interests and rights pending court time being made available for a substantive hearing.

EMERGENCY PROTECTION ORDERS

The primary provision governing the emergency protection of children is set out in section 44 Children Act 1989:

(1) Where any person ('the applicant') applies to the court for an order to be made under this section with respect to a child , the court may make the order if, but only if it is satisfied –
  (a) there is reasonable cause to believe that the child is likely to suffer significant harm if –
    (i) he is not removed to accommodation provided by or on behalf of the applicant; or
    (ii) he does not remain in the place in which he is then being accommodated;
  (b) in the case of an application made by a local authority –
    (i) enquiries are being made with respect to the child under section 47(1)(b); and
    (ii) those enquiries are being frustrated by access to the child being unreasonably refused to a person authorised to seek access and that the applicant has reasonable cause to believe that access to the child is required as a matter of urgency; or
  (c) in the case of an application made by an authorised person –
    (i) the applicant has reasonable cause to suspect that a child is suffering, or is likely to suffer, significant harm;

---

[8] As soon as is reasonably practicable: section 46(3) Children Act 1989.
[9] Under section 47 Children Act 1989 the local authority has a duty to investigate the circumstances of every child who is the subject to police protection or an emergency protection order.

    (ii) the applicant is making enquiries with respect to the child's welfare; and

    (iii) those enquiries are being frustrated by access to the child being unreasonably refused to a person authorised to seek access and that the applicant has reasonable cause to believe that access to the child is required as a matter of urgency.

An 'authorised person' in section 44(1)(c) means a person authorised for the purposes of section 31 of the Act, presently limited to the NSPCC.

The main test to be applied by the court in determining an application for an emergency protection order is whether the applicant has reasonable cause to believe that the child in question is suffering or is likely to suffer significant harm. The term 'harm' is defined in section 31(9) of the Act to mean ill-treatment or the impairment of health or development. Section 31(10) provides that where the question of whether harm suffered by a child is significant turns on the child's health or development, his or her health or development shall be compared with that which could reasonably be expected of a similar child.

In determining an application for an emergency protection order the justice or justices (next section) will have regard to the key principles of the Children Act including the welfare principle, the welfare checklist (*Chapter 7*) and the presumption of no order (*Chapter 7*). This 'steering by the minimum' is an important approach to this or any other application under the Children Act where an order would interfere with the right to family life under Article 8 of the European Convention. It properly reflects the test of whether an intervention by the state in family life is necessary in a democratic society.

Emergency protection order procedure

An application for an emergency protection order may be made to a court with notice to the parents or at the opposite extreme to a single justice without any notice being given. The majority of applications are made in this latter way, i.e. *ex parte* - after a justices' clerk has been persuaded that there is a sufficient emergency to allow the application to proceed without giving notice to the child's parents.

Some concern has been expressed that emergency protection orders may be sought in circumstances short of a real and pressing emergency. It is the function of the justices' clerk in the first place to filter out poorly timed or unreasoned applications and in any event the justice should always consider the nature and gravity of the emergency when considering the application. The decision to allow an application to proceed without notice is an exercise of judicial discretion and justices' clerks should generally ensure they have sufficient information on which to base their decisions and should provide reasons for them in order to comply with the minimum standards of a fair trial in Article 6 of the European Convention.

In any application for an emergency protection order the court will usually appoint a solicitor for the child from the Law Society's Children Panel and children's guardian from CAFCASS (*Chapter 4*). Sometimes it is impractical to appoint either or both; in such circumstances the child will have no voice in the proceedings.

Naturally, the parents of a child who is the subject of an *ex parte* application will have no notice of the proceedings - and no opportunity to test the grounds put forward or to otherwise make representations. Alternatively, where the application proceeds on notice the minimum period of notice is 24 hours. It is not usual practice for the local authority to provide disclosure of the case other than in the general terms required by the application forms. Instead a parent may have to wait until the social worker gives evidence before discovering the allegation he faces. Where the procedure takes place without notice having been given, a parent may have to wait until a full hearing of the case which may take as long as seven days to be convened. Given what is at stake for the parents in either situation, such a procedure may not accord with their right to a fair trial under Article 6 of the European Convention. However a UK national court has recently affirmed[10] the use of the *ex parte* procedure in private law cases (*Chapter 8*) and it seems unlikely that the public law equivalent will be found to violate the Convention. Department of Health Guidance provides:

> An emergency protection order will usually be heard *ex parte* - that is, without other persons having to be given notice of the hearing and allowed to attend and make representations. Rules of court provide for applications to be heard *inter partes* (at a full hearing with others who wish to attend able to do so) but the very fact that the situation is considered to be an emergency requiring immediate action will make this inappropriate or impracticable in most cases.

Duration and effect of an emergency protection order

The order operates as a direction to any person who is in a position to do so to comply with any request to produce the child to the applicant and authorises his or her removal to (or prevention of removal from) accommodation provided by or on behalf of the applicant. The order may be made for a maximum of eight days in the first instance. If the order was made on an *ex parte* basis there may be no hearing to discharge the order for at least 72 hours. Where the parents were in attendance or had notice of the application there is no right to apply to discharge the order at all. Nor is there an appeal against the making of the order.[11] An emergency protection order may be extended for a further seven days on application with notice so long as the court is satisfied that the applicant still has reasonable cause to believe that the child has suffered or is likely to suffer significant harm.

The emergency protection order gives the applicant limited parental responsibility for the child concerned. The limitation applies to the power to remove the child and the applicant may only do so in order to safeguard and promote the welfare of the child. The child should also be

---

[10] *Re J (Wrongful Abduction) (2000)* (unreported).
[11] Section 45(9) and (10) Children Act 1989.

returned home if it appears to be safe to do so. Arrangements for adequate contact between the child and his or her parents should also be made. Often justices will be anxious to know what arrangements are being made for the child's placement as well as contact during the period of the order.

In many cases the applicant may also wish to have the child medically examined or assessed and specific provision exists to allow the court to make directions in an emergency protection order situation for just such a purpose. Indeed without the leave of the court such examinations may not take place.[12] However where the child requires examination and treatment for a medical or psychiatric disorder the local authority will have sufficient powers as a function of parental responsibility to consent to such treatment without the leave of the court.

Emergency protection orders and exclusion requirements
In some cases the risk of harm to a child may be attributable to only one of his parents or to one person within, or visiting the home where he lives. The emergency protection order, as originally drafted was a blunt instrument for dealing with such circumstances as it allowed the removal of the child from home whereas the issue could be better, and less intrusively dealt with by removing the relevant adult from home. Schedule 6 of the Family Law Act 1996 (FLA) introduced the power to include an exclusion requirement[13] in an emergency protection order (and in an interim care order). Such a requirement may not be included in a final order. An exclusion order may:

- require the relevant person to leave the home in which he or she is living with a child
- prohibit the relevant person from entering a home in which the child lives; and
- exclude the relevant person from a defined area in which a home in which a child lives is situated.

Enforcement
The court may attach a power of arrest to an exclusion order. This allows a police constable to arrest someone whom he reasonably suspects to be in breach of the requirement.[14] Exclusion requirements may be of specified duration or for as long as the substantive order is in force. However the purpose of such a measure is to allow the child to remain at home. If the local authority then removes the child for a continuous period of more than 24 hours, the exclusion requirements are automatically extinguished. There are also powers whereby exclusion requirements to be varied, extended or discharged.

---

[12] Section 44(6) Children Act 1989.
[13] Section 38A Children Act 1989.
[14] As a somewhat lesser measure, the court can accept from the relevant person an undertaking, for example to leave the home within a specified period.

When an exclusion requirement can be made

As far as an emergency protection order is concerned the court may include an exclusion requirement if certain grounds are met.[15] These are:

(a) there is reasonable cause to believe that if a person ('the relevant person') is excluded from a dwelling-house in which the child lives, then -
   (i) in the case of an order based on section 44(1)(a), the child will not be likely to suffer significant harm, even though the child is not removed or, as the case may be, does not remain; or
   (ii) in the case of an order based on section 44(1) (b) or (c), the inquiries will cease to be frustrated; and
(a) another person living in the dwelling-house (whether or not a parent of the child) –
   (i) is able and willing to give the child the care which it would be reasonable to expect a parent to give him, and
   (ii) consents to the inclusion of the exclusion requirement.

CARE ORDERS

A care order in respect of a child of under 17 years of age (or 16 in the case of a child who is married) may be made by a court[16] on the application of either the local authority or an authorised person. Currently, the NSPCC is the only 'authorised person'. There is a two-stage test. The court must be satisfied that:

- the criteria in section 31(2) Children Act 1989 are met - often referred to as 'the threshold test'; and
- the child's welfare must demand that a care order be made as opposed to either no order or some lesser order available to the court.

The statutory criteria in section 31(2) are that:

(a) the child concerned is suffering, or is likely to suffer, significant harm; and
(b) the harm, or likelihood of harm, is attributable to –
   (i) the care given to the child, or likely to be given to him or her if the order were not made, not being what it would be reasonable to expect a parent to give to him or her; or
   (ii) the child being beyond parental control.

In the context of care proceedings the word 'harm' means ill-treatment or the impairment of health or development. 'Development'

---

[15] Section 44A(2) of the Children Act 1989.
[16] Either the family proceedings court, the county court or the High Court. Generally care proceedings are dealt with in the main by the first two of these courts.

means physical, intellectual, emotional, social or behavioural development. Health means physical or mental health and ill-treatment includes sexual abuse and forms of ill-treatment which are not physical. Where the question of whether harm suffered by a child is significant turns on the child's health or development, his or her health or development must be compared with that which could reasonably be expected of a similar child.[17]

In determining the second stage of this two-test process – whether the child's welfare demands a care order - the starting point is the welfare principle in section 1(1) of the 1989 Act, which is informed by reference to the welfare checklist in section 1(3) (*Chapter 7*). The court is also required to consider the presumption of no order principle and should also have regard to the range of other orders available under the Children Act 1989.

Care Proceedings and the Human Rights Act 1998

Making a care order represents a substantial interference with the right to respect for family life under Article 8 of the European Convention. Accordingly when the court is determining an application for a care order it should do so in the light of the principles recognised by the Court of Human Rights. In *Johansen v. Norway* (1996), 23 EHRR 33 the following principles were laid down:

- taking a child into care should normally be regarded as a temporary measure to be discontinued as soon as circumstances permit;
- any measure taken to implement a decision to place a child in temporary care should be consistent with the ultimate aim of reuniting the natural parent and child;
- therefore a fair balance must be struck between the interests of the child in remaining in public care and those of the parent in being reunited with the child;
- when assessing whether a fair balance has been struck, particular importance attaches to the best interests of the child which, depending on their nature and seriousness, may override those of the parent;
- in particular, a parent cannot be entitled under Article 8 to have measures taken that would harm the child's health and development;
- the Convention does not rule out placing a child in care with a view to adoption or that contact between a child and his parents should be terminated. However such measures should only be taken in exceptional circumstances and only if they are based on an overriding requirement pertaining to the child's best interests.

Despite these principles the Court of Human Rights has generally been reluctant to interfere with decisions taken in respect of children in public

---

[17] Section 31(9) and (10) Children Act 1989.

law cases. In *Scott v. UK* (2000) 2 FCR 560 it said that the Court's role was not to take the place of the competent national authorities in the exercise of their responsibilities for the regulation of the public care of children, but to review under the Convention the decisions taken by those authorities fall within a state's 'margin of appreciation' (in other words the court should give some deference to the choice made by a local authority as to what is in the interests of the child and how it is to be best achieved). Authorities enjoy a wide margin of appreciation in assessing the necessity of taking a child into care, restrictions placed on parental rights and access by those authorities require stricter scrutiny.

It is against these minimum Convention standards that courts are required to interpret the Children Act. In general terms the scheme providing for the public protection of children is broadly compatible with Convention rights. However, Article 2 (the right to life) and Article 3 (prohibition of torture, or inhuman or degrading treatment) may create a positive obligation on the state to have measures in place to protect children from abuse. In general terms the Children Act provides such measures but they are only realisable by the courts upon application by the local authority. Where a court is of the opinion that a child is suffering significant harm it has no powers of its own motion to either make a protective order in respect of that child or to direct the local authority to bring proceedings. If concerned, the only option for the court is to direct an investigation of the child's surroundings under section 37 of the Act (above). Once a local authority forms the view that no application for care or supervision should follow the court has exhausted its powers. In *Nottinghamshire County Council v. P* (1993), 2 FLR 134 the Court of Appeal expressed its concerns over the impotence of the court in such a case. Taking into account the decisions of the Court of Human Rights, the Divisional Court decided that a local authority could be liable in negligence where it had failed to take the steps required of it to remove a child from circumstances which amounted to inhuman or degrading treatment. The extent of this positive obligation to seek to protect children is bound to lead to further litigation.

Effect and duration of a care order
A care order lasts until the child concerned attains the age of majority. A care order may be discharged on application to an appropriate court and relevant persons may apply for an order defining contact with a child in care. Otherwise the issue of contact is a matter for the local authority subject to a statutory requirement to facilitate and permit reasonable contact between a child and his or her parents under section 34 of the Act.

The local authority shares parental responsibility with people who had parental responsibility prior to the order. It remains possible for an unmarried father to obtain parental responsibility even where his child is in care through a parental responsibility agreement. A care order acts to discharge any existing orders under section 8 of the Act.[18] The authority

---

[18] e.g. residence, contact, specific issues or prohibited steps orders.

has power to place a child in a variety of forms of accommodation including foster care or residential placements, or to return the child to live at home.[19] A child in care may also be considered for adoption (*Chapter 2*) where rehabilitation with natural parents has been effectively ruled out.

It is important to recognise the different roles of the local authority and the court in the public protection of children at risk. The local authority has two main roles:

- to bring proceedings under the Children Act and to seek to prove to the relevant standard that the child concerned has suffered or is likely to suffer significant harm, and to establish the need for the court to make a care order in the best interests of the child; and
- to take responsibility for the upbringing of the child after an order has been made including the duty to work towards stabilising the child through rehabilitation or, as the case may be, adoption.

The court's role is to provide an independent, impartial, fair and judicial setting in which an assessment can be made of the harm suffered or likely to be suffered by the child and whether an order is in the best interests of the child's welfare.

It is not the role of the court to exercise control or supervision over the local authority's management of the child's care. The court is expected to assess and make findings as to the threshold criteria and if satisfied they are met to scrutinise the care plan put forward by the local authority and, if it is satisfied that the plan meets the welfare needs of the child, to make an order. The order entrusts the local authority to act appropriately.[20]

A problem arises with this 'once and for all' principle where the local authority, for whatever reason, is unable to proceed with the care plan approved by the court. It must in the alternative manage the child's care but where is the effective scrutiny of that process? Arguably an aggrieved parent may be able to apply to discharge the care order or to seek an order for contact but in many cases such options are simply not appropriate. These applications do not provide an adequate remedy to ensure that the local authority complies with its own care plan. It is possible that Article 8 of the European Convention (right to private and family life) and the duty of the local authority to act compatibly with it may allow parents, at the very least, a greater voice in post-care decision-making and, at its highest, allow a court to scrutinise the management of a child's care by the local authority via judicial review.[21]

---

[19] See the Placement of Children with Parents etc. Regulations 1991.
[20] *Re J (Minors)(Care: Care Plan)* (1994) 1 FLR 253; *Re T (A Minor)(Care Order: Conditions)* (1994) 2 FLR 423.
[21] Or under section 7 Human Rights Act 1998.

Care plans

Within care proceedings the local authority has to show to the court that making an order is in the best interests of the child's welfare. The court must be satisfied of course that the threshold criteria have been met but in considering the welfare part of the two stage test the local authority will be expected to produce a care plan outlining, in some detail, its arrangements for the care of the child after the proceedings have finished. The care plan should contain details of rehabilitation or adoption arrangements, assessments or programmes to be followed by the child or his or her parents and how the process of contact and education is to be managed. It is usual now for a care plan to be provided to accompany interim care orders.

In 1999 the Secretary of State issued guidance (under section 7 Local Authority Social Services Act 1970) on care plans.[22] It states:

> The guidance in this circular seeks to address concerns that care planning, although considered to have steadily improved during the 1990s, lacks consistency between and within authorities across the country. These differences may be in the style, format and level of detail set out in the care plan but also who contributes to its completion, including family members. There are also believed to be continuing uncertainties about the status of the contents of care plans, particularly regarding key decisions and timetable. This in turn gives rise to differing expectations from those involved in the court proceedings, including the judiciary, about the strictness with which the care plan should be implemented. There is general acceptance that family circumstances do change and that plans may well need to be adjusted to reflect the changing needs of the child who is the subject of the care order. Typically, this will be one of the main tasks of the statutory reviews which are required to be undertaken for all looked after children.

The guidance covers practice and policy matters including the aim of the care plan, the child's needs including contact, the views of others involved in the management of the child's care, placement details and timetables and management and support by the local authority. The importance of the care plan should not be underestimated as it provides the only comprehensive statement of how the child's rights and welfare are to be balanced, maintained or changed in respect of the rights of his or her parents.

Parental involvement post-care

A parent does not lose rights towards his or her child by the making of a care order. This position is recognised in both national and international law. The local authority shares parental responsibility with the child's parents after the order is made and accordingly retains an important role in making decisions in respect of the child's future. In addition to the practical aspects of sharing parental responsibility a parent's right to

---

[22] Local Authority Circular LAC (99) 29, 'Care Plans and Care Proceedings Under The Children Act 1989' (12 August 1999).

family life under Article 8 of the European Convention is not lost when a care order is made. In particular parents must be properly involved in proceedings concerning the care and custody of, and access to/contact with their children. The same rights have been recognised in relation to any administrative determination of issues encompassed within the right to family life. The decision-making process must be procedurally fair which includes the right of the parent's to be consulted on important decisions and to be given disclosure of the material on which the decision-maker is proposing to rely.[23] The importance of the care plan becomes apparent in the context of protecting parental rights after a care order has been made. Where the contents of the care plan are crucial to the decision of the court whether to make an order or not, a procedure now exists to enable the judge or magistrates to star certain milestones in the care plan. If the local authority fails to meet a starred milestone, the children's guardian or a parent has the power to reactivate the professional conference of experts originally involved in the proceedings to review the position. If agreement is not then reached, the case may be referred back to the court which made the original decision for directions. The court (not the family proceedings court) may then enforce the starred milestones through injunctions, damages or directions in order to protect the child's and parents' human rights: *Re W and B (Children) (Care Plan)* (2001) EWCA CIV 757.

SUPERVISION ORDERS

A court may make a supervision order either on specific application by a local authority or as an alternative to a care order. The threshold test and the welfare test both apply to the making of a supervision order. The order lasts for a period of one year but may be extended on application to the court for a period of up to three years.

A local authority does not acquire parental responsibility for the child under a supervision order and accordingly has no power to remove a supervised child from his or her home. If such a child becomes at risk the local authority would have resort to an emergency protection order or to bringing care proceedings to safeguard the child (both above). A supervision order is generally made out to a named individual - the supervising officer - and it is his or her main duty to advise, assist and befriend the supervised child and to take such steps as are reasonably necessary to give effect to the order. The supervising officer may, if authorised by the order itself give directions to the child to require him or her to take part in certain activities or to report at a particular location. The aim of the directions must of course relate to issues relevant to the child's protection.

---

[23] *W v. UK* (1987) 10 EHRR 29; *McMichael v. UK* (1995) 20 EHRR 205. But *cf. Scott v. UK* (2000) 2 FCR 560.

Differences between care and supervision

The differences between a care order and supervision order were summarised in *Re S (J) (A Minor) (Care or Supervision Order)* (1993) 2 FLR 919:[24]

- When deciding whether to make a care order or a supervision order the court needs to be clear as to what the future risks are. This requires a careful scrutiny of what has happened in the past so that a view of the future risks can be formed.
- A supervision order is capable of providing a great deal of protection. It can guarantee access into the child's home, supported by a warrant if necessary. There can be a care plan. An emergency protection order is available if there is a need to remove the child in an emergency. The child can be kept on the 'at risk' register (see the start of this chapter) so that the local authority is required to conduct periodic reviews.
- The concept of parental responsibility is at the heart of the difference between a care order and a supervision order. A care order means that a local authority can take over virtually all parental responsibility functions if satisfied that it is necessary to do so in order to safeguard or promote the child's welfare. A supervision order does not deprive the parents of parental responsibility and does not endow the local authority with parental responsibility. Section 34 Children Act 1989 enables the local authority to control contact between the child and other people where a care order has been made.
- When a care order is made a duty is imposed on the local authority under section 22 Children Act 1989 to safeguard the welfare of the child. A supervision order carries with it no such duty, and the obligation to keep the child safe remains with the parent who has parental responsibility.
- Under a supervision order the supervisor has a duty under section 35 of the 1989 Act to advise and assist the supervised child but not the parents.
- A care order places a local authority in a better position to enforce its requirements than a supervision order. For example, it has power to remove the child when it is no longer considered to be safe. Under a supervision order, information and access must be given to the supervisor, which can be enforced by a warrant; that is the only part of the arrangement which is given any specific sanction. Thus where a grave risk exists in relation to a child the court should make a care order.
- The court must look at the case as a whole and determine its views as to the risk of both physical and emotional harm to the child, and then decide whether, in the light of the gravity of the case, the local authority ought to have extra duties imposed on it.

---

[24] After *A Practical Approach to Family Law*, 5th Edition, Black J, Bridge J and Bond T, London: Blackstone Press, 2000.

SEARCH AND REMOVAL

A range of other orders exists under the Children Act 1989 to facilitate the public care of children at risk. These include:

- an order for the discovery of a child in respect of whom an emergency protection order has been granted and whose whereabouts are unknown. The order requires any person with knowledge of the child's location to deliver him or her up. The order allows premises to be entered and searched. Obstruction of such an order is an offence;[25]
- a warrant to enter and search of premises may be issued to a police constable where there are grounds to believe that someone has been prevented, or will be prevented, from exercising the powers available under an emergency protection order. The authority allows a constable to use reasonable force to gain access to any premises and the court may direct that the constable is accompanied by a registered medical practitioner, nurse or health visitor in addition to the person named in the emergency protection order;[26]
- a discovery order relating to children found at the premises but in respect of who no emergency protection order is in force. If such an authority is granted and the applicant is satisfied that the grounds for making an emergency protection order exists in respect of such children the order may be treated as an emergency protection order;[27] and
- a recovery order may be granted by a court in respect of a child who is in care or the subject of an emergency protection order if there is reason to believe that the child has run away, is staying away from the person responsible for his or her care or is missing. A recovery order may only be made on application by a person with parental responsibility for the child by virtue of a care order or emergency protection order or, where the child is in police protection, the designated officer. The order requires anyone with knowledge of the child to disclose his or her whereabouts and allows the search of premises and extends to the use of reasonable force if necessary.

SECURE ACCOMMODATION

Under section 25 Children Act 1989 the local authority may seek permission from a court to place a child in secure accommodation for a

---

[25] Section 48 Children Act 1989.
[26] *ibid.*
[27] *ibid.*

certain period. Without the sanction of a court the local authority may not place a child in such accommodation.

The court to which the application is made depends on the status of the child. In the first place the child must be accommodated by the local authority. This may mean after the making of a care order (including an interim care order), under a voluntary arrangement between the local authority and the child's parents, or after a remand by a youth court (either on bail or with a condition to reside as directed by the local authority), or after a remand to accommodation provided by the local authority following a refusal of bail (see *Chapter 6* where this aspect of secure accommodation is more fully explained).

Remands

Where a child is on remand to the local authority in criminal proceedings after a refusal of bail the application for secure accommodation may only be made to the youth court under section 23(5) Children and Young Persons Act 1969.[28] The maximum period of remand in such cases is 28 days and accordingly this is also the maximum period of secure accommodation. In those rare cases of a child defendant being committed to the Crown Court for trial (*Chapter 6*) and this period being exceeded prior to sentence the youth court loses jurisdiction to deal with further applications for the use of secure accommodation. Instead the Crown Court has power to deal with an application for a further remand but the use of secure accommodation is a matter for the family proceedings court. Where the child is remanded on bail with a condition to reside where directed by the local authority,[29] or in any other case, the application must be made to the family proceedings court.

Secure accommodation and the family proceedings court

In the family proceedings court a child may not be kept in secure accommodation unless it appears to the court:

(a) That –
  (i) he or she has a history of absconding and is likely to abscond from any other description of accommodation; and
  (ii) if he absconds, he is likely to suffer significant harm; or

(b) that if he is kept in any other description of accommodation he is likely to injure himself or other persons.[30]

An order allows the local authority to place a child in secure accommodation for up to three months. This period may be extended by

---

[28] See *Chapter 6* generally for remands and for the use of secure accommodation in criminal proceedings.

[29] *Re W (A minor) (Secure Accommodation: Jurisdiction)* (1995) 2 FCR 708; *Re C (Secure Accommodation: Bail)* (1994) 2 FCR 1153.

[30] Section 25 Children Act 1989.

a further court order for up to another three months.[31] The local authority also has power under the Children (Secure Accommodation) Rules 1991 to hold a child in such accommodation for up to 72 hours in any given period of 28 days without having obtained the authority of the court.

In *Re K (A Child) (Secure Accommodation Order: Right to Liberty)* (2001) 1 FCR 249 the Court of Appeal refused to make a declaration of incompatibility in respect of section 25 Children Act 1989 and the use of secure accommodation. The challenge the court was determining was based on Article 5 of the European Convention (right to liberty). It was accepted in principle that the use of secure accommodation engaged the right to liberty. The question for the court was whether the legislation could be read compatibly with one or more of the exceptions to the right to liberty listed in Article 5(1)(a) to (f). It was decided that section 25 could be read compatibly with the exception set out in Article 5(1)(d) which permits a minor's liberty to be restricted as part of supervision for an educational purpose.

Accordingly the court declined to make a declaration of incompatibility but noted that - whilst the legislation was Convention compliant - there was a distinction to be drawn with the exercise of the powers granted under the Children Act. In other words, the Convention could still have a bearing on whether the use of secure accommodation was lawful without rendering the legislative provision itself unlawful. This distinction between legality and lawfulness remains an area of forensic development.

In *Re K* the Court of Appeal confirmed that a child subject to an application for the use of secure accommodation enjoyed the protection afforded by Article 5 of the Convention but that the proceedings should not be classified as criminal for the purposes of the right to a fair trial under Article 6. Nevertheless, the court affirmed the principle that a child's rights to be heard and procedural fairness should lead a court to ensure that his or her rights were protected in the same way as the rights of someone charged with a criminal offence should be protected under the right to a fair trial.

Applications for secure accommodation may proceed in the absence of the child. However, it is a requirement of the legislation that the child be informed of his or her right to be legally represented in the proceedings. The right to be so represented includes the right to be informed of the case against the child, to provide instructions and in all but exceptional circumstances to have a children's guardian appointed.[32] Whilst the provision of a voice for the child is sufficient to discharge the state's duties under the UN Convention On the Rights of the Child it must in future be interpreted in the light of the right to a fair trial under Article 6 of the European Convention and in particular the right of access to the court recognised in *Golder v. UK* where it was said that courts must ensure that the child has an opportunity to consult with an independent solicitor and to give and receive instructions including the power to

---

[31] Regulations 10 and 11 of the Children (Secure Accommodation) Regulations 1991.
[32] *Re AS (Secure Accommodation Order)* (1999) 1 FLR 103.

instigate or participate in proceedings that affect him or her either directly or indirectly.

Although regulations provide for the maximum duration of a secure accommodation order case law confirms that the order should be no longer than is necessary and unavoidable.[33] Justices are also required to provide reasons for the length of the order.[34] It would seem to be at least good practice for a local authority seeking permission to use secure accommodation to provide the court with a plan of work to be undertaken by the child whilst subject to such a placement. The plan should make clear provision for the regime of contact with his or her parents, siblings and for education.

CHILDREN AND MENTAL HEALTH

In certain cases children suffering from a mental illness for the purposes of the Mental Health Act 1983 may require protection. The *Code of Practice* issued under section 118(4) of the 1983 Act provides guidance to those authorities charged with the functions of supervising mentally disordered children. In some cases a child may require the protection of the schemes established under both the Children Act and the Mental Health Act. The purpose of the intervention should dictate under which statutory scheme the child falls to be dealt with. Where the objective of the intervention is to provide assessment or treatment for a mental condition the procedure for voluntary or compulsory admission to hospital under the Mental Health Act may be more appropriate than using powers under the Children Act 1989. In practice the choice between procedures may not be as simple as that. Mental health law is complex and professionals need to have access to specialist sources of advice and information. As far as the rights of the child are concerned the general guidance applicable to adults in the *Codes of Practice* applies equally to them with the following particular considerations to be taken into account:

- children should be kept as fully informed as possible about their care and treatment, and their views and wishes should be ascertained and taken into account, having regard to their age and understanding;
- any intervention considered necessary by reason of their mental disorder should be the least restrictive possible and result in the least possible segregation from family, friends, community and school; and
- all children should receive appropriate education whilst in hospital.

---

[33] *Hereford and Worcester County Council v. S* (1993) 2 FLR 360.
[34] *W v. North Yorkshire County Council* (1993) FCR 693.

A central weakness in the mental health provisions is that they are only engaged in respect of people whose disorder is treatable as a mental illness. A child displaying a personality disorder or other form of disturbed behaviour may not fall within the definition of a mentally disordered person to whom the hospital admission programme can apply. In such circumstances the 1989 Act procedures may be the only effective way of protecting the child from a serious risk of harm or injury.

WARDSHIP

The power to make a child a ward of court is an ancient power exercisable only by the High Court. The term describes the legal process by which parental responsibility for a child is vested in the court. The management of a ward's care is usually delegated by the court to either his parent or the local authority but no important step can be taken without the leave of the court.

The Children Act 1989 has significantly reduced the importance of the High Court's wardship powers. The range of orders available under the Act has all but made redundant the need for the intervention of the court. However wardship remains an effective intervention in the interests of a child where the Children Act is either unavailable or inappropriate, for example, where a local authority wishes to resolve an issue which but for the prohibition on the local authority seeking a specific issues order or prohibited steps order (*Chapter 8*) would usually be resolved by seeking such an order.[35]

Wardship may also have a role to play in private law (*Chapter 8*). However generally the orders available under section 8 Children Act are sufficient to cover the majority of instances where the inherent jurisdiction of the High Court has previously been invoked. The Abduction of children or proceedings for the recovery of children unlawfully removed from the UK jurisdiction may be areas where the use of wardship remains the most effective method of protecting children and their welfare.

CHILD SAFETY ORDERS

A local authority may apply to a family proceedings court for a child safety order with respect to a child aged under ten years.[36] The order places the child under the supervision of a responsible officer of the local authority and requires that child to comply with certain specified

---

[35] e.g. where the wishes of the child are not in accordance with the local authority's preferred course of management; where there is an issue over sterilisation; where there are issues relating to the exercise of parental responsibility; proceedings to determine whether essential and life preserving medical treatment should be withdrawn.
[36] Section 11 and 12 Crime and Disorder Act 1998.

requirements. The order may only be made where one or more of the following conditions are satisfied, i.e. where:

(a) the child has committed an act, which, if he had been aged ten or over, would have constituted a criminal offence;

(b) a child safety order is necessary for the purpose of preventing the commission by the child of such an act;

(c) the child has contravened a ban imposed by a curfew order;[37] and

(d) the child has acted in a manner that caused or was likely to cause harassment, alarm or distress to one or more people not of the same household as himself or herself.

The order may contain such requirements as the court thinks desirable in the interests of securing that the child receives appropriate care, protection and support and is subject to proper control, or of preventing any repetition of the kind of behaviour which led to the child safety order being made. The order may only be made after the court has obtained and considered a report on the child's home circumstances and the likely effect of the order on them. The court should also consider making a parenting order (*Chapter 6*).

A child safety order does not set out to address the protection of the child. Its aim is to provide protection for the community from children out of control. The measure directly confronts the child with a restriction on his or her liberty and makes the parent subject to an order requiring him or her to receive guidance and counselling on how to take steps to prevent further misbehaviour. In this way the child's welfare is promoted and the community in which he or she lives is protected.

ANTI-SOCIAL BEHAVIOUR ORDER (ASBO)

The Crime and Disorder Act 1998 introduced a range of civil orders to equip a local authority, working with the police, with an armoury of measures to prevent anti-social behaviour. The measures rely on the premise that prevention is better than cure and accordingly seek to prevent an incident happening in the first place rather than to provide a solution after the event. In earlier chapters of this book reference has been made to sex offender orders, child safety orders (also mentioned above) and child curfew orders. The anti-social behaviour order is a further order concerning behaviour. Its placement in this chapter on the public law protection of children at risk is not ideal but the order fits comfortably nowhere else within the text.

---

[37] The Crime and Disorder Act 1998 empowered local authorities to apply for a child curfew order. If granted, such an order would prohibit children of an age specified in the order from remaining abroad in certain specified districts without an adult during certain hours. The power initially related to children under ten but has been extended to children under 16. It merits only the briefest of mentions as no orders have been made in the UK since the legislation was introduced.

An ASBO can be made by the magistrates' court for a minimum of two years or until further order on the application of a local authority or the police. It must be shown, *in civil proceedings,* that the person against whom the order is sought has acted or conducted himself or herself in such a way as to cause or be likely to cause harassment, alarm or distress to one or more persons from further anti-social acts by that individual.

The order can be made against anyone aged ten years or over, and if convicted of breaching the order *in criminal proceedings* the person against whom the order was made may be fined up to £5,000 (subject also to the youth court limits set out in *Chapter 6*) or imprisoned for up to six months if convicted in the magistrates' court or up to five years imprisonment in the Crown Court (in effect such proceedings would, in the case of a juvenile, normally limited to the youth court in the case of a juvenile, unless, possibly, where jointly charged with adults: *Chapter 6*). At the time of writing, many ASBOs have been made against both adults and juveniles; some, for example, have been addressed to persistent shoplifters and have banned them from going into retail areas in certain towns; others against so-called 'problem families' who act against the public good in residential areas.

It is important to remember that criminalisation of behaviour which as a result of an ASBO can only occur vis-à-vis to children aged ten (the age of criminal responsibility) or over. Below ten years of age the comparable—and non-criminal route—is the child safety order (above).

CHILDREN'S COMMISSIONER

The Care Standards Act 2000 established the office of Children's Commissioner for Wales. The role of the Commissioner is to review and monitor arrangements made by the providers of regulated children's services in Wales for the purpose of ascertaining whether, and to what extent, they are effective in safeguarding and promoting the rights and welfare of children. The power extends to include the review of arrangements made for ensuring that proper action is taken in response to any disclosure of information which tends to show that a crime has been committed, that legal obligations have not been complied with, that health and safety has been endangered or that information relating to any of these has been deliberately concealed.

The remit of the Children's Commissioner is widely drawn and provides for the first time a single administrative body through which children's services can be effectively reviewed and monitored. It is unfortunate that the Government has so far rejected proposals to establish a similar office in England.

CHAPTER 8

Emergency Protection of Children: *Private Law* Safeguards

Children may be in need of protection in situations falling short of circumstances that would trigger the involvement of the local authority under the Children Act 1989 as described in the last chapter. The Law Commission considered the extent and adequacy of the position in 1992 and the Family Law Act 1996 (FLA) consolidated legislation protecting both children and parties to a matrimonial or similar arrangement where one adult party presents a risk of harm. The FLA now provides a simple, unified system of protection against domestic violence[1] although the scheme is also supplemented by legislation aimed at harassment. The resulting position is certainly better than it was when Lord Scarman observed in *Richards v. Richards* [1983] 2 All ER 807:

> The statutory provision is a hotchpotch of enactments of limited scope passed into law to meet specific situations or to strengthen the power of specified courts. The sooner the range, scope and effect of these powers are rationalised into a coherent and comprehensive body of statute law, the better.

International obligations

The UN Convention On the Rights of the Child (*Chapter 1*) provides generally that a child has the right to be brought up safely. The right is made up of a series of obligations falling upon the state to ensure that a child is protected from abuse of all kinds and that systems are in place to ensure that he or she is able to remain with a non-abusive parent during his or her upbringing.[2]

The European Convention On Human Rights imposes a similar obligation on the state to take measures to protect citizens - including a child - from treatment amounting to inhuman or degrading treatment.[3] Also, under Article 8 of the Convention the right to private life includes a right to physical integrity and accordingly the state may be under a duty to ensure that adequate protection is available within the law and to intervene where a child's physical integrity is in some way compromised.

The duty to provide protection against domestic violence has been of importance in a number of cases decided by the Court of Human Rights. In *Airey v. UK* (1979) 2 EHRR 305 the Court found a violation of Article 8

---

[1] For detailed information see *Domestic Violence and Occupation of the Family Home*, Bazell C and Gibson B, Winchester: Waterside Press, 1999.

[2] e.g. Article 9 of the UN Convention.

[3] See *A v. UK* in *Chapter 2*.

based on the lack of legal aid in separation proceedings. Of great relevance to the Court was the recognition that the applicant needed protection from her drunk and violent husband. In *Whiteside v. UK* (1994) 76-A DR 80 the Commission was sympathetic to the complaint that the absence in the UK at that time of a tort of harassment meant that the applicant was not adequately protected against the violence of her former partner. The Commission recognised an appropriate level of harassment engaged the responsibility of the state to secure the applicant's rights under Article 8 by providing adequate protection against such abuse. This case contributed to the Protection From Harassment Act 1997 (see later in this chapter).

Domestic violence

Domestic violence is a social problem without magic solutions. Its primary impact is statistically likely to be on women. Children suffer as a result of domestic violence, either directly or indirectly. It is also clear that men may suffer from domestic violence although the incidence is far lower than that against women. In 1999[4] the government noted:

> Violence against women is a serious crime with serious consequences. One in four women experience domestic violence at some stage in their lives, thousands of children live in fear in their own home, witnessing or experiencing violence ... All across the UK, there are people working at the sharp end dealing with the consequences of violence against women. Volunteers, community organizations, probation officers, police, social workers and others have been working hard for many years to help and support women who experience violence. But help is still not comprehensive enough or easily accessible. In some cases, women are sent to up to ten different places before they get the help they need. And often how you are treated is entirely a matter of where you live. In some places, the service is extremely good and efficient; in others it simply does not exist ... It is time to change that. We have moved on from the days when no one wanted to intervene in a domestic situation. Just as, as a society, we have woken up to the horrors of child abuse, it is time to act to change attitudes and make sure women are not subject to violence in their own home or anywhere else.

In the legal system domestic violence may be addressed through a number of orders considered below. The overall scheme provides the kind of protection required by victims in order to properly enforce their international rights to safety. This is of particular importance where children are involved.

However the existence of legal machinery can only be one half of the story. The remainder of the tale requires domestic violence to be taken

---

[4] *Living Without Fear: An Integrated Approach to Tackling Violence Against Women*, 1999, London: Cabinet Office/Home Office.

more seriously. It requires a different approach.[5] The Court of Appeal[6] has issued guidance on the relationship between domestic violence and contact with a child. On hearing a contact application in which allegations of domestic violence are established, the court should consider the conduct of both parties towards each other and the children, the effect on the children and on the residential parent and the motivation of the parent seeking contact, ensuring, as far as it can do, that any risk of harm to the child is minimised and the safety of the child and the residential parent is secured.

The need for courts, and society to take the problem of domestic violence more seriously reflects the significant harm suffered by partners and also children. The legal system is structured so that the impact of violence between adults may easily overlook the indirect consequences to children. Domestic violence, like other forms of breakdown, leads to a much broader spectrum of social and economic consequences than just the issue of physical and psychological harm. Not only must the problem be discussed in this wider context but so must the availability of remedies take into account specifically these consequences.

The remainder of this chapter describes the orders available to a court dealing with issues of domestic violence and harassment to the extent that they provide protection to the child against domestic violence.

EMERGENCY PROTECTION ORDERS

As explained in *Chapter 7* - which looks at emergency protection orders sought by a local authority to discharge its duty to protect children - any person may apply to a court for an emergency protection order. In the case of an applicant who is not a local authority or an authorised person the application may only be made under section 44(1)(a) as set out in that chapter. As a measure of child protection the emergency protection order is limited in its effectiveness. Firstly, it is quite rare for an individual or his or her representative to be aware of the power let alone make the application. Secondly - and in any event - the order is for a maximum of eight days in the first instance. It may be extended for a further period of seven days. Thirdly, an individual cannot seek to apply for a care order

---

[5] It remains the case that the majority of domestic assaults are treated less seriously than other assaults of equivalent harm between strangers. There is an anecdotal perception that a complainant is unlikely to pursue her complaint and that such assaults are somehow part and parcel of an otherwise equal and non-abusive relationship. This misinformation is upheld by the failure of courts to sentence cases of domestic violence appropriately. Yet the offence is likely to be *more* serious; it is a breach of trust, the trust created by the commitment of relationship and it is an assault on a vulnerable class of people for the same reason. It is unfortunate that the government is able to send out a clear message to those people using violence against a member of an ethnic minority (the offence of racially aggravated assault) but cannot send out a similar message to perpetrators of domestic violence. For a general treatment see *Domestic Violence and Occupation of the Family Home*, Bazell C and Gibson B, Winchester: Waterside Press, 1999.

[6] In *Re L (a Child)(Contact: Domestic Violence)* (2000), *The Times*, June 21.

and – unless the local authority decided to intervene as described in *Chapter 7* - any child protection issues would have to be dealt with in the course of private law proceedings. There is, however, power to include an exclusion requirement in the order – again as described in that chapter.

The emergency protection order may be of assistance where a child is unsafe in his or her home and there is an appropriate relative able and willing to take him or her away from that insecure environment for a short period. Clearly a court faced with an application by someone whose connection with the child is ambiguous, tenuous or otherwise suspect may prefer to make a direction to the local authority, under section 37 Children Act 1989, to investigate the child's circumstances.

NON-MOLESTATION ORDERS

A non-molestation order is available under section 42 FLA 1996. Application may be made to either the family proceedings court (i.e. to magistrates) or the county court.[7] Practice and experience suggests that by far the majority of these applications are made to the county court. A non-molestation order means an order containing either or both of the following terms:

- a provision prohibiting the respondent from molesting another person who is associated with the respondent
- a provision prohibiting the respondent from molesting a relevant child.

In practice a non-molestation order is a routine device in the case of domestic breakdown.[8] Few practitioners would accept criticism that the focus of such orders is more often the partner as victim as opposed to the children as victims. Culture stands in the way of progress. Molestation must be prevented, but the interests of children are often seen as secondary in circumstances where they should have at least equal weight with the interests of the molested victim. But at the same time if an order fails adequately to protect the victim of molestation there will be a serious risk of yet further harm to the children as a consequence of the cycle of fear, risk and harm.

---

[7] The order is available in family proceedings which include proceedings under the inherent jurisdiction of the High Court, Parts II and IV of the Family Law Act 1996, the Matrimonial Causes Act 1973, the Adoption Act 1976, the Domestic Proceedings and Magistrates' Courts Act 1978, Part III of the Matrimonial and Family Proceedings Act 1984, Parts I, II and IV of the Children Act 1989 and section 30 Human Fertilisation and Embryology Act 1990. In *any such proceedings* the court has power to make a non-molestation order.

[8] Whereas the availability of undertakings (below) often leads to issues of domestic violence being 'fudged' in order to produce a compromise order.

Molestation

The purpose of a non-molestation order is to prohibit the other party – the respondent - from pursuing a certain course of conduct and to protect the party or child who has endured such conduct. There is, in fact, no need to establish *a course of conduct* as such, as there is for a similarly drafted order under the Protection from Harassment Act 1997 (see later). A single event may be sufficient to found both an application for a non-molestation order and its grant.

The word 'molestation' is not defined in the legislation. In *C v. C (Application for Non-molestation Order)* (1998) 1 FCR 11 it was held that the word implies some quite deliberate conduct which is aimed at a high degree of harassment of the other party such that the court ought to intervene. It does not therefore follow that the act complained of must be unlawful in itself. It is the effect of the conduct rather than its nature that is important for the purposes of the legislation. This approach was approved of in a case under the previous law, *Davis v. Johnson* (1979) AC 264, where Viscount Dilhorne said that violence is a form of molestation, but that molestation may take place without the threat or use of violence and still be serious and inimical to mental or physical health.

Associated person

A non-molestation order is only available as between parties who are associated with each other.[9] The aim of the FLA was, amongst other things to provide protection for people whose relationships are based on and characterised by an emotional commitment of however brief duration. It was not the purpose of the legislation to allow strangers, business or work-place acquaintances to seek redress in a family proceedings court. Sadly the UK legal system is ill-equipped to deal with statutes of principle and accordingly several pages of the FLA are given over to defining associated persons.[10] People are associated if they:

- are married or have been married
- are cohabitants
- are former cohabitants
- live in the same household
- have lived in the same household other than by one of them being the other's employee, tenant, lodger or boarder
- are relatives (a concept is again complicated by definition: below)
- have agreed to marry each other
- are the parents of the same child; or
- have or have had parental responsibility for the same child; and
- are parties to the same family proceedings.

---

[9] However a child may also bring an application provided he or she has obtained the leave of the court to do so. Leave may only be granted if the child has sufficient understanding to make the application: section 43(1) FLA 1996.

[10] Sections 62 and 63 FLA define 'associated person', 'relative' and 'relevant child'.

The legislation does not require the relevant relationship to be between heterosexuals. Accordingly, gay or lesbian people who are part of, or formerly part of, one of the relationships described above may obtain an order against their partner or former partner.

Relative

Section 63 FLA defines the term 'relative'. It includes the following familial relationships: father, mother, stepfather, stepmother, son, daughter, stepson, stepdaughter, grandmother, grandfather, grandson, granddaughter of a person or of that person's spouse or former spouse; and brother, sister, uncle, aunt, niece, or nephew (whether of the full blood or of the half blood or by affinity) of a person or of that person's spouse or former spouse.

Relevant child

A relevant child in relation to any proceedings under the FLA 1996 means any child:

- who is living with either party to the proceedings;
- who might reasonably be expected to live with either party to the proceedings;
- to whom an order under the adoption Act 1976 is in question in the proceedings;
- to whom an order under the Children Act 1989 is in question in the proceedings; and
- any other child whose interests the court considers relevant.[11]

Grounds for making a non-molestation order

Once a court is satisfied that someone associated with the respondent or a relevant child has suffered molestation the court may make a non-molestation order. The order is discretionary and the court should have regard to all the circumstances of the case, including the need to secure the health, safety and well-being of the applicant or the person for whose benefit the order would be made and any relevant child.

A non-molestation order may be made so as to be of specific duration or until further order. In either case the order may be discharged or varied on application. If the order was made on an *ex parte* basis (i.e. in the absence of the respondent: see below) section 45(3) FLA requires the court to give the respondent an opportunity to make representations at a full hearing of the issue as soon as is just and convenient.

The respondent, of course, has a raft of rights arising out of Article 6 of the European Convention as to the fairness of the procedure. Such rights are broadly encompassed by the doctrine of equality of arms which implies that everyone should have a reasonable opportunity to present his or her case on a level playing field. This minimum right includes a right to disclosure of the case both for and against an accused

---

[11] Section 62(2) FLA 1996.

person. In practice these requirements may place a significant burden on the party seeking to enforce the order.

Ex parte applications

A non-molestation order may be obtained on an *ex parte* basis where the court considers this just and convenient. Section 45(2) FLA prescribes the factors which the court must take into account:

- all the circumstances of the case
- any risk of significant harm to the applicant or a relevant child attributable to the conduct of the respondent if the order is not immediately made
- whether the applicant is likely to be deterred or prevented from pursuing the application if the order is not immediately made; and
- whether there is any reason to believe that the respondent is aware of the application but is deliberately evading service and that the applicant or a relevant child will be seriously prejudiced by the delay involved in effecting service of the proceedings.

Enforcement of non-molestation orders: power of arrest

Section 47(2) FLA requires the court to attach a power of arrest to the order if it appears that the respondent has used or threatened violence against the applicant or a relevant child unless the court is satisfied that in all the circumstances the applicant or child will be adequately protected without such a power of arrest. The power of arrest may also be attached to an ex parte order so long as it appears to the court that the respondent has used or threatened violence against the applicant or a relevant child and there is a risk of significant harm to the applicant or child attributable to conduct of the respondent if the power is not attached immediately.

A power of arrest allows a constable to arrest someone - on suspicion of having breached the terms of such an order - without a warrant. The order is then enforced by the applicant in proceedings which may result in the court committing the respondent to imprisonment, or suspending such an order. Where a respondent has appeared in court on suspicion of having breached the order the court has power to remand him or her on bail or in custody. Release may be conditional. The court also has power to order a medical examination or to make a disposal under the Mental Health Act 1983 where appropriate.

Undertakings

Under section 46 FLA a court may accept an undertaking from a respondent to comply with the terms of a non-molestation order. The court cannot however attach a power of arrest to an undertaking. Accordingly the undertaking and the order may only be enforced through a further application for a warrant of arrest under section 47(8) and (9) of the Act. Such a procedure may be slow and may not provide an adequate protective response to violation of the order.

The use of the undertaking procedure has a number of attractions. It saves time for both parties and the respondent does not have a formal order issued against him or her. However, as the legislation effectively requires the court to attach a power of arrest where violence has been used or threatened, and the court cannot attach such a power to an undertaking, there are few occasions where the nature of the molestation includes domestic violence but where an undertaking will be acceptable to the court.

PROTECTION FROM HARASSMENT

People falling outside the definition of 'associated person'[12] (above) may obtain protection from harassment under the Protection from Harassment Act 1997. In a unique twin-track approach, the 1997 Act (when fully in force) sets out both civil procedures and remedies which—if breached—have criminal consequences, as well as a separate code of criminal offences and sanctions. The philosophy underlying the 1997 Act shares much in common with the approach to a number of the orders under the Crime and Disorder Act 1998[13] and illustrates a trend towards controlling conduct through the civil law but with default punishable by the criminal law. This kind of enforced social engineering seems to be the current vogue and a favoured device of government to supplement or replace more traditional or educational approaches to changing behaviour and attitudes. The alleged perpetrator of harassment may thus be dealt with in one of two ways under the Protection from Harassment Act 1997. His or her conduct may amount to a crime dealt with in either the magistrates' court or the Crown Court, or be sufficient to lead a civil order dealt with in the county court.

Prohibition of harassment
Section 1 of the 1997 Act provides:

> 1(1) A person must not pursue a course of conduct –
>   (a) which amounts to harassment of another, and
>   (b) which he knows or ought to know amounts to harassment of the other
>   (2) For the purposes of this section, the person whose course of conduct is in question ought to know that it amounts to harassment of another if a reasonable person in possession of the same information would think the course of conduct amounted to harassment of the other.
>   (3) Subsection (1) does not apply to a course of conduct if the person who pursued it shows –
>   (a) that it was pursued for the purpose of preventing or detecting crime,

---

[12] The 1997 Act also applies to people who are associated, and criminal sanctions may be the only appropriate measure in some instances.
[13] e.g. anti-social behaviour orders.

(b) that it was pursued under any enactment or rule of law or to comply with any condition or requirement imposed by any person under any enactment, or

(c) that in the particular circumstances the pursuit of the course of conduct was reasonable.

Criminal harassment

The criminal law may not generally become engaged by behaviour amounting to molestation, although clearly some forms of molestation may amount to criminal offences of assault or other forms of personal abuse. Whatever, the effect of criminal proceedings on children is more a consequence than a driver – and in order adequately to protect the victim of harassment or other forms of criminal abuse from further injury or harm, the interests of children in maintaining an independent relationship with another adult – the perpetrator - may have to yield. Sometimes the interests of the victim and children will coincide. Where they do not the criminal law focuses more on protection of the victim than the rights of the child.

If this is a criticism of the choices made by society and Parliament it is one made without any desire to protect or excuse the actions of those who transgress the criminal or civil law and visit both fear and injury on others. But it is important to note the apparent inadequacy of the legal system to simultaneously protect victims and promote the interests of children.

Summary harassment

Anyone pursuing a course of conduct in breach of section 1 of the 1997 Act (above) is guilty of a criminal offence[14] punishable on summary conviction by imprisonment of up to six months or a fine of up to £5,000.

Aggravated version of harassment

Section 4 of the 1997 Act deals with the use or threat of violence in harassment. Anyone guilty of an offence under section 4 may be punished on indictment by imprisonment of up to five years or a fine. On summary conviction he or she may be imprisoned for up to six months or fined £5,000. The section 4 offence is as follows:

4(1) A person whose course of conduct causes another to fear, on at least two occasions, that violence will be used against him is guilty of an offence if he knows or ought to know that his course of conduct will cause the other so to fear on each of those occasions.

(2) For the purposes of this section, the person whose course of conduct is in question ought to know that it will cause another to fear that violence will be used against him on any occasion if a reasonable person in possession of the same information would think the course of conduct would cause the other so to fear on that occasion.

---

[14] Section 2(1) Protection from Harassment Act 1997.

Restraining orders

A criminal court sentencing a defendant for an offence contrary to either section 2 or 4 of the Act may also make a restraining order.[15] The order prohibits the offender from further conduct which amounts to harassment or which will cause a fear of violence. The purpose of such an order is specifically linked to the protection of the victim of the offence empowering the court to make the order, or the protection of any other person mentioned in the order (e.g. a child). The order may be made to last for a specified period or until further order and may include particular requirements to govern the kind of harassment forming part or all of the criminal conduct.

A breach of a restraining order is itself a criminal offence and is punishable on conviction on indictment by up to five years imprisonment or a fine, and on summary conviction imprisonment of up to six months or a fine of £5,000.

Sentencing under the Protection from Harassment Act 1997

Quite apart from whether the offence is one under section 2 or section 4 above, the court determining sentence the court should have regard to the following kinds of considerations:

- whether there is a history of disobedience to court orders, whether orders under the Act or civil orders;
- the seriousness of the defendant's conduct which can range from actual violence through to threats and down to letters expressing affection rather than any wish to harm the victim;
- whether there has been persistent misconduct or a solitary instance of misbehaviour;
- the physical or psychological effect upon the victim, whether the victim requires protection, and the level of risk that the defendant poses to the victim or to the victim's children or family;
- the defendant's mental health and whether he or she is ready to undergo treatment or receive any necessary help from the probation service; and
- the defendant's reaction to the court proceedings particularly whether he or she has pleaded guilty, whether there is remorse and whether there is a recognition of any need for help.

Where the offence is so serious that only a custodial sentence can be justified, it has been said that in general terms a first offence should be dealt with by way of a short sharp sentence. A second offence, however, must be treated more seriously and – for an offence under section 4 - a sentence of 15 months upon a guilty plea is likely to be the appropriate starting point.[16]

---

[15] Section 5 Protection from Harassment Act 1997.
[16] *R v. Liddle* [1999] 3 All ER 816.

Bail conditions: a note

An effective measure of protection may be afforded to a victim of criminal conduct by the imposition of conditions on a defendant's bail.[17] Conditions may be imposed on the grant of bail where the court perceives a real and not fanciful risk that the offender may either commit further offences, abscond or interfere with witnesses without such conditions.[18] The court has a wide discretion to restrict bail but in order to properly give effect to the right to liberty in Article 5 of the European Convention On Human Rights it is likely that such conditions should be relevant to the risk presented by the defendant and no more than is necessary to ensure he or she does not fulfil that risk. Where a defendant is charged and released pending his court appearance, a police custody sergeant may impose conditions of bail.

A defendant may be arrested by a police officer under section 7 Bail Act 1976 if the officer has reasonable grounds for believing that the person in question will not surrender to the court at the appropriate time or either has or is likely to breach any of his or her conditions of bail.

Civil harassment

Alternatively, an actual or apprehended breach of section 1 may be the subject of a claim in civil proceedings by the person who is or may be the victim of the course of conduct in question.[19]

The county court and the High Court both have power to award damages against the perpetrator of conduct encompassed by section 1 of the Act. However the main remedy is an injunction prohibiting the perpetrator from continuing with his or her course of conduct or other harassment. Breach of an injunction may be dealt with as a contempt of court or, in time,[20] as a criminal offence punishable by imprisonment of up to five years or a fine in the Crown Court.

Harassment: Statutory defences

It is a defence for a person charged with an offence under section 1 to show that –

- his or her course of conduct was pursued for the purpose of preventing or detecting crime
- his or her course of conduct was pursued under any enactment or rule of law or to comply with any condition or requirement imposed by any person under any enactment; or

---

[17] Or, where there are substantial grounds to believe that the defendant will commit further offences or interfere with witnesses a court may refuse bail and remand an offender in custody during the course of the proceedings.
[18] *R v. Mansfield Justices ex parte Sharkey* [1985] 1 All ER 193.
[19] Section 3(1) Protection From Harassment Act 1997.
[20] At the time of writing the power of the criminal court to deal with breaches of civil injunctions under this Act had not been brought in to force.

- the pursuit of his course of conduct was reasonable for the protection of himself or another or for the protection of his or another's property.

Limitations of harassment law

As a criminal measure proceedings under the 1997 Act have to be reactive. They cannot be taken in respect of an apprehended course of conduct and accordingly the criminal consequences of the Act may only be visited upon a perpetrator once the damage has been done. The civil procedure of the Act allows a preventative approach, but evidentially it may be difficult to establish a case. The more serious an allegation, the greater the weight of evidence needed to establish it. This principle may be further affected by the risk of making an order in civil proceedings which may, on breach, give rise to criminal liability (when in force).

The investigation of offences may also be difficult where the acts complained of are either in themselves quite lawful or upon the evidence of the complainant's alone or his or her close circle. A restraining order may also be difficult to enforce where an established relationship exists between the perpetrator and the victim. To this extent the forensic difficulties are analagous to those experienced in securing convictions for domestic violence.[21]

A restraining order may also interfere with arrangements made or being made in respect of children. It is difficult to anticipate the many forms of harassment that may occur where former partners are in conflict but maintaining contact with children or otherwise exercising parental responsibility.

OCCUPATION ORDERS

An occupation order is available under the FLA 1996 to regulate the right of occupation of certain dwelling-houses by associated persons (see the definition already given in relation to 'non-molestation' above). Housing is a major practical issue on breakdown of a matrimonial or quasi-matrimonial relationship. Where one party has assumed the role of parent with care of a child the issue becomes one of child protection. It becomes yet more complicated where both parties have assumed the primary care role for different children. The law has not only to determine the rights of such parties to occupy the former home but also to identify which parent and child association has precedence. The law deals with five situations and provides the courts with a range of powers which differ depending on the situation in which they arise.[22] The five situations are where an applicant is:

---

[21] See further *Domestic Violence and Occupation of the Family Home*, Bazell C and Gibson B, Winchester: Waterside Press, 1999.

[22] For the purposes of this text the framework described is that in place for making regulatory orders rather than declaratory orders. The court has power under the FLA to make orders declaring occupation rights of parties—something beyond the scope of this

- entitled to occupy the property;
- a former spouse with no existing right to occupy the property;
- a cohabitant or former cohabitant with no existing right to occupy the property;
- a spouse or former spouse and neither the applicant nor the respondent has a right to occupy the property; and
- a cohabitant or former cohabitant and neither the applicant nor the respondent has a right to occupy the property.[23]

The rights of a relevant child

In proceedings for a non-molestation order or an occupation order the rights of the child are protected by the requirement that a court take into account factors appropriate to the relevant child. The legislation uses similar to terms to those in the Children Act 1989. Both the FLA and the 1989 Act refer to the likelihood of significant harm attributable to the conduct of a perpetrator or respondent and the welfare of the child is crucial. In proceedings under the Children Act welfare is paramount; under the FLA a vital factor in applying the balance of harm test. The child's right to be safe, provided with accommodation and a safe environment and to have access to education and doubtless a stable social and family circle are all rights and interests courts must balance against the right of adults to act as adults in conflict are wont to do.

---

work: see *Domestic Violence and Occupation of the Family Home,* referred to in the previous footnote.
[23] Section 33 to 38 FLA 1996.

CHAPTER 9

If Adult Relationships Break Down

The primary legislative method by which the rights of children affected by parental conflict are protected is that provided by the Children Act 1989. In general terms the Act imposes the frontline responsibility to protect children at risk on the local authority and provides, in a number of regulations, rules and notes of guidance a very detailed framework to facilitate the care of those children remaining at risk of harm. Where children are not at risk, at least not of the kind of risk envisaged by the definitions which otherwise trigger the local authority's intervention, the Children Act again sets out the orders available to a court to facilitate whatever is in the best interests of the child.

Breakdown in the relationship between parents can take many forms from the most amicable to the most hostile. It is often the perception of practitioners that the interests of the children play a secondary role to the ongoing conflict between adults. It is an over used but largely accurate description to say that children are merely pawns in the end game of family life. Where parents are able to reconcile their interpersonal difficulties in order to settle the arrangements for the children on an amicable basis it is unlikely that the measures under the Act will need to be engaged. There are also a number of other avenues available to parents to bring about the same end without embarking on the rougher road to court proceedings. The availability of alternative dispute resolution schemes, mediation on either a voluntary or professional basis or the use of the voluntary or charitable sector offer a cost effective and arguably more flexible approach to families in trouble.

Where such other mediums of resolution are either inappropriate or ineffective the road eventually leads to court proceedings and the Children Act 1989. Court based resolution may be a costly and a lengthy process. Ultimately, it may prove unsatisfactory. Parents generally lose control. An order of the court often imposes unwelcome obligations or restrictions on parents which may offset the benefit to them of having the issue decided by someone else. There is a strong sense amongst practitioners that the most successful orders made by the family courts are those in which the parties have invested; usually by compromise and negotiation, perhaps facilitated by their advocates, officers, CAFCASS or the court itself.

International obligations

The UN Convention On the Rights of the Child contains a number of obligations and rights relating to children's rights with regard to parental conflict. However, in general terms and in the main, the Convention addresses issues between state and child (*Chapter 3*) rather than the relationship between individuals. Article 7(1) provides the starting point:

The child shall be registered immediately after birth and shall have the right from birth to a name, the right to acquire a nationality and, as far as possible, the right to know and be cared for by his or her parents.

Article 9 provides the limited grounds for intervention in the family by the state:

(1) State Parties shall ensure that a child shall not be separated from his or her parents against their will, except when competent authorities subject to judicial review determine, in accordance with applicable law and procedures, that such separation is necessary for the best interests of the child. Such determination may be necessary in a particular case such as one involving abuse or neglect of the child by the parents, or one where the parents are living separately and a decision must be made as to the child's place of residence.

(2) In any proceedings pursuant to paragraph 1 of the present article, all interested parties shall be given an opportunity to participate in the proceedings and make their views known.

(3) State Parties shall respect the right of the child who is separated from one or both parents to maintain personal relations and direct contact with both parents on a regular basis, except if it is contrary to the child's best interests.

The right of the child to express his or her views is recognised in Article 12. Proceedings under the Children Act also require that the court take into account the views of the child concerned. The child's voice however may be heard through the children and family reporter whose dual role[1] may not comfortably fit with the scheme envisaged by Article 12(2):

12(1) States Parties shall assure to the child who is capable of forming his or her own views the right to express those views freely in all matters affecting the child, the views of the child being given due weight in accordance with the age and maturity of the child.

(2) For this purpose, the child shall in particular be provided with the opportunity to be heard in any judicial and administrative proceedings affecting the child, either directly, or through a representative or an appropriate body, in a manner consistent with the procedural rules of national law.

The final piece of the international code is set out in Article 18 and provides for the recognition of parental responsibility:

18(1) States Parties shall use their best efforts to ensure recognition of the principle that both parents have common responsibilities for the upbringing and development of the child. Parents or, as the case may be, legal

---

[1] i.e. to provide an objective recommendation to the court of where the welfare of the child best lies and to adequately express the child's views on the case.

guardians, have the primary responsibility for the upbringing and development of the child. The best interests of the child will be their basic concern.

The Children Act 1989 was passed against the background of, amongst other things, the development and ratification of the UN Convention. Accordingly its basic private law framework reflects the international scheme in principle. The Act establishes the detailed rules against which these principles and others peculiar to domestic law are set. For example concepts of parental responsibility, contact or residence contained in the Children Act reflect similar principles outlined in the Convention.

The welfare principle

Section 1(1) of the Act provides:

> 1(1) When the court determines any question with respect to:
> (a) the upbringing of the child; or
> (b) the administration of the child's property or the application of any income arising from it,
> the child's welfare shall be the court's paramount consideration.

This fundamental statement of the overarching principle of the Act governs the approach all courts and tribunals take in the determination of any issue impacting upon the life of a child. It applies not only in proceedings under the Children Act. The following proceedings have been held to involve the paramount principle of the child's welfare:

- wardship[2]
- non-Convention child abduction cases[3]
- the High Court's inherent jurisdiction[4]
- disputes between parents and other individuals;[5] and
- disputes over a child's religious upbringing.[6]

However the courts have also identified a number of instances where the child's welfare is not paramount, i.e.:

- proceedings under Part III of the Act[7]
- proceedings for secure accommodation[8]
- proceedings under Schedule 1 for maintenance[9]

---

[2]   *J v. C* (1970) AC 668.
[3]   *Re J A (Child Abduction: Non-Convention Country)* (1998) 1 FLR 231.
[4]   *Re W (A Minor)(Medical Treatment: Court's Jurisdiction)* (1992) 4 All ER 627.
[5]   *Re W (A Minor)(Residence Order)* (1993) 2 FLR 625.
[6]   *Re J (Child's Religious Upbringing and Circumcision)* (1999) 2 FCR 345.
[7]   Section 22 Children Act 1989.
[8]   *Re M (A Minor)(Secure Accommodation Order)* (1995) 1 FLR 418.
[9]   *K v. H (Child Maintenance)* (1993) 2 FLR 61.

- directions for taking blood tests to establish paternity[10]
- determination of applications for leave to bring proceedings under section 8[11]
- applications for leave under section 91(17)[12]
- certain procedural and interlocutory applications determined on a case by case basis;[13] and
- publicity in the media of issues not directly relating to the child's upbringing.[14]

In cases where there is more than one child involved and there is a conflict between their interests it is not always possible to use the welfare principle in its purest form to resolve the issue. In *Re T and E (Proceedings: Conflicting Interests)* (1995) 1 FLR 581 Wall J commented:

> … where a number of children are all the subject of an application or cross-application to the court in the same set of proceedings, and where it was impossible to achieve what was in the paramount interests of each child, the balancing test [of balancing the children's interests to find a preponderance of benefit or detriment] had to be undertaken, and the situation of least detriment to all the children achieved …

Welfare is not defined in the Act. The welfare checklist (below) provides a range of issues the court must have regard to when determining cases. Commentators tend to approve the simple definition of welfare given by Hardie Boys J in New Zealand:

> 'Welfare' is an all-encompassing word. It includes material welfare, both in the sense of adequacy of resources to provide a pleasant home and a comfortable standard of living and in the sense of adequacy of care to ensure that good health and due personal pride are maintained. However, while material considerations have their place they are secondary matters. More important are the stability and the security, the loving and understanding care and guidance, the warm and compassionate relationships, that are essential for the full development of the child's own character, personality and talents.[15]

The welfare checklist is set out in section 1(3) of the Act. Whilst it is not exhaustive the checklist is the main standard against which the court welfare service provides reports to the court and against which the courts endeavour to discover where the best interests of the child lie. The checklist includes:

---

[10] *Re H (A minor)(Blood tests: parental rights)* (1997) Fam 89.
[11] *Re A (Minors)(residence Orders: Leave to Apply)* [1992] 3 All ER 872.
[12] *Re T (Minors)(Termination of Contact: Discharge of order)* (1997), 1 FLR 517.
[13] e.g. the issue of a witness summons: *Re P (Witness Summons)* (1997) 2 FLR 447.
[14] *R v. Central Television Plc* [1994] 3 All ER 641.
[15] 1981 NZ Recent Law 257.

- the ascertainable wishes and feelings of the child concerned (considered in the light of his or her age and understanding);
- his or her physical, emotional and educational needs;
- the likely effect on the child of any change in his or her circumstances;
- his or her age, sex, background and any characteristics of the child which the court considers relevant;
- any harm which he or she has suffered or is at risk of suffering;
- how capable each of his or her parents, or any other person in relation to whom the court considers the question to be relevant, is of meeting the child's needs; and
- the range of powers available to the court under the Act in the proceedings in question.

The welfare checklist applies in:

- all contested section 8 applications;[16] and
- all care and supervision applications.[17]

However whilst there is no requirement to apply the checklist to other applications it is clearly a most useful tool to be used to direct the judicial mind to the important issues relating to the case. Accordingly judicial approval for its use has been given in relation to applications for parental responsibility, the appointment of a guardian and for leave to change the child's surname.[18] Where such applications are contested the use of the checklist would be uncontrovertibly prudent.

The presumption against intervention

An important principle of the 1989 Act and one often overlooked by practitioners is the presumption *against* orders. Section 1(5) provides:

> Where a court is considering whether or not to make one or more orders under this Act [with respect to] a child, it shall not make the order or any of the orders unless it considers that doing so would be better for the child than making no order at all.

Article 8 of the European Convention On Human Rights provides that any interference with the right to respect for family life must be no more than is necessary in a democratic society. The element of proportionality introduced into the way courts must now read the Children Act suggests that the presumption against making orders will become vastly more significant in future.

---

[16] Section 1(4) of the Act.

[17] *Ibid.*

[18] *Re B (Change of Surname)* (1996) 1 FLR 791. The position should be contrasted with an application for a specific issues order or prohibited steps order under section 8 where the checklist is mandatory: *Dawson v. Wearmouth* (1999) 1 FCR 625.

Volume 1 of *The Children Act 1989 Guidance* and regulations published by the Department of Health explains the major objective of this principle:

> ... the first is to discourage unnecessary court orders being made, for example as part of a standard package of orders. If orders are restricted to those cases where they are necessary to resolve a specific problem this should reduce conflict and promote parental agreement and co-operation. The second aim is to ensure that the order is granted only where it will positively improve the child's welfare and not simply because the grounds for making the order are made out as, for example, in care proceedings where the court may decide that it would be better for a particular child not to be in local authority care.

Applications and parties

The Children Act recognises that the parents of a child may be treated differently depending on their status at the time of the child's birth. An unmarried father is in a less advantageous position when compared with a father who was married to the child's mother. A married father has parental responsibility automatically. An unmarried father does not but may acquire it in a variety of ways (most often by court order or through a parental responsibility agreement signed by mother and father and registered in the High Court under section 4 Children Act 1989). Parental responsibility may be shared between individuals including with the local authority.

Someone with parental responsibility has the right to bring proceedings under the Children Act and to be a party to applications brought by any other person including the local authority. A person without parental responsibility may be entitled to receive notice of certain applications but has no automatic right to be a party to them. An unmarried father may bring applications under section 8 of the Act without first requiring leave. Other people – such as grandparents - require leave before they are able to commence proceedings.[19]

The difference in treatment between married and unmarried fathers has been the subject of litigation in the Court of Human Rights. As a general rule it has been accepted that the difference in treatment is a justified interference with the father's right to respect for family life under Article 8 of the Convention and is a legitimate discrimination for the purposes of Article 14. The basis of this lawful discrimination reflects the range of circumstances in which a child may be conceived. It is legitimate to distinguish between a father by commitment (within an enduring relationship) and a father by circumstance (in an independent and isolated relationship) and across the spectrum of relationships in between. The requirement however that other members of the child's family (such as grandparents) seek leave from the court raises other issues under article 8. The test that such persons must have an arguable case may be thought to impose too high a hurdle for such individuals to

---

[19] See section 10 of the Act for a full description of the statutory scheme.

case may be thought to impose too high a hurdle for such individuals to clear before they are able to make applications for contact with the child for example. The test exists to protect children from the risk of unmeritorious litigation but this must be balanced against the rights of the applicant under Article 8. Where the interests of adults and children cannot be reconciled the Court of Human Rights has generally put the best interests of the child first. It is interesting to note that in applications for leave under section 8 the English courts are *not* required to apply the welfare principle.

The Children Act provides the following orders to resolve conflicts which relate to the child's upbringing:

- parental responsibility;
- residence orders;
- contact orders;
- specific issues orders;
- prohibited steps orders; and
- family assistance orders.[20]

Parental responsibility
Section 4 provides:

> 4(1) Where a child's father and mother were not married to each other at the time of his birth—
> - (a) the court may, on the application of the father, order that he shall have parental responsibility for the child; or
> - (b) the father and mother may by agreement ('a parental responsibility agreement') provide for the father to have parental responsibility for the child.

In an application for parental responsibility the court will usually consider the following (matters which will often focus on the father):

- the level of commitment by parent towards the child;
- the level of attachment between the parent and the child; and
- parent's motive for making his application.

Generally the notion of parental responsibility implies the acquisition by the applicant of an undefined set of obligations and responsibilities, powers and rights the exercise of which is characteristic of parenthood. The exercise of rights over the child is the least of the concepts implied within the term.

Section 8 orders
Section 8 contains the four major orders available to a court in private law child proceedings. A mother, father, person with parental

---

[20] The power to change a child's surname (section 13 of the Act) has been considered in *Chapter 2*.

responsibility or any other person with the leave of the court may apply for the orders. A child with the leave of the court may also do so. The court itself also has power to make any of the orders available of its own motion. Under the scheme applications for section 8 orders may be commenced in either the county court or the family proceedings court. In certain circumstances applications may be commenced in the High Court. The Children Act (Allocation of Proceedings) Order 1991 contains rules for the commencement of proceedings and their transfer between the courts. Applications by children however should always be determined by the High Court and accordingly transferred there by lower courts seized of such proceedings. It should be re-emphasised that the welfare principle and checklist apply in the determination of any proceedings under section 8. The orders are as follows:

- a contact order: an order requiring the person with whom a child lives, or is to live, to allow the child to visit or stay with the person named in the order, or for that person and the child otherwise to have contact with each other;
- a prohibited steps order: an order that no step which could be taken by a parent in meeting his or her parental responsibility for a child, and which is of a kind specified in the order, shall be taken by any person without the consent of the court;
- a residence order: an order settling the arrangements to be made as to the person with whom a child is to live: and
- a specific issues order: an order giving directions for the purpose of determining a specific question which has arisen, or which may arise, in connection with any aspect of parental responsibility for a child.

Residence orders
The purpose of a residence order is to settle the arrangements to be made as to the person with whom the child is going to live. There is a quality of permanence about the making of a residence order although in time such an order may be discharged or brought to an end by operation of law.[21] A residence order may be made:

- in respect of more than one person
- comes to an end if the child's parents live with each other for more than six months[22]
- may not be made in favour of the child himself or herself[23]
- may be shared between two (or more) people, even if they do not live together for example to accommodate arrangements where separated parents share the custody of the child at weekends or during the week[24]

---

[21] E.g. on making a care order or the child reaching the age of majority.
[22] Section 11(5).
[23] *Re M (Minors)(Interim Residence Order)* (1997) 2 FCR 28.
[24] *A v. A (Children: Shared Residence Order)* (1995) 1 FCR 91.

- may be made on an interim basis although in law its effect is the same as making a final residence order but for a very short period. Thus, an interim residence order discharges any existing care order (see, generally, *Chapter 7*). Practitioners need to be aware of the consequences of such orders especially where they purport to run alongside interim or final care orders[25] and
- a residence order may, in exceptional circumstances be made without notice.[26] Generally *ex parte* residence orders should be for the shortest period and be made only where there are compelling reasons to do so, for example where there is a fear of abduction.

Contact orders

The purpose of a contact order is to settle arrangements by which a child has contact with his or her absent parent. The issue of contact is often the most difficult of issues to resolve where there is conflict between parents. It is also probably the most crucial and needs to be resolved in order to allow the child to exercise his right to know an absent parent and to establish those essential ties which characterise family life.

Contact may also be difficult to facilitate. An absent parent may be a risk to the child; he or she may be violent either towards the child or towards the parent with care. The absent parent's absence may be enforced through an order of the court, ranging from short-term injunctions to long-term restraining orders, or enforced through his or her receipt of a sentence of custody in criminal proceedings. Similar practical difficulties may arise from the parent with care's hostility to contact as a principle or hostility to the absent parent. A new family for either parent may also create apparently irreconcilable barriers to contact.

None of these issues should, in a perfect world hinder the proper enjoyment of contact between a child and his absent parent. In the real world however the courts have been required to devise a number of strategies to deal with them.

The right to respect for family life under Article 8 of the European Convention On Human Rights has led the Court of Human Rights to identify the existence of a positive obligation on the state (and this includes the courts) to take measures to ensure that contact orders are properly enforced.[27] The Human Rights Act 1998 imposes a duty on courts to act compatibly with the Convention and to give effect to Convention rights by taking into account the decisions of the Court of Human Rights. The extent to which existing enforcement procedures are able to protect the absent parent's right to ongoing contact is an issue to be considered. A contact order:

---

[25] *S v. S (Custody: Jurisdiction)* (1995) 1 FLR 155.
[26] Rule 4(4) Family Proceedings Rules 1991 as amended to take into *account Re B (Minors)(Residence Order)* [1992] 3 All ER 867.
[27] *Hokkanen v. Finland* (1994) 19 EHRR 139.

- may include elements of, or be restricted to direct or indirect contact. Indirect contact may be by telephone, letter and doubtless e-mail[28]
- may provide for contact with any person named in the order and not only the applicant
- may provide for reasonable contact or contain directions under section 11(7) to define contact
- will be brought to an end if the parents of the child live with each other for a period of more than six months
- may be made on an interim basis
- could, in theory, be made without notice but would probably be impossible to enforce
- may be expressed so as to prohibit contact.[29] The court has the power to make an order for no contact and an order that there shall be no order as to contact. By whatever means the result is achieved prohibiting contact between a child and his absent parent is a serious step. Only where there are cogent reasons for concluding that contact would be against the welfare of the child should it be prohibited.[30] The principle of continuing contact set out in Article 9(3) of the UN Convention On the Rights of the Child has received express judicial approval.[31] Where direct contact is either impractical or inappropriate the approach appears to be that indirect contact should be tried or considered.

As a general expression of the state of English law, Wall J summarised the principles as follows:

- Overriding all else, as provided by section 1(1) of the Act, the welfare of the child is the paramount consideration, and the court is concerned with the interests of the mother and the father only in so far as they bear on the welfare of the child.
- It is almost always in the interests of the child whose parents are separated that he or she should have contact with the parent with whom the child is not living.
- The court has powers to enforce orders for contact, which it should not hesitate to so exercise where it judges that this will, overall, promote the welfare of the child.
- Cases do, unhappily and infrequently - but occasionally - arise in which a court is compelled to conclude that in existing circumstances an order for immediate direct contact should not be ordered, because so to order would injure the welfare of the child.
- In cases in which, for whatever reason, direct contact cannot for the time being be ordered, it is ordinarily highly desirable that there should be indirect contact so that the child grows up knowing of

---

[28] *A v. L (Contact)* (1998) 1 FLR 361.
[29] *Nottingham County Council v. P* (1993) All ER 815.
[30] *Re H (Minors)(Access)* (1992) 1 FLR 171.
[31] *Re R (A Minor) (Contact)* (1993) 2 FLR 762.

the love and interest of the absent parent with whom, in due course, direct contact should be established.[32]

Two particular issues present intractable problems to the proper facilitation of contact. In both cases the degree of difficulty caused may, in extreme cases, justify the refusal or prohibition of contact. These two areas are: 'implacable hostility' from the parent with care; and situations involving domestic violence.

Implacable hostility
Implacable hostility should not generally deter a court from making an order for contact.[33] In practice however an order made against a parent's hostility is likely to be an unenforceable order and many absent parents may withdraw from the process of repeated applications and repeated court proceedings. In *Re P (Contact: Discretion)* (1999) 1 FCR 566 three different situations from which hostility may arise were identified by Wilson J, i.e. where:

- there is no rational basis for the parent's hostility. In such a case the court should only refuse to make a contact order if to do so would create a serious risk of emotional harm to the child;
- the parent with care is able to advance grounds disclosing sufficient reason to displace the usual presumption that contact is in the child's best interests; and
- those grounds exist but there are also sound arguments the other way. In such cases the hostility itself may be of importance, occasionally of determinative importance, when it is measured against what is in the child's best interests.

Where a parent with care presents grounds falling within either the first or third categories above the court is faced with an almost irreconcilable problem. It would be wrong in principle to deny a child his right to know and have contact with the absent parent. But if the order is to be effective it must be enforced. The enforcement of such orders presents as many problems. Generally the court has a limited range of options and can only take those measures which are in the best interests of the child. Such measures include:

- making a defined contact order
- making a family assistance order (see below)
- the transfer of residence from the hostile parent to the parent willing and able to care for the child and facilitateing contact with the other
- treating the refusal to comply with the order as a contempt and attaching to it the sanction of a fine

---

[32] *Re P (Contact: Supervision)* (1996) 2 FLR 314.
[33] *Re J (A Minor)(Contact)* (1994), 1 FLR 729

- treating the refusal to comply with the order as a contempt and attaching to it penal consequences, probably suspended in the first instance; or
- committing the parent at fault to custody.

Transfer of residence is a measure of last resort and is dependent on the ability of the absent parent to provide a home for the child. The committal to prison of an otherwise exemplary parent for resisting a court order for contact seems both disproportionate and undesirable. The lack of practical effective measures to enforce contact on behalf of, and as a right of, the child is likely to present further difficulties to the court in light of the decision in *Hokkanan v. Finland* (1994) 19 EHRR 139.

Domestic violence
The existence of domestic violence in the family background is not a reason on its own to refuse to make a contact order between a child and his or her absent parent.[34] It may inform the exercise of the court's discretion but cannot override the principle that a child is entitled to contact with his or her parents so long as it is in the child's best interests. However it has long been accepted that domestic violence presents the courts with a challenge. Wall J emphasised that too little weight has been attached by the courts to the need for a violent parent to change his behaviour so as to demonstrate his fitness for contact.[35]

In 1999 the Advisory Board on Family Law Children Act Sub-Committee published an open report to the Lord Chancellor on the question of parental contact where there is domestic violence. It made several recommendations and set them out as follows:

1. In every case in which domestic violence is put forward in a statement to the court as a reason for refusing or limiting contact the court should consider the allegations made at the earliest opportunity (and any answer to them) and decide whether the nature and effect of the violence alleged by the complainant (or admitted by the respondent) is such as to make it likely that the order of the court for contact will be affected if the allegations are proved.

2. Where the allegations are disputed and the court forms the view that the nature and effect of the violence alleged is such as to make it likely that the order of the court will be affected if the allegations are proved the court should:

(a) consider what evidence will be required to enable the court to make findings of fact in relation to the allegations;

(b) ensure that appropriate directions are given at an early stage in the application under section 11(1) Children Act 1989 to enable the matters in issue to be heard as speedily as possible;

---

[34] *Re H (Minors)(Contact:Domestic Violence)* (1983) 3 FCR 385.
[35] *Re M (Minors)(Contact: Violent parent)* (1999) 2 FCR 56.

(c) consider whether an order for interim contact pending the final hearing is in the interests of the child;

(d) direct a report from a court welfare officer on the question of contact unless satisfied that it is not necessary to do so in order to safeguard the child's interests;

(e) subject to the seriousness of the allegations made and the difficulty of the case consider whether or not the children in question need to be separately represented in the proceedings; and, if the case is proceeding in the family proceedings court whether or not it should be transferred to the county court; if in the county court whether or not it should be transferred to the High Court for hearing.

3. Where the court orders a welfare officer's report under section 7 of the Children Act 1989 in a disputed application for contact in which it considers domestic violence to be a relevant issue, the order of the court should contain specific directions to the court welfare officer to address the issue of domestic violence; to make an assessment of the harm which the children have suffered or which they are at risk of suffering if contact is ordered; and to make particular efforts to ascertain the wishes and feelings of the children concerned in the light of the allegations of violence made.

4. In deciding any question of interim contact pending a full hearing the court should:

(a) specifically take into account the matters set out in section 1(3) of the Children Act 1989 ('the welfare check-list')

(b) give particular consideration to the likely effect on the child of such contact and any risk of harm, physical and / or psychological, which the child is likely to suffer as a consequence of such contact being ordered;

(c) consider, if it decides such contact is in the interests of the child, what directions are required about how it is to be carried into effect and, in particular, whether it should be supervised, and if so, by whom; and generally, in so far as it can, ensure that any risk of harm to the child is minimised.

(d) consider whether the parent seeking contact should seek advice and/or treatment as a precondition to contact being ordered or as a means of assisting the court in ascertaining the likely risk of harm to the child from that person at the final hearing.

5. At the final hearing of a contact application in which there are disputed allegations of domestic violence:

(a) the court should, wherever practicable, make findings of fact as to the nature and degree of the violence which is established on the balance of probabilities and its effect on the child and the child's mother;

(b) in deciding the issue of contact the court should, in the light of the findings of fact which it has made, apply the individual items in the welfare checklist with reference to those findings; in particular, where relevant findings of domestic violence have been made, the court should in every case consider the harm which the child has suffered as a consequence of that violence and the harm which the child is at risk of suffering if an order for contact is made;

6. In each case where a finding of domestic violence is made, the court should consider the conduct of both parents towards each other and towards the children; in particular, the court should consider;

(a) the effect of the domestic violence which has been established on the child and on the parent with whom the child is living;

(b) whether or not the motivation of the parent seeking contact is a desire to promote the best interests of the child or as a means of continuing a process of violence against or intimidation or harassment of the other parent;

(c) the likely behaviour of the parent seeking contact during contact and its effect on the child or children concerned;

(d) the capacity of the parent seeking contact to appreciate the effect of past and future violence on the other parent and the children concerned;

(e) the attitude of the parent seeking contact to past violent conduct by that parent; and in particular whether that parent has the capacity to change and/or to behave appropriately.

7. Where the court has made findings of domestic violence but, having applied the welfare checklist, nonetheless considers that direct contact is in the best interests of the child or children concerned, the court should consider (in addition to the matters set out in paragraphs 5 and 6 above) what directions are required to enable the order to be carried into effect under section 11(7) of the Children Act 1989 and in particular should consider:

(a) whether or not contact should be supervised, and if so, by whom;

(b) what conditions (for example by way of seeking advice or treatment) should be complied with by the party in whose favour the order for contact has been made;

(c) whether such contact should be for a specified period or should contain provisions which are to have effect for a specified period;

(d) whether or not the operation of the order needs to be reviewed, and if so the court should set a date for the review and give directions to ensure that the court at the review has full information about the operation of the order.

8. The court should also take steps to inform itself (alternatively direct the court welfare officer or the parties to inform it) of the facilities available locally to the court to assist parents who have been violent to their partners and / or their children, and, where appropriate, should impose as a condition of future contact that the violent parent avail himself of those facilities.

9. In its judgement or reasons the court should always explain how its findings on the issue of domestic violence have influenced its decision on the issue of contact; and in particular where the court has found domestic violence proved but nonetheless makes an order for contact, the court should always explain, whether by way of reference to the welfare check-list or otherwise why it takes the view that contact is in the best interests of the child.

10. Although not part of our formal guidelines, we think that all courts hearing applications where domestic violence is alleged should review their

facilities at court and should do their best to ensure that there are separate waiting areas for the parties in such cases and that information about the services of Victim Support and other supporting agencies is readily available'[36]

In *Re L (a Child)(Contact: Domestic Violence), The Times,* 21 June 2000 the Court of Appeal tackled the issue of domestic violence head on. Waller LJ summarised the key points as follows:

- That the effect of children being exposed to domestic violence of one parent as against the other might up until now have been underestimated by judges and advisers alike.
- That alleged domestic violence was a matter which should be investigated and findings of fact should be made because, if it was established, its effect on the children exposed to it and the risk to the residential carer were highly relevant factors in considering orders for contact and their form.
- That in assessing the relevance of past domestic violence it was likely to be highly material whether the perpetrator had shown an ability to recognise the wrong he, or less commonly she, had done and the steps taken to correct the deficiency in that perpetrator's character.
- That there should, however, be no presumption against contact simply because domestic violence was alleged or proved. It was one highly material factor among many which might offset the assumption in favour of contact when the difficult balancing exercise was carried out.

Specific issues orders

The purpose of a specific issues order is to allow a specific question about the exercise of parental responsibility to be brought to a court for decision. The order may be used in conjunction with other orders under section 8 and may be made on an *ex parte* basis. By their nature such orders are unlikely to lend themselves to interim orders. The court has power to impose detailed terms and conditions in any order made.

Prohibited steps orders

The purpose of a prohibited steps order is to empower the court to make an order prohibiting a parent from doing what would otherwise be a lawful exercise of parental responsibility. The order can be made on an *ex parte* basis and may be directed against non-parties in appropriate circumstances. The court again has power to impose detailed terms and conditions in any order made.

Neither a prohibited steps order or a specific issues order may be used to oust a parent from the matrimonial home or indeed any home where the child lives. The only power to oust a parent arises under the

---

[36] For a detailed commentary on these issues see *Domestic Violence and Occupation of the Family Home*, Bazell, C and Gibson B, Winchester: Waterside Press, 1999.

Family Law Act 1996 (see *Chapter 8*). Section 9(5) of the Act prevents the making of either order with a view to achieving a result which could be achieved by a residence or contact order (above).

Family assistance orders

Section 16 FLA provides:

16(1) Where, in any family proceedings, the court has power to make an order under this part with respect to any child, it may (whether or not it makes such an order) make an order requiring—
 (a) a probation officer to be made available; or
 (b) a local authority to make an officer of the authority available,
to advise, assist and (where appropriate) befriend any person named in the order.

The purpose of a family assistance order is to provide short-term help to a family to overcome the problems and conflicts associated with separation and divorce.[37] The two major requirements to be satisfied before a court may make a family assistance order are that the circumstances of the case are exceptional and that the consents of all people named in the order have been obtained. This last requirement provides the weak link in what could be a most useful order. The usefulness of the order lies in the supervisory and advisory role assigned to a professional to assist and facilitate the section 8 order (more often than not, contact) usually associated with it. The requirement for consent from everyone named in the order allows one party to thwart and frustrate the intention of the court. Given that orders are, in any event, reserved for use only in exceptional circumstances it is not really surprising to discover that few family assistance orders have found their way into the law reports.

An element of compulsion would arguably extend the powers of the local authority to become involved in the supervision of children who are not at risk of suffering serious harm. Resources of course come into this issue and it is often the case that the consent of the local authority is as hard to obtain as that of the parties. Nevertheless the family assistance order may become more frequently considered by courts in the effort to provide an effective remedy or enforcement measure to a parent whose rights are improperly frustrated by the other parent. Until the requirement for all parties to consent is removed the order has but a limited place in the protection of the rights of children in cases of parental breakdown because breakdown inevitably involves the withdrawal of consent to joint decision-making by one party or another.

Children and divorce

Where a marriage is to be brought to an end by divorce the court has a duty to ensure that suitable arrangements exist for any children of the family. The petitioner for divorce files at the court his or her petition

---

[37] Guidance ante Vol. 1.

together with a Statement of Arrangements for Children. This procedure is followed only where the children concerned are under 18 years of age or still in full time education. The statement sets out the following information:

- details of the child and his or her accommodation
- arrangements for the day-to-day care of the child
- what contact arrangements exist between the child and his or her absent parent
- maintenance arrangements for the child.

In determining the application for the decree *nisi* the District Judge will also consider the statement. Generally if content with the arrangements for the child he or she will issue a certificate under section 41 Matrimonial Causes Act 1973 that no orders are required under the Children Act. In those very few cases where the arrangements are unsatisfactory the District Judge has power to make directions leading towards the resolution of issues under the procedures in the Children Act. Usually, however, the arrangements are approved and the District Judge certifies accordingly.

Where parents in divorce are also in conflict over the child's residence or contact arrangements it would be usual to expect applications to have already been made under the Children Act within the divorce proceedings. Once an application is made for an order under section 8 the procedure for determining how the interests of the child are to be upheld is the same as for freestanding applications.

However the arrangements before the District Judge are merely submitted for information. They do not constitute an enforceable order for either party and the courts' powers are limited to approving them or otherwise. Where the court is seized of an application under the Children Act those proceedings are capable of being determined both before and after the final grant of the divorce.

Divorce court powers are effectively limited to approving the arrangements for the children. If a party seeks an order - even an order giving effect to the arrangements - he or she must do so via a separate application which may or may not be capable of determination in the same proceedings depending on the allocation of proceedings rules. Thus the rights of the child are a secondary issue and are not either protected or promoted in divorce proceedings which are solely concerned with the dissolution of marriage.

CHAPTER 10

Financial Matters

Responsibility for the financial support of children falls on either parents, guardians or the state. The child's right to receive financial support in his or her own name is limited and there are large gaps in the provision of state support, especially for children who have left full-time education at 16 but have not commenced employment or a training scheme. This chapter describes generally the major sources of financial provision for children in the UK: sources of crisis provision to families and children. The arrangements between children and their parents in stable family life are generally a private concern attracting few legal consequences.

An uninformed reader might reasonably have anticipated that financial assistance for children and their families in the UK is at the least adequate. However, a report by UNICEF on *Child Poverty in the Rich Nations* listed the UK at fourth from bottom in the league table for relative child poverty and in the bottom quartile of the table for absolute poverty.[1] The report noted that children who grow up in poverty tend to live lives that perpetuate poverty and disadvantage into succeeding generations. Poverty leads to exclusion both socially and economically and often includes exclusion from opportunity and from the benefits which arise from equal access policies followed by successive governments. Poverty impacts on housing, health, education and expectation; all issues which form the subject matter of those basic rights possessed by children as a birthright. No one would try to argue that being born into poverty is the fault of the child. It is merely the lottery of birth and fundamental to concepts of progress and civilisation that an accident of birth should not be allowed to circumscribe the quality of a child's life.

Present policy in the UK - as judged by adjustments introduced in the tax and benefits systems and from the local authority's obligation towards children after care - is characterised by the principle of supportive self-reliance

International obligations
Article 27 of the UN Convention On the Rights of the Child states:

(1) States Parties recognise the right of every child to a standard of living adequate for the child's physical, mental, spiritual, moral and social development.

(2) The parent(s) or others responsible for the child have the primary responsibility to secure, within their abilities and financial capacities, the conditions of living necessary for the child's development.

---

[1] Published 14 June 2000 and available from UK Committee for UNICEF, 55 Lincolns Inn Fields, London WC2A 3NB.

(2)   The parent(s) or others responsible for the child have the primary responsibility to secure, within their abilities and financial capacities, the conditions of living necessary for the child's development.

(3)   States Parties, in accordance with national conditions and within their means, shall take appropriate measures to assist parents and others responsible for the child to implement this right and shall in case of need provide material assistance and support programmes, particularly with regard to nutrition, clothing and housing.

(4)   States Parties shall take all appropriate measures to secure the recovery of maintenance for the child from the parents or other persons having financial responsibility for the child, both within the State Party and from abroad. In particular, where the person having financial responsibility for the child lives in a State different from that of the child, States Parties shall promote the accession to international agreements or the conclusion of such arrangements as well as the making of other appropriate arrangements.

As far as the child's right to state assistance is concerned Article 26 provides:

(1) States Parties shall recognise for every child the right to benefit from social security, including social insurance and shall take the necessary measures to achieve the full realisation of this right in accordance with their national law.

(2)   The benefits should, where appropriate, be granted, taking into account the resources and the circumstances of the child and persons having responsibility for the maintenance of the child, as well as any other considerations relevant to an application for benefits made by or on behalf of the child.

The obligations under the UN Convention operate in international law and require the UK government to take those steps necessary to give effect to the Convention. However it does not provide a source of directly enforceable rights. A child's rights to financial support are limited to those recognised under national law.

The European Convention On Human Rights does not expressly provide a right to welfare benefit and entitlements. Where national law does provide such a right their enjoyment may be treated as the enjoyment of property under Article 1 of the First Protocol to the Convention. The determination of applications for benefits is also likely to fall within the determination of a civil right and accordingly the fair trial requirements of Article 6 apply to any procedure relating to their grant or refusal.

Several complaints have been made to the Court of Human Rights concerning maintenance payments to a child by an absent parent. In *Logan v. UK*[2] the Court rejected a petition that the level of child maintenance set by the Child Support Agency was such that it left no money for the father to continue contact with his son and that this

---

[2] (1992) 2 EHRR CD 178.

amounted to a violation of his rights under Article 8 of the Convention. The Court also rejected a complaint against a maintenance order where it was alleged that the child was being brought up contrary to the absent parent's religious views. The Court was satisfied that the obligation to pay maintenance was a general obligation and had no implications for the child's religious upbringing.[3]

STATE PROVISION[4]

The present government's response to the issue of social security has been to develop a range of measures and incentives designed to encourage people into (or to return to) work. This welfare to work approach has been characterised by a dramatic shift in social policy away from dependence to self-reliance. UNICEF's recent report on child poverty estimated that these policies could reduce child poverty in the UK by no more than two thirds. The shortfall was accounted for by the fact that half of poor children live in households where parents are unavailable for work—through sickness, disability or because a child is below school age—and because one in ten entering work would earn too little to lift them out of poverty. The poor provision of state funded pre-school facilities and the high cost of private sector facilities also acts as a disincentive to parents in receipt of benefit to enter the workplace.

A danger of building a welfare benefits regime around the ability of certain sections of its community to move from dependence upon it to self-reliance through welfare supported employment is that it fails to provide a sufficiency of support for those who are genuinely unable to work. The children of such people are at risk of further marginalisation and exclusion and it is in this area that the government has an increasing duty - and an increasing reluctance - to intervene.

Income support
Income support is the main welfare benefit. It is payable to people who are not in work and not entitled to job seeker's allowance, or one of the range of statutory sick or disability benefits. A single parent with sole responsibility for the care of a dependent child is eligible for income support. One claim may be made per household. The purpose of the benefit is to provide a weekly allowance designed to cover day-to-day expenses. Someone in receipt of income support is also likely to qualify for a series of 'premiums', such as an additional allowance for a dependant child, and will be eligible for other state help in the form of housing benefit and free prescriptions amongst others.

Whilst in receipt of income support the recipient may earn money from a range of sources although all monies received are taken into account to calculate both the entitlement to and sum of income support.

---

[3] *Karakuzey v. Germany* (1996) 23 EHRR CD 92.
[4] Details of current rates and allowances can be found at http://www.dss.gov.uk/ba

Certain sums of money, to a maximum of £25 per week may be disregarded for the purposes of the calculation. Similarly the possession of capital below a maximum of £8,000 will not disentitle a claimant from receiving income support but between £3,000 and £8,000 the claimant will be treated as receiving £1 per week income per £250 of capital. Accordingly the amount of income support paid will be reduced. Capital of less than £3000 is disregarded as is any capital sum held by a child except that if the child's savings exceed £3,000 it will not be possible for the claimant to claim an allowance in respect of the child.

Income support and children
A child must be aged 16 years or over in order to claim income support. Such a claim would be limited to where a child also falls within those categories that would permit an adult to claim the benefit. To be eligible the child would have to be incapable of work, pregnant, a full-time carer, a lone parent or within one of a number of restrictive categories. Otherwise a 16/17 year old is not able to claim as an unemployed person as he or she is guaranteed a Youth Training place.

Job seeker's allowance
Job seeker's allowance is a benefit with two parts: contribution-based and income-based. It is available to all people not working but actively seeking work. The main rates are the same as the personal allowances for income support. Job seeker's allowance may be suspended if someone fails to take part in certain government training schemes and work related initiatives. It may also be reduced or suspended altogether if the claimant has brought about his or her own unemployment.

Job seeker's allowance and children
A child must be aged 16 years or over in order to claim job seeker's allowance. However such a person is not able to claim as an unemployed person as he is guaranteed a Youth Training place (below). However if the claimant is classed as being in a vulnerable group he or she may be eligible for job seeker's allowance but only where the child will suffer severe hardship if it is not paid. Examples of vulnerable groups include those forced to live away from their parents or home, couples with children and those released from custody or care.

Youth Training schemes
All 16/17 year olds are guaranteed a Youth Training place. The training is for skills and qualifications which will make the claimant a better prospect on the labour market. A standard allowance of £40 per week is payable to a trainee. A young person failing to take part in the scheme is not eligible for the allowance nor is he or she is eligible to make a claim as an unemployed person for either income support or job seeker's allowance unless within the class of other people so entitled to make such claims. Youth training is a relatively new concept in compulsory training for the youth unemployed and until such times as proper studies have been completed it is difficult to asses its success or otherwise.

Child benefit
Child benefit is payable to every family with dependent children aged under 16 years or under 19 years and in full time education. The benefit is not means tested and is payable weekly at the rate of £15 for the eldest child and £10 for each subsequent child. The benefit is payable to the parent with care of the child.

Working Family Tax Credits
The Working Family Tax Credits scheme is administered by the Inland Revenue and not the Benefits Agency. It provides a tax credit by way of a range of allowances depending on the circumstances of a family where a parent works at least 16 hours per week.

Welfare to Work incentives
The government's focus on returning people - and parents especially - to work getting them off the benefits roundabout has been supported by the creation of a number of other financial incentives. For example the cost of childcare may be taken into account in the calculation of Working Family Tax Credit. A parent with care of a child and in receipt of child maintenance from the absent parent moving from benefit to work may qualify for a payment of up to £1,000 under the Child Maintenance Bonus Scheme.

Tax incentives
In his pre-budget statement in November 1999, the Chancellor of the Exchequer affirmed the government's ambition to reduce child poverty and to eliminate it within 20 years. As part of the raft of welfare benefit measures in this regard he introduced a children's tax credit to replace the married couples tax allowance from April 2001. At the same time the Treasury published a paper describing in more detail the adjustments to the tax system which had and would continue to facilitate the reduction in child poverty.[5]

Liable relatives
Sections 78(6) and 105(3) Social Security Administration Act 1992 impose a statutory duty on liable relatives when their dependants claim various welfare benefits. The liability falls on wives, husbands and the parents of dependent children. Where income support is claimed the duty is to provide financial support for the claimant in place of him or her receiving the income support allowance. If the liable relative does not maintain his or her dependent the Benefits Agency will pursue the liable relative and in the first place enter into a voluntary agreement under which he or she

---

[5] *Supporting Children through the Tax and Benefit System.* The report is available from the Treasury Website at http://www.hm-treasury.gov.uk/ The paper estimated that by the general election of May 2001 at least 800,000 children would have been removed from poverty. This figure has been supported by the recent UNICEF report on child poverty in the rich nations.

maintains the dependent claimant. If such an arrangement fails the dependent person, or indeed the Benefits Agency, can take steps to seek an order for maintenance in the family proceedings court.

CHILD SUPPORT MAINTENANCE

The Child Support Act 1991 was a somewhat hasty measure to ensure that absent parents were called to account for the financial support of their children and to reduce the burden on the taxpayer in terms of the amount of public funds being spent on providing such support. There was at the time a quite justifiable perception that the courts were ill-equipped and ill-prepared to make realistic assessments of child maintenance and that the enforcement of such orders as there were was arbitrary, half-hearted and inadequate. Many of the criticisms of the way courts dealt with the question of child maintenance were justified, others perhaps unfair.

The response from Parliament was the Child Support Act which effectively transferred the power to make maintenance orders and to enforce them from the courts to a new agency (with relatively Draconian powers) called the Child Support Agency. In order to achieve consistency the calculation of child maintenance was reduced to a rigid formula which allowed little in the way of discretion to adjudicating officers within the agency to take into account, for example, the costs of contact visits for the absent parent or the expenses associated with his[6] new family. As a result of pressure from many agencies and interest groups, the worst features of the Act were mitigated by the Child Support Act 1995. The Child Support, Pensions and Social Security Act 2000 comes into force in April 2002 and makes a range of changes to the operation of the child support system. In particular Schedule 1 changes the formula for calculating the basic rate of child maintenance. The basic rate is calculated as a percentage of the non-resident parent's net weekly income: 15 per cent for one child; 20 per cent for two and 25 per cent for three or more. Adjustments are avialable to deal with second families or where the net income is below £200.

The scheme under the Child Support Act 1991
The basic scheme provides for the calculation of maintenance by the agency as against an absent parent. If the order is not complied with the agency has power to seek from the magistrates' court a liability order empowering it to take a number of enforcement measures. Continued non-payment after a liability order allows the agency to apply again to the magistrates' court for an order committing the defaulter to prison. Under section 16 Child Support, Pensions and Social Security Act 2000, the court is also empowered to order a defaulter to be disqualified from holding or obtaining a driving licence. A ban from driving may seem an

---

[6] It was generally the absent father who became associated with the rigidity of the 1991 Act.

odd response to non-payment of child maintenance but reflects a perception of the recalcitrant parent's priorities.

The natural or adoptive parent of a child whose other parent lives elsewhere in England, Scotland, Wales or Northern Ireland may apply for child support maintenance. Similarly, someone other than a parent (e.g. a grandparent or other relation, or a guardian who has the care of a child whose parents live elsewhere) may also apply.

Child support maintenance is the amount of money that non-resident parents pay regularly as a contribution to the financial support of their children. The money is payable to the parent etc. with care - meaning a parent etc. who lives with the children for whom maintenance is required. If the child stays with both parents, the non-resident parent is the one who provides fewer nights of care than the other parent.

A parent with care who claims or receives (or whose current partner claims or receives):

- income support; or
- job seeker's allowance

may be required to give their authority for child support to be sought. Exceptionally, some people may not be required to apply if the Secretary of State (through an appropriate decision-maker) considers that they, or any child living with them, would be at risk of harm or undue distress if they were to apply. If a parent with care fails to comply with the requirement to give their authority or fails to give information required by the Child Support Agency their benefit may be reduced by 40 per cent.

Any other person falling within the definition of a parent with care may also apply to the Child Support Agency for a maintenance assessment to be made against an absent parent. The element of compulsion to make such an application falls only on those parents with care who are on benefits. However, a parent with means seeking to recover maintenance from an absent parent has also to apply through the Child Support Agency as the court has very limited power to exercise jurisdiction over an application for maintenance (see later in this chapter).

Since 5 April 1993 most new maintenance assessments in respect of children have been dealt with by the Child Support Agency instead of the courts. Courts, however, continue to be involved in certain circumstances dealt with later in this chapter.

Parents with care in receipt of benefits will generally be written to by the Benefits Agency and invited to apply for a maintenance assessment. Others who do not receive income support or job seeker's allowance (which is income based), and do not have an existing written maintenance agreement or a court order for periodical payments of maintenance in respect of their children may apply at any time.

The amount of child maintenance prior to the implementation in April 2002 of the Child Support, Pensions and Social Security Act 2000 is worked out in accordance with a statutory formula, taking into account:

- the day-to-day cost of maintaining a child

- the income of the parent with care and the non-resident parent after making allowances for tax, national insurance, half of any pension and basic living expenses, including rent or mortgage costs. The income of the parent with care can serve to reduce the non-resident parent's payments but in most cases is not high enough to do so; and
- any other children either parent may have.

New partners of either parent will not be expected to pay anything towards the child support maintenance of children who are not their own. However, partner income details are required because where the parent with care and their current partner or the non-resident parent and their current partner have a child of their relationship it needs to be established whether the partner can contribute to the upkeep of that child. In the case of a non-resident parent, information is required to check that the income of the non-resident parent's household does not fall below certain limits if the maintenance liability were to be met in full.

A formula is used to work out how much child maintenance is payable. It takes account of each parent's income and essential expenses. The formula has six elements:

- *the maintenance requirement:* this is the basic amount which all parents are required to contribute to the maintenance of their children if they can afford to; it represents the weekly cost of maintaining each child based on the weekly allowances in the Income Support Scheme;
- *exempt income:* this represents the weekly amount which parents are deemed to need for their own essential living expenses. This 'exempt income' figure is deducted from net income to arrive at a figure for 'assessable income' which is the income from which maintenance is deducted;
- *the deduction rate:* maintenance is deducted at the rate of 50 per cent from 'assessable income' until the maintenance needed is met;
- *the additional element:* an extra payment required from parents who have assessable income left after they have met the maintenance required for their children;
- *protected level of income:* this is the minimum amount which non-resident parents must retain after meeting their maintenance obligations. It ensures that non-resident parents and any second family are significantly better off after paying maintenance than they would be if receiving income support; and
- *a minimum amount:* if the formula produces a figure which is less than a prescribed minimum amount then the non-resident parent will pay that minimum amount unless exempt, for example because he or she has a dependent in his or her household or is disabled.

In addition, there are safeguards to ensure that non-resident parents keep more money than they would get if they were receiving income support or job seeker's allowance and do not pay more than 30 per cent of

CHAPTER 11

Education and Employment

The majority of a child's life is taken up with education. Education prepares and develops the child and moves his or her intellectual and physical character towards that required of an adult. The majority of an adult's life is taken up with employment. This chapter looks at the measures in place to protect and promote the child's rights in education and employment. Education is a basic and positive right for all children aimed at facilitating the child's intellectual and emotional development. The right to employment as far as an adult is concerned is not generally recognised, mainly because this would be impossible to secure within society. As far as children are concerned the rights surrounding employment are of a negative or protective nature, and aimed at preventing exploitation and setting minimum standards to ensure that where work is available it is properly regulated to promote the welfare of young workers.

Education and employment have a direct interface in the case of 16 and 17 year olds who have left school but have been unable to secure work. Such people are guaranteed a Youth Training place for which an allowance of £40 per week is payable by the state. The training programme is aimed at training for skills and qualifications that will make the claimant a better prospect in the labour market. In providing an alternative to beginning adult life reliant on state benefits, the Youth Training scheme is commendable, but in too many cases it amounts to much the same thing [as being on benefits.]

The employment of children conjures up many unsavoury images drawn either from the Victorian era of Henry Mayhew and the mudlarks of London, or from the abusive labour regimes established in many Third World and undeveloped countries. The exploitation of labour especially of children often appears to be a function of society's own economic development. There is a danger therefore of neglecting child employment issues in the UK.

PART I: EDUCATION

International obligations

The UN Convention On the Rights of the Child and the European Convention On Human Rights recognise the right to education. Article 28 of the UN Convention provides:

(1) States Parties recognise the right of the child to education, and with a view to achieving this right progressively and on the basis of equal opportunity, they shall, in particular:

(a) make primary education compulsory and available free to all;
(b) encourage the development of different forms of secondary education, including general and vocational education, make them available and accessible to every child, and take appropriate measures such as the introduction of free education and offering financial assistance in case of need;
(c) make higher education accessible to all on the basis of capacity by every appropriate means;
(d) make educational and vocational information and guidance available to all children;
(e) take measures to encourage regular attendance at schools and the reduction of dropout rates.

(2) States Parties shall take all appropriate measures to ensure that school discipline is administered in a manner consistent with the child's human dignity and in conformity with the present Convention.

(3) States Parties shall promote and encourage international cooperation in matters relating to education, in particular with a view to contributing to the elimination of ignorance and illiteracy throughout the world and facilitating access to scientific and technical knowledge and modern teaching methods. In this regard, particular account shall be taken of the needs of developing countries.

Article 29 of the Convention provides guidance as to the content of the educational system outlined in Article 28 above:

(1) States Parties agree that the education of the child shall be directed to:
(a) the development of the child's personality, talents and mental and physical abilities to their fullest potential;
(b) the development of respect for human rights and fundamental freedoms, and for the principles enshrined in the Charter of the United Nations;
(c) the development of respect for the child's parents, his or her own cultural identity, language and values, for the national values of the country in which the child is living, the country from which he or she may have originated, and for civilisations different from his or her own;
(d) the preparation of the child for responsible life in a free society, in the spirit of understanding, peace, tolerance, equality of sexes and friendship among all peoples, ethnic, national and religious groups and persons of indigenous origin;
(e) the development of respect for the natural environment.

(2) No part of the present Article or Article 28 shall be construed so as to interfere with the liberty of individuals and bodies to establish and direct educational institutions, subject always to the observance of the principle set forth in paragraph 1 of the present article and to the requirements that the education given in such institutions shall conform to such minimum standards as may be laid down by the state.

The European Convention On Human Rights also contains provision for the right to education. The inclusion of the right within a charter designed to protect against interference by the state with the basic and fundamental rights of the individual was controversial. In the *Belgian Linguistics Case (No 2)* (1968) 1 EHRR 252 the Court of Human Rights interpreted the right to education as including a right of access to education facilities that already exist, a right to have the opportunity to draw benefit from the education received and a right to official recognition of any qualification received on the completion of studies. The right however did not extend to a right to require the state to set up a particular type or level of education. In *X v. UK*, 1 December 1986 (unreported) the Commission rejected a complaint based on the right to education where the state had closed down a local school thereby necessitating the transfer of pupils to another school. Accordingly the right does not imply a right of access to a particular school.

Article 2 of the First Protocol to the European Convention states:

No person shall be denied the right to education. In the exercise of any functions which it assumes in relation to education and to teaching, the State shall respect the right of parents to ensure such education and teaching in conformity with their own religious and philosophical aims.

The UK has entered a reservation in respect of this right in the following terms:

... in view of certain provisions of the Education Acts in the United Kingdom, the principle affirmed in the second sentence of Article 2 is accepted by the United Kingdom only in so far as it is compatible with the provision of efficient instruction and training, and the avoidance of unreasonable public expenditure.

In *SP v. UK* (1997) 23 EHRR 139 the Commission expressed the view that in the light of developments in case-law on reservations the reservation may be susceptible to challenge.

The Court of Human Rights has given education a wide definition. In *Campbell and Cosans v. UK*[1] it held that:

... the education of children is the whole process whereby, in any society, adults endeavour to transmit their beliefs, culture and other values to the young, whereas teaching or instruction refers in particular to the transmission of knowledge and to intellectual development.

The Court has also recognised that the right to education by its very nature calls for regulation by the state.[2] The question that arises is the extent to which any restrictions on access to education are justified in accordance with principles of Convention law. However it does not

---

[1]   (1982) 4 EHRR 293.
[2]   *The Belgian Linguistics Case* above.

follow that the state has exclusive responsibility for the provision of education. The Court has not found the existence of private schools to be incompatible with the Convention.[3] The right to run private schools is not unlimited and a private education system must be subject to regulation by the state in order to ensure a proper educational system as a whole.[4]

The provision of education for children with special needs has been considered by the Commission in very few cases and in those reported the Commission has allowed each state a wide margin of appreciation in the way resources are made available for disabled children generally.[5] A similar degree of discretion has been recognised by the Court in disciplinary matters. In *Valsamis v. Greece*[6] it observed:

> The imposition of disciplinary penalties is an integral part of the process whereby a school seeks to achieve the object for which it was established, including the development and moulding of the character and mental powers of its pupils.

However a disciplinary measure should not be imposed if it conflicts with the parent's religious or philosophical convictions, amounts to a breach of one of the other Convention rights or violates the principle of equal opportunity. The suspension or exclusion of a pupil from school may engage the right to education where no other provision has been made for the child's education.[7] Although the Court has found that such measures do not amount the determination of a criminal charge[8] there remains a convincing argument to suggest that education is a civil right and therefore the determination of disciplinary proceedings engages Article 6 and the right to a fair trial. Even if this suggestion overstates the position the Court of Human Rights has consistently affirmed the principle that where decisions are made affecting an individual there must be procedural fairness in the decision-making process. The duty on public authorities under the Human Rights Act 1998 seems likely to require at least a hearing in accordance with general principles of fairness informed by Convention case law under Article 6.[9]

Article 5 (right to liberty) allows a minor to be detained for an educational purpose as provided for by law. This provision may found the basis of secure accommodation orders made in the family proceedings court (*Chapter 7*) where the care plan includes educational requirements. However the power for national courts to make a care order on the basis of inadequate education was removed by the Children

---

[3]   *Kjeldsen, Busk Madsen and Pedersen v. Denmark* (1976) 1 EHRR 711.

[4]   *Jordebo v. Sweden* (1987) 51 DR 125.

[5]   *Simpson v. UK* (1989) 64 DR 188.

[6]   1996) 24 EHRR 294.

[7]   *Yanasik v. Turkey* (1993) 74 DR 14.

[8]   *ibid.*

[9]   In *R (on the application of B) v. Head Teacher of Alperton Community School* 2001 All ER (D) 312 the Administrative Court held that Article 6 was not applicable to pupil disciplinary measures leading to expulsion.

Act 1989 and replaced instead by a power to make an education supervision order.[10] The use of an order permitting a child to be placed and kept in the secure estate may as a consequence appear to be disproportionate.[11]

The statutory scheme

The provision of education in the UK is governed primarily by the Education Act 1996. Its foundation is supported on two pillars of responsibility[12]; the duty of the Secretary of State, the local authority and the local education authority to provide facilities for education and those other resources necessary to meet that provision; and the duty on a child's parents to ensure that their child is educated to a suitable standard. Section 1(1) of the 1996 Act provides:

> The statutory system of public education consists of three progressive stages: primary education, secondary education and further education.

Primary and secondary education is compulsory in the case of children of compulsory school age (below). Further education is available in respect of children and other people who are no longer of compulsory school age.[13]

Primary education means full-time education suitable to the requirements of junior pupils[14] who have not attained the age of ten years and six months and for pupils of such an age but in respect of whom it is expedient to educate together with junior pupils under that age.[15]

Secondary education means full-time education suitable to the requirements of pupils of compulsory school age who are either senior pupils or junior pupils who have attained the age of ten years and six months and whom it is expedient to educate with senior pupils of compulsory school age.[16] The Act recognises six types of school:

- *primary schools:* providing primary education;
- *secondary schools:* providing secondary education;
- *middle schools:* providing education for children of a specified age below ten years and six months and over 12 years;
- *nursery schools:* providing education for children between two and five years of age;

---

[10] An education supervision order is one which can be made in the family proceedings court on the application of the local authority. It places the child under the supervision of the local authority for the purpose of securing his or her attendance at school.

[11] However, the Court of Appeal in *Re K* (above: *Chapter 7*) found that the use of secure accommodation in accordance with the regulations was not disproportionate.

[12] In *R v. Neale, ex parte S* (1995) ELR 198 Turner J observed that a child's education was a three way partnership between the child, the school and his or her parents.

[13] Further education falls outside the scope of this work.

[14] Section 3(2) Education Act 1996 defines a 'junior pupil' as a child under the age of 12 years and a 'senior pupil' as a child aged between 12 and 18 years.

[15] Section 2(1) Education Act 1996.

[16] Section 2(2) Education Act 1996.

- *special schools:* providing education for children with special educational needs; and
- *grammar schools:* providing education based on a selective admissions policy at the beginning of the 1997/98 school year and which are so designated by the Secretary of State.

A further categorisation of schools exists. An 'independent school' is defined in section 463 of the Act as 'any school at which full-time education is provided for five or more pupils of compulsory school age … which is not a school maintained by a local education authority or a special school not so maintained'. The local authority maintains schools that are not independent. This work is generally concerned with the protection and promotion of child rights within the public provision of education at maintained schools.

Compulsory school age
A child has no legal obligation to attend school. The duty to ensure that he or she does so lies with his or her parents. Whilst the education system deals directly and exclusively with the provision of suitable education for a child, it invests very little responsibility for him or her. Education is *done to* and not *with* children. This is the source of little difficulty in the case of the majority of children but where a child is excluded from education, by act or omission the difficulties become more apparent. Broadly speaking children are expected to be educated when they are of compulsory school age. A child is of compulsory school age between the ages of five and 16 years. Regulations determine the precise start date and leaving date for a specific child.[17]

Parental obligations
Section 7 Education Act 1996 provides:

> The parent of every child of compulsory school age shall cause him to receive efficient full-time education suitable –
> (a) to his age, ability and aptitude, and
> (b) to any special educational needs he may have,
> either by regular attendance at school or otherwise.

A parent is therefore free to determine how education is to be provided including a right to educate the child at home. However a parent not causing a child to attend school must be able to satisfy the local education authority that the child is receiving suitable education as defined in section 7. Where the local education authority is not satisfied as to the suitability of a parent's educational provision it has power to serve on the parent a school attendance order requiring the child to be registered at a school. The authority also has power in the criminal court

---

[17] The Education (Start of Compulsory School Age) Order 1998 and the Education (School Leaving Date) Order 1997. See also *Chapter 1*.

to enforce the order and the child's attendance at the school at which he or she is registered.[18]

The Secretary of State's primary obligations

The general duties of the Secretary of State are set out in sections 10 and 11 of the 1996 Act. His or her primary function is to promote the education of the people in England and Wales. Those powers available to him must be exercised in particular with a view to improving standards, encouraging diversity and increasing opportunities for choice.

Education: the Local Education Authority's primary obligations

The local education authority is under a duty to provide sufficient schools to enable a child of compulsory school age to receive efficient full-time and suitable education.[19] In discharging this function the local education authority must have regard for its general responsibility for education under section 13 of the Act which provides:

> (1) A local education authority shall (so far as their powers enable them to do so) contribute towards the spiritual, moral, mental and physical development of the community by securing that efficient primary education, secondary education and further education are available to meet the needs of the population of their area.

The rights of parents to have a child educated in accordance with their own set of values is a further factor to which the local education authority must have due regard. Section 9 of the Act provides:

> In exercising or performing all their respective powers and duties under the Education Acts, the Secretary of State, local education authorities and the funding authorities shall have regard to the general principle that pupils are to be educated in accordance with the wishes of their parents, so far as that is compatible with the provision of efficient instruction and training and the avoidance of unreasonable public expenditure.[20]

In addition to its general function the local education authority has responsibilities, duties and liabilities in the following areas:

- the establishment and maintenance of a suitable standard of education delivered through a head teacher and teaching staff at its schools;
- the assessment of children for special educational needs and the provision thereof;

---

[18] See below.

[19] Section 14(1) Education Act 1996. The administration of schools and provision for the welfare of a child are discussed below.

[20] It is this provision which triggered the UK's reservation against the right to education and in particular the second sentence thereof in Article 2 of the First Protocol to the European Convention On Human Rights.

- a duty to promote high standards including the formulation and publication of an education development plan;
- to make arrangements for the provision of suitable education to children not at school for example by virtue of exclusion, pregnancy or child care;
- to make arrangements for the provision of suitable education to children who are ill or injured and unable to go to school;
- to secure facilities for recreation and social and physical training;
- to provide transport or such facilities as will enable a child to attend school where it is necessary to do so; and
- to make arrangements in respect of a child's welfare while at school which are ancillary to the provision of suitable education. This duty may include assistance for clothing, school meals, board and lodging where appropriate, the payment of certain expenses and fees and arrangements for medical, dental and basic hygiene services.

School governors

Each school must have a governing body. The School Standards and Framework Act 1998 makes provision for the appointment of governors to a governing body which is a body corporate. The number of governors required depends on the size and type of school but generally includes a number of parent governors, local education authority governors, teacher governors, staff governors, foundation governors, co-opted governors and additional governors. The governing body must have its own constitution prescribing the functions and administration of the body and the school. The governing body must also hold an annual parents' meeting at which there is opportunity to discuss:

- the governors' report
- the discharge by the governing body, the head teacher and the local education authority of their functions in relation to the school
- the aims and values of the school
- how the spiritual, moral, cultural, mental and physical development of pupils is to be promoted at the school
- how pupils are to be prepared for the opportunities, responsibilities and experiences of adult life and citizenship
- the standards of educational achievement of pupils; and
- how the governing body is to promote the good behaviour, discipline and wellbeing of pupils.[21]

In general terms the conduct of the school is the preserve of the school governing body. The role of the governors includes:

- establishing and publicising a complaints procedure
- ensuring that policies designed to promote good behaviour and discipline are pursued at the school and in particular to make a

---

[21] Section 43 School Standards and Framework Act 1998.

written statement of general principles to which the head teacher is to have regard and to provide guidance on particular measures[22]

- controlling the use of the school premises;
- determining the times of school and the school terms and holidays (within an existing framework set by the local education authority);
- holding an annual parents' meeting; and
- meeting any target set by the Secretary of State for reducing the level of unauthorised absences by pupils.

The curriculum

The curriculum taught in schools is set by the National Curriculum. A discussion of the full implications of the National Curriculum falls outside the scope of this work. However religious education must be included alongside the National Curriculum. There is also a requirement for a daily act of collective worship. The religious syllabus must first be approved by a conference (Agreed Syllabus Conference) consisting of representatives of a number of bodies including the Church of England, the other major religious traditions in the area, teacher's associations and members of the local education authority. Section 375 Education Act 1996 provides that 'every agreed syllabus shall reflect that the religious traditions in Great Britain are in the main Christian whilst taking account of the teaching and practices of the other principal religions represented in Great Britain.' The aim of collective worship is

... to provide the opportunity for pupils to worship God, to consider spiritual and moral issues and to explore their own beliefs; to encourage participation and response, whether through active involvement in the presentation of worship or through listening to and joining in the worship offered; and to develop community spirit, promote a common ethos and shared values, and reinforce positive attitudes.[23]

In the case of religious education and collective worship a parent of a child may request that his or her child be withdrawn from attendance and the School Standards and Framework Act 1998 makes provision for such withdrawal. A parent is also entitled to make personal arrangements for his or her child to be provided with religious education elsewhere so long as it does not interfere with remainder of the school day. A child does not have a personal right to seek to be withdrawn. Where such a child is of the age and understanding to form an opinion

---

[22] School policies may address issues such as encouraging respect for others in and outside school, schemes for the reward and punishment of appropriate and inappropriate behaviour, truancy, bullying and equal opportunity reflecting principles of racial and sexual equality. Now that the Disability Discrimination Act 1998 is in force, guidance may be relevant on equal treatment for the disabled. It is unlikely, given the restrictions of section 2A Local Government Act 1986 (which prohibits the promotion of homosexuality), that any sophisticated guidance will be capable of being set in place to prevent discrimination based on sexual identity or orientation.

[23] Department of Education Circular, 1/94.

on his religious beliefs it would seem that an issue under Article 9 of the European Convention (right to freedom of thought, religion and conscience) may arise. The statutory provisions governing the religious education and daily worship provided in schools have to be applied sensitively especially given the rights of parents to have their children educated in accordance with their own wishes and Article 9.[24]

The syllabus established by the local education authority must not permit the political indoctrination of the pupils. Section 406 Education Act 1996 prohibits the pursuit of partisan political activities by junior pupils or their promotion by teaching staff. The curriculum must also include an element of sex education.[25] The governing body and head teacher are under a duty under section 403 of the Act to take such steps as are reasonably practicable to secure that where sex education is given to pupils at school it is given in such a manner as to encourage those pupils to have due regard to moral considerations and the value of family life. The promotion of homosexual relationships is prohibited under the Local Government Act 1986.[26]

Parents may withdraw their children from sex education save to the extent to which it is a requirement of the National Curriculum. Advice on sex education to parents should be available from the governing body on request.[27]

Admissions procedures and parental choice

It is lawful, and probably necessary for a local education authority to have a policy as to admissions to their schools. In *R v. Greenwich London Borough Council, ex parte Governors of the John Ball Primary School* (1990) 1 Fam Law 469 the Divisional Court said that a local education authority might have any reasonable policy that it thinks fit, provided it does not conflict with duties under section 86 School Standards and Framework Act 1998 or any other enactment. Accordingly an admissions policy must not be in violation of anti-discrimination legislation and should take proper account of the rights of parents and children alike under the Human Rights Act 1998.

In general terms the local education authority is obliged to allow parents to express a preference as to the school at which they would like their child to be educated.[28] To facilitate parental choice the local education authority must publish statements of policy on a range of ancillary matters such as the payment of fees, arrangement of free

---

[24] In particular since the enjoyment of such a freedom must be without discrimination under Article 14.

[25] Advice on which is set out in Department of Education Circular 5/94.

[26] Recent government proposals to remove this prohibition were rejected in the House of Lords. However, as a public authority the LEA has a duty to act compatibly with the European Convention on Human Rights under the Human Rights Act 1998. This includes the duty to provide access to education (Article 2, First Protocol) without discrimination (Article 14) (see *Chapter 3*). The prohibition under the Local Government Act 1986 may create difficulties in fulfilling this aspect of the Human Rights Act.

[27] Section 352(3) Education Act 1996.

[28] Section 86 School Standards and Framework Act 1998.

transport, and the curriculum or subject choices taught at the maintained schools for which it is responsible. The publication of national league tables provides parents with additional information upon which to base their preference.

The local education authority is under a duty by virtue of section 9 of the Education Act 1996 to have regard to the parents rights to have their child educated in accordance with their wishes. However parental choice may be limited where:

- compliance with the preference would prejudice the provision of education or the efficient use of resources;
- the preferred school is a foundation or voluntary aided school and compliance with the preference would be incompatible with the arrangements between the local education authority and the governors; or
- where the admission arrangements for the preferred school are based on aptitude or ability and compliance with the preference would be incompatible with the admissions policy.

Where a school is over-subscribed the local education authority may decline to comply with the stated preference of parents. In respect of such schools the local education authority may adopt an admissions policy which is reasonable and not inconsistent with its duties under section 86 School Standards and Framework Act 1998. In *R v. Richmond upon Thames London Borough Council and Another, ex parte JC (A Child)* (2000), *The Times,* August 10 the Court of Appeal confirmed that restrictions on the size of infant school classes had restricted the right of a parent to appeal against the refusal of his or her preferred school to admit a child.

The School Standards and Framework Act 1998 requires the local education authority to set up a procedure by which a parent may appeal against the refusal of the local education authority or the governors of a maintained school to admit a child in accordance with the exercise of parental choice. The appeal panel must consist of three to five members appointed by the local education authority.[29] The decision of the panel is binding on the governors or the authority but not on the parents who have a right to petition the Secretary of State on the basis that the original decision was unreasonable. The High Court also has powers exercisable on judicial review.

School attendance
The attendance of a child of compulsory school age is secured under the Education Act 1996 through a series of measures that may be taken by the local education authority or, in appropriate circumstances, by a court:

---

[29] Schedule 24 School Standards and Framework Act 1998.

- informal approaches to the child's parents
- serving a notice on parents to satisfy the authority that the child is receiving suitable education
- serving a notice of intention to make a school attendance order
- a school attendance order
- prosecution in the criminal courts for failing to comply with a school attendance order
- prosecution for failing to ensure the attendance of a child at school;
- a parenting order
- an application to a family proceedings court for an education supervision order; and
- prosecution for failing to comply with an education supervision order.

Notice of concern

Where it appears to a local education authority that a parent is failing to ensure that his or her child is receiving suitable education, whether by regular school attendance or otherwise it may serve on the parent a notice of its concern.[30] In this context a parent includes any person who is not a parent but who has parental responsibility for the child or who has care of him or her.[31]

A parent has a specified period of not less than 15 days in which to satisfy the local education authority that the arrangements in place for the child's education are suitable taking into account the child's age, ability and aptitude. If the authority is not so satisfied it may serve on the child's parents a school attendance order but only after giving notice of its intention to do so.

School attendance orders

The school attendance order specifies a school at which the child should be registered as a pupil by the parents. In the notice of intention to serve a school attendance order the local education authority are required to identify the school and any alternative schools in order to allow the parents to exercise their preference, or to make their own arrangements to satisfy the concerns of the authority.

If the school identified in the order is a maintained school the governing body must admit the child although it retains a power to exclude the child as appropriate.[32] Once a child attendance order has been made the parents have a responsibility to ensure that the child concerned is registered as a pupil of the specified school. Failure to comply with a school attendance order is a summary offence punishable by way of a fine.[33]

The school attendance order remains in force until the child ceases to be of compulsory school age. The order may be amended or revoked by

---

[30] Section 437 Education Act 1996.
[31] Section 576 Education Act 1996.
[32] Section 431 Education Act 1996.
[33] Section 443 of the Education Act 1996.

the local education authority at any time on the application of the child's parents. It may also be brought to an end if a court, having acquitted a parent of an offence under section 443 of the Act so directs.[34]

Prosecution of parents in the magistrates' court

Where a child is of compulsory school age and registered at a school it is the duty of his or her parents to ensure that he or she attends school regularly. Failure to do so is an offence under section 444 of the Education Act 1996, punishable by way of a fine. The offence is one of an absolute nature. There exist a number of situations where, in accordance with section 444(3) to (4), a child is not to be regarded as having failed to attend regularly. In effect these grounds provide the only substantive defences to proceedings under this part of the legislation. The grounds are where:

- the absences were with the leave of a person authorised by the governing body or proprietors of the school;
- the absences were due to sickness or any unavoidable cause;
- the absences were on any day exclusively set apart for religious observance by the religious body to which the parents belong;
- the parents can prove on a balance of probabilities that the school is not within walking distance of the child's home;[35] and
- no suitable arrangements have been made by the local education authority for the child's transport to school, boarding or for his or her transfer to another school closer to home.

A parent must be acquitted of an offence under section 444 if he or she can prove on a balance of probabilities that he or she is engaged in a trade or business of such a nature as to require him or her to travel from place to place; that the child has attended as regularly as the trade or business permits and, in the case of a child aged over six years, that child has made at least 200 appearances in the immediate 12 months.

Parenting orders

Where the court convicts a parent of an offence under section 443 or 444 Education Act 1996 (above) it is under a duty to consider a parenting order requiring the parent to attend certain counselling programmes as may be specified in the order aimed at preventing a repetition of the conduct leading to conviction. Parenting orders are discussed in more detail elsewhere in (*Chapter 6*). In general terms experience suggests that the prosecution of parents under the Education Act is usually a measure of last resort and that a parenting order is not a popular disposal with justices faced with parents who have already either rejected or failed to comply with the raft of support put in place before such a step is taken by the local education authority.

---

[34] Section 443(2) of the Education Act 1996.

[35] In the case of a child less than eight years this distance is two miles; in the case of a child over eight years, the distance is three miles.

Education supervision order

In such circumstances the way forward may lie with a direction to the local education authority under section 447(2) of the Act to apply for an education supervision order. Such an application may only be made to a family proceedings court.

The local education authority which is directed to make such an application must report back to the court making the direction within eight weeks. If the local education authority, having consulted with the local authority, is of the opinion that the child's welfare will be satisfactorily safeguarded without such an order they may decline to bring proceedings in the family court. Otherwise the legislation contemplates an application being made without delay. The Department of Health guidelines[36] set out the aims of the order:

> ... to provide an effective means of guiding parents and children so as to ensure that all children receive a satisfactory education. Supervisors are responsible for ensuring that an education supervision order brings about the required improvement, and for taking further action in the event that it fails to do so. In doing so, they need to keep in mind the best interests of the child, the requirements of the law on school attendance, and their responsibility to the court for the effective discharge of the order.

Where an education supervision order is in force it is the duty of the supervising officer to advise, assist and befriend and to give appropriate directions to the child and his or her parents to secure a proper education for the child. Before making any direction the supervising officer must, as far as practicable, ascertain the wishes and feelings of the child and his or her parents. He must give due weight to these views. It is only at this stage that the feelings and wishes of a child of appropriate age and maturity come directly into play. At all earlier stages of the legal process the enforcement of education is something done to a child rather than in partnership.

As indicated, where the terms of an education supervision order are persistently flouted a parent may be prosecuted in the criminal courts. The supervisor should also in such circumstances consider whether to refer the matter to the local authority for an assessment of whether it is appropriate to engage other powers available in respect of children in need or at risk under Part IV of the Children Act 1989 (see, generally, *Chapter 7*).

The welfare of children in school

The welfare of children at maintained schools is a matter for the local education authority working in partnership with the local authority under the general provisions of the Children Act 1989. The school and its teaching staff are often a vital resource in the protection of children from abuse or neglect. Often the school will pick up the first warning that a

---

[36] *Children Act 1989, Guidance and Regulations*, Vol. 7, 'Guardians ad litem and other Court related Issues'.

child is at risk. A teacher may be the person to whom a child turns in times of distress or anguish. The Department of Education has issued guidance[37] on the role of the education service the main points of which are:

- all staff should be alert to signs of abuse and know to whom they should report any concerns or suspicions;
- all schools and colleges should have a designated member of staff responsible for co-ordinating action within the institution and liasing with other agencies, an area Child Protection Committee (CPC);[38]
- all schools and colleges should be aware of the child protection procedures established by the CPC and, where appropriate, by the local education authority;
- all schools and colleges should have procedures (of which all staff should be aware) for handling suspected cases of abuse of pupils or students, including procedures to be followed if a member of staff is accused of abuse;
- staff with designated responsibility for child protection should receive appropriate training;
- in every local education authority a senior officer should be responsible for co-ordinating action on child protection across the authority.

Not only should teachers be vigilant for signs of abuse or neglect but also of indications that a child is failing to develop or that he or she has special educational needs, which may require the use of the school's or the local education authority's particular powers.

As far as independent and non-maintained schools are concerned the welfare of pupils again falls within the general duty of the local authority towards children in its area under the Children Act 1989. To this end there is a non-specific obligation on all people providing educational facilities to safeguard and promote the welfare of children provided with such services. Volume 5 of *The Children Act Guidance* provides detailed advice on independent schools. The local authority is under a specific duty under section 87 Children Act 1989 to take reasonably practicable steps to enable it to determine whether a child's welfare is adequately safeguarded whilst at an independent school. The Inspection of Premises, Children and Records (Independent Schools Regulations) 1994 govern the power of the local authority to inspect and police independent and non-maintained schools in this regard.

Discipline in school
It is the responsibility of the governors of a maintained school to set school policies on a number of matters including behavioural standards but the drafting of school rules and the setting of regulations for the

---

[37] 'Protecting Children From Abuse: The Role of the Education Service:', DFEE 10/95.
[38] Part of the child protection strategies mentioned at the start of *Chapter 7*.

conduct of school pupils are the responsibility of the head teacher. The power to exclude a child may only be exercised by the head teacher.

Under the School Standards and Framework Act 1998 the head teacher must develop the code of conduct which gives overall effect to the governor's policy. The code, which should be in writing and be actively publicised, should promote self-discipline and proper regard for authority, encourage good behaviour and respect for others, secure acceptable behaviour and generally regulate the conduct of pupils. The Department of Education has issued guidance to head teachers and others on 'Pupil Behaviour and Discipline' dealing with issues such as bullying and racial and sexual harassment.[39]

Of particular concern is the adoption of a clear set of rules relating to bullying and victimisation. The school bully has an almost mythical place in an adult's recollection of schooldays. However the misery that a bully may cause his or her victim is extreme and a failure by a public authority to take adequate steps to protect a child from such a course of conduct may amount to a violation of the state's duty under Article 3 of the European Convention to prevent inhuman or degrading treatment. In any event a failure to tackle bullying is morally reprehensible.

The duty of course goes beyond the protection of the victim and extends to taking measures against the bully in order to prevent a repetition of his or her behaviour and to secure the completion of his or her own education.

The responsibility for enforcing the code of conduct and taking such measures as are necessary to secure adherence to it rests with the head teacher. There are four main methods by which misconduct may be addressed other than an informal warning or through resort to parents:

- restraint
- detention
- corporal punishment; and
- exclusion.

Restraint

In certain circumstances a child may be restrained by a teacher. Section 550A Education Act 1996 provides:

> 550A (1) A member of staff of a school may use, in relation to any pupil at the school, such force as is reasonable in the circumstances for the purpose of preventing the pupil from doing (or continuing to do) any of the following, namely –
> (a) committing any offence; or
> (b) causing personal injury to, or damage to the property of, any person (including the pupil himself) or
> (c) engaging in any behaviour prejudicial to the maintenance of good order and discipline at the school or among any of its pupils, whether that behaviour occurs during a teaching session or otherwise.

---

[39] DES Circular 8/94.

(2) Subsection (1) applies where a member of the staff of a school is –

(a) on the premises of the school; or

(b) elsewhere at a time when, as a member of its staff, he has lawful control or charge of the pupil concerned:

but it does not authorise anything to be done in relation to a pupil which constitutes the giving of corporal punishment within the meaning of [this Act].

Department of Education Circular (DFEE 10/98) provides further guidance on the use (and misuse) of the power to restrain a pupil as envisaged by section 550A.

Detention

Detention of a child during school hours or outside them is a recognised punishment for infringements of school rules. Section 550B Education Act 1996 prescribes the use of detention after the school session in maintained schools. Detention at other times during the school day and detention at any time in the case of independent schools is governed by the common law.

Detention during the ordinary hours of the school day may be lawful at common law where it is reasonable and necessary. Detention that is not reasonable and necessary may amount to false imprisonment. The duty on public authorities to act compatibly with the right to liberty in Article 5 of the European Convention may cloud the issue further. Certainly the grounds for imposing a 'within hours' detention should be both clear and accessible to avoid any suggestion of arbitrariness. Factors that might dictate whether the use of such a detention is just and reasonable include:

- the nature of the rule infringed
- the opportunity for the child to either exonerate himself or herself or to make reparation for the transgression;
- the age of the child
- the environment in which the detention is served
- the period of the detention; and
- the opportunity for the child to obtain adequate refreshment and rest before the remainder of the school day.

Detention outside the normal school hours is governed by section 550B. Detention otherwise than within the statutory grounds is unlawful and may give rise to civil liability. The power to use such detention flows from the assumed transfer of parental rights (*Chapter 2*) to the head teacher by the child's parents. The position thus depends on the reasonable exercise of those rights by the head teacher. Where a parent expressly withdraws his or her consent to the exercise of those powers the head teacher may be acting unlawfully by going against parental wishes. Section 550B(3) seeks to establish a degree of protection where parental consent is absent (but not where it has been withdrawn).

The position in relation to a child's right not be deprived of liberty under Article 5 of the European Convention may yet be an issue to be resolved.[40] However the absence of a procedure by which the child can participate in the decision-making process or challenge the decision taken against him or her appears to lack a proper degree of procedural fairness. Again detention within an educational setting appears to be something *done to* a child and does not necessarily reflect the importance of the child's wishes, feelings or welfare.

It is interesting to note that the detention of a child in accommodation that amounts to secure accommodation is permitted in the UK only in those circumstances set out in section 25 Children Act 1989. Although school premises are not generally within the definition of secure accommodation for the purposes of the Children Act there is perhaps a fine line to be drawn between what is lawful punitive detention in an educational setting and what amounts to the unlawful deprivation of liberty. This is an issue that may be of more concern with regard to detention imposed as a punishment in non-maintained schools or in respect of detention during the school day where the position is governed by an uncertain common law. Section 550B provides so far as it is relevant:

> 550B(1) Where a pupil to whom this section applies is required on disciplinary grounds to spend a period of time in detention at his school after the end of any school session, his detention shall not be rendered unlawful by virtue of the absence of his parent's consent to it if the conditions set out in subsection (3) are satisfied . . .
>
> (3) The conditions referred to in subsection (1) are as follows:
> (a) the head teacher of the school must have previously determined, and have –
>> (i) made generally known within the school, and
>> (ii) taken steps to bring to the attention of the parent of every person who is for the time being a registered pupil there,
>
> that the detention of pupils after the end of the school session is one of the measures that may be taken with a view to regulating the conduct of pupils;
> (a) the detention must be imposed by the head teacher or by another teacher at the school specifically or generally authorised by him for the purpose;
> (b) the detention must be reasonable in all the circumstances; and
> (c) the pupil's parent must have been given at least 24 hours' notice in writing that the detention was due to take place.

In determining whether detention is reasonable the following factors should be taken into account:

- the age of the child
- any special educational needs he or she may have
- any religious requirements affecting him or her

---

[40] See generally the discussion of secure accommodation measures in *Chapter 7*.

- travel arrangements to travel home or those reasonable and suitable alternative means of transport his parents can arrange; and, most importantly; and
- whether the detention constitutes a proportionate punishment in the circumstances of the case.

Corporal punishment

The use of physical correction by a parent has traditionally been held to be lawful so long as it is done in a reasonable manner.[41] As a teacher was deemed to be *in loco parentis* the right to use corporal punishment was said to travel with that designation. It was thus lawful to use such punishment for an infringement of a school rule. What was to be considered to be reasonable punishment was a mater to be judged by the standards prevailing in contemporary society at the time.[42]

The position is now clear as far as teachers are concerned. The School Standards and Framework Act 1998 abolished the use of corporal punishment in all schools whether maintained by a local education authority or in the independent sector. The position of parents using corporal punishment remains unclear in the light of *A v. UK (1999)* dealt with in more detail in *Chapter 2*.

The prohibition on the use of corporal punishment does not however prevent the use of restraining force under section 550A Education Act 1996 or anything done for reasons that include averting an immediate danger of personal injury to, or an immediate danger to, the property of any person including of the pupil concerned.[43]

Exclusion

The exclusion of a child from education is a drastic step that should only be taken where is it absolutely necessary and no other form of discipline is appropriate. The local education authority retains a duty towards children who have been excluded to ensure that proper and adequate provision is made for their education. Experience shows that there is a clear link between exclusion from school and offending behaviour. Young people not attending school are more than three times as likely to offend than those attending school.[44] Up to 65 per cent of youth offenders sentenced in court are non-attendees or have been excluded from school.[45] Excluded pupils are twice as likely to receive custodial sentences

---

[41]   Section 1(7) Children and Young Persons Act 1933.

[42]   *Costello-Roberts v. UK* (1994) 1 FCR 65

[43]   Section 131(5) School Standards and Framework Act 1998.

[44]   Graham J. and Bowling B., *Young People and Crime*, Research Study No. 145, London: Home Office, 1995.

[45]   *Misspent Youth*, Audit Commission, 1996.

as those not excluded[46] and almost 60 per cent of youths on supervision orders were outside mainstream education or training.[47]

The power to exclude a pupil can be exercised only by the head teacher having regard to the governor's statement of policy on conduct and his or her duty to take into account any guidance issued by the Secretary of State. The School Standards and Framework Act 1998 contains detailed provisions concerning the exclusion of a pupil from school.[48] An exclusion may be for either a specified period not exceeding 45 days in any one school year or permanent. The use of indeterminate periods of exclusion is no longer permitted although many professionals might hold the view that a more flexible approach would allow a head teacher to wield his or her powers more effectively.

The head teacher has a duty to investigate the circumstances surrounding the conduct in question. In *R v. Roman Catholic Schools, ex parte S* (1998) Education Law Report 304 the Divisional Court identified a number of principles relevant to the discharge of this function:

- the overriding principle is that a pupil must have a fair opportunity to exculpate himself or herself
- whether such an opportunity has been afforded will depend upon the issues raised in the inquiry
- those conducting the inquiry must decide what critical issues of fact they should resolve and what inquiries could reasonably be made to resolve those issues
- they must give careful and even-handed consideration to all the available evidence in relation to those issues; and
- those conducting an inquiry do not need on every occasion to carry out searching inquiries involving calling of bodies of oral evidence.

Where a child has been permanently excluded he or she may seek to persuade the governing body of the school to order his or her reinstatement. Where such representations are unsuccessful there is a right of appeal to the local education authority. No particular procedure is required to be followed by the appeals panel but it must act in accordance with principles of fairness.[49] Such a common law requirement seems likely to be influenced by the European Convention standard of procedural fairness contemplated by Article 6. However it seems unlikely that Article 6 will directly apply to the procedure given that Article 2 of the First Protocol guarantees a right of access to education generally and not a right of access to a particular educational facility.

---

[46] *Schools, Disruptive Behaviour and Delinquency*, Research Study No. 96, London: Home Office, 1988.

[47] Figures supplied by INCLUDE, the national charity dedicated to securing the inclusion of all young people in mainstream education, employment and training: www.include.org.uk

[48] Sections 64 to 68 and Schedule 18 of the School Standards and Framework Act 1998.

[49] Where the appeals panel fails to act reasonably an appeal to the High Court by way of judicial review may exist.

A successful appeal may result in an order to the head teacher to reinstate the child. Many head teachers have found this mandatory order difficult to accept and accordingly further guidelines have been issued by the Department of Education in August 2000 to assist and support the initial decision of the head teacher. The local education authority remains responsible for ensuring that a child thus excluded from school is educated. To fulfil this obligation the authority may arrange for the child's admission to an alternative maintained school or make other provision at a special school. Parental choice is, at this stage lost where the child has been excluded from two or more schools in the preceding two years.

Special educational needs

The local education authority has specific duty to provide suitable and sufficient places in education for children with special needs. The duty does not extend to requiring the authority to educate such a child to his or her maximum potential nor to provide a Utopian system.[50] However such provision must be appropriate to the child's needs and against the statutory background of education being made available in mainstream as opposed to special schools.

Section 312 Education Act1996 provides that a child has special educational needs if he or she has a learning difficulty that calls for special educational provision to be made for the child. A learning difficulty means where the child:

- has a significantly greater difficulty in learning than the majority of children of his or her age; or
- has a disability that either prevents or hinders the child from making use of educational facilities of a kind generally provided for children of his or her age in schools within the area of the local education authority.

The Secretary of State has issued guidance on the assessment of special educational needs.[51] The procedure provides for five stages of assessment. The first three take place within the school and involve the school and parents in working together to make arrangements for the child within mainstream schooling. Where adequate provision for the child cannot be made the local education authority's direct responsibility comes into play in stages four and five of the statutory procedure below:

- In *Stage One* the initial assessment of a child's needs is taken by the class teacher and, in consultation with the appointed SEN co-ordinator and the head teacher, special and suitable arrangements are put into place to meet those needs.
- In *Stage Two* the child's needs are managed, monitored and reviewed by the special educational needs (SEN) co-ordinator.

---

[50] *R v. Surrey County Council Education Committee, ex parte H* (1984) 83 LGR 219.
[51] *Code of Practice on the Identification and Assessment of Special Educational Needs.*

- In *Stage Three* specialist staff from outside the school may be used to support a child with more specialist educational needs. If the arrangements are not adequate those specialists will assist the school in assessing whether the statutory procedure by the local education authority is appropriate.
- In *Stage Four* the local education authority assumes primary responsibility to make an assessment of the child's needs and decide if a statement of his or her needs is necessary and desirable.
- In *Stage Five* if it is necessary for the local education authority to make a statement of a child's special educational needs it must do so in accordance with the legislation.[52]

The statement sets out the conclusions of the local education authority's assessment, the special educational needs of the child and the special educational provision needed to meet them. Additionally the statement must include details of any proposed placement for the child and provision for non-educational needs as may exist. The local education authority is under a duty to execute its educational plan for the child and to monitor and review the child's progress and the evolution of the special educational provision.

At all stages of the process the local education authority is under a duty to engage the support and co-operation of the child's parents. Where practicable the child's needs should be met in mainstream education and proper regard should be had to parents' wishes and preferences. The Code of Practice provides detailed guidance on what parents may expect a local education authority to do and the procedure leading to the making of relevant decisions.

Where a local education authority makes a decision in respect of a child's special educational needs a right of appeal lies to the Special Educational Needs Tribunal. An appeal may be made in respect of:

- refusal to make an assessment
- refusal to issue a full statement of needs after an assessment
- the description of the child's needs in a statement
- the description of the provision to meet those needs in the statement
- the failure to name the school in the statement
- the refusal to change the name of the school in the statement
- the refusal to reassess the child if no assessment has been made for six months; and
- the refusal to maintain a statement.

The procedure for an appeal is set out in the Special Educational Needs Tribunal Regulations 1995. The child has no personal right to appeal against any of the relevant decisions of the local education authority and is not a party to the proceedings. Accordingly the

---

[52] Section 324 Education Act 1996, the Education (Special Needs Education) Regulations 1994 and the *Code of Practice*.

promotion of his or her rights lies in the hands of the parents. A child with special educational needs may have a sufficient understanding, and be of suitable age and maturity to bring the child's views to the appeal process and the procedure may therefore leave some children at a disadvantage.

Decisions taken by the tribunal may be the subject of a further appeal within the education legislation to the Secretary of State or to the High Court on a point of law or by way of judicial review.[53] The tribunal otherwise has power on appeal to dismiss the application, order the local education authority to amend the statement or order the authority to cease to maintain the statement. The power of the tribunal to order a local education authority to substitute a different school where the special educational provision is to be made is limited.

PART II: EMPLOYMENT

The employment of children is regulated in UK national law to reflect the principle that children have a right to special treatment. The extent to which employment is permitted depends on the age of the child. The employment of children under the age of 14 years is generally prohibited save to the extent to which statute allows, and between 14 years and 18 years employment is statutorily regulated. The chart which starts at page vi of this work contains some examples of specific instances where age determines whether a child can pursue a particular employment activity.

International obligations
The UN Convention On the Rights of the Child provides in Article 32:

(1) States Parties recognise the right of the child to be protected from economic exploitation and from performing any work that is likely to be hazardous or to interfere with the child's education, or to be harmful to the child's health or physical, mental, spiritual, moral or social development.

(2) States Parties shall take legislative, administrative, social and educational measures to ensure the implementation of the present article. To this end, and having regard to the relevant provisions of other international instruments, States Parties shall in particular:

(a) provide for a minimum age or minimum ages for admission to employment;

(b) provide for appropriate regulation of the hours and conditions of employment;

(c) provide for appropriate penalties or other sanctions to ensure the effective enforcement of the present article.

---

[53] Generally the court will defer to the Secretary of State in matters relating to striking the right balance between the appellant, another parent and the local education authority. *R v. London Borough of Brent, ex parte F* (1999) [ELR 32]. Accordingly judicial review is better confined to procedural impropriety.

Other international instruments include those issued by the European Union which are directly enforceable in the UK by virtue of the European Communities Act 1972 and those issued by the International Labour Organisation upon which the UK has collaborated which are effective only to the extent to which legislation has been enacted to bring their content into force.

The Employment of Women, Young Persons and Children Act 1920 gives effect in UK law to the Washington Convention which regulates the employment of children in factories, industrial undertakings and at sea. The minimum age for such employment is 14 years with special provisions governing the employment of children aged less than 16 years in industry and factories. Nothing in the Act however makes it unlawful for a child to receive training in such placements in accordance with government or local authority approved schemes.[54]

Regulation of child employment in national law

Subject to a very few exceptions explained below, no child may be employed:

- so long as he or she is under the age of 13 years; or
- before the close of school hours on any day on which he or she is required to attend school; or
- before 7 a.m. or after 7 p.m. on any day; or
- for more than two hours on any Sunday; or
- where employment on a ship is permitted, to lift, carry or move anything so heavy as to be likely to cause injury to him or her.[55]

These restrictions are in addition to the restrictions on the employment of children in factories and industrial undertakings by virtue of the 1920 Act, above. This legislation is prospectively amended or repealed by the Employment of Children Act 1973 (not yet in force).

The local education authority is able to make byelaws with respect to the employment of children. The power to make such byelaws is likely to be abolished by the Employment of Children Act 1973 which will empower the Secretary of State to make similar orders in subordinate legislation. At present byelaws may be made to prohibit or prescribe:

- the minimum age for employment
- the number of hours in a day or week when a child may be so employed and the days on which he or she may be employed
- the periods of rest and meal breaks
- the holidays and half-holidays allowed; and
- any other conditions to be observed in relation to employment.

---

[54] This would include certain work experience schemes or other training schemes of an educational nature.

[55] Section 18 Children and Young Persons Act 1933.

The byelaws may distinguish between children of different ages and sexes and between localities, trade, occupations and circumstances.[56] The local education authority may not however interfere with the basic statutory scheme unless it is to permit the employment of children either by their parents or guardians in light agricultural or horticultural work while the children are less than 13 years of age, or for not more than one hour before the commencement of school hours on a school day.

Street trading

No child[57] may be engaged or employed in street trading unless the local authority has made a byelaw authorising children who have attained the age of 14 years to be employed by their parents in such undertakings.

Enforcement

Where a child is employed contrary to the general restrictions on employment or in violation of any byelaws or regulations made under them the employer and any other person to whose act or default the contravention is attributable is liable to criminal prosecution depending on the type of regulation or bye-law concerned and, on summary conviction, to a fine.

An officer of the local authority or a constable may apply to a justice of the peace for authority to enter premises where there are grounds to believe that any of the regulations, byelaws or general provisions as to employment are being breached. The purpose of entry is to make inquiries into the suspected violation and any person who obstructs such an authorised officer is liable on summary conviction to a fine.

Performances by children

A child may not take part in any performance unless a local authority[58] has issued a licence permitting such engagements. The following performances require licensing:

- any performance in connection with which a charge is made
- any performance in licensed premises or a registered club
- any broadcast performance
- any other such performance included in a programme service within the meaning of the Broadcasting Act 1990,[59] and
- any performance recorded with a view to its use in a broadcast or such a service or in a film intended for public exhibition.

---

[56] Section 18(2) Children and Young Persons Act 1933.
[57] Defined as a child of compulsory school age (see earlier in the chapter).
[58] The local education authority.
[59] If the Internet can be brought within the definition of a broadcast, a licence would probably be required under the Broadcasting Act 1990. The difficulty, inherent in anything seeking to regulate the Internet, would be in the practical problem of enforcement against operations outside the jurisdiction of the English courts.

A licence is not required if the child has not taken part in such a performance in the preceding six months on more than three days or if the performance is given under arrangements made by a school or authorised by the Secretary of State or a body acting on his or her behalf. The Secretary of State has made regulations dealing with the maximum hours of work, rest and daily meals for children taking part in performances not requiring a licence.[60]

Licences

The local authority has power to grant licences in respect of performances by children.[61] Where the child concerned is under the age of 14 years a licence may not be granted unless:

- the licence is for acting and is accompanied by a declaration by the applicant that the child's part cannot be taken except by a child of about his or her age;
- the licence is for dancing in a ballet; or
- the nature of his or her part in the performance is wholly or mainly musical or the performance consists only of ballet or opera.

Section 37 Children and Young Persons Act 1933 makes provision for the grant of licences; procedural matters are set down in the Children (Performance) Regulations 1968. A local authority may not grant a licence unless it is satisfied that the child is fit to take part in such a performance, that proper provision has been made to secure the child's health and kind treatment and that his or her education will not suffer. Where the authority is so satisfied it may not refuse to grant the licence.

Anyone who causes or procures any child or, being his or her parent or guardian allows him to take part in an unlicensed performance or in breach of any of the terms of a licence duly granted under section 37 of the Act is liable on summary conviction to a fine of up to £1,000 or imprisonment of up to three months. Where a licence is in force, upon conviction the court may revoke it.

Dangerous performances

It is an offence to cause, procure or allow a child to take part in any performance to which certain provisions restricting such performances apply under section 37 of the Act, and in which his life or limbs are endangered. The prosecution of such an offence may only be instituted by or with the authority of the chief officer of police and is punishable on summary conviction by a fine of up to £1,000.

The local authority may grant a licence to allow a child of 12 years or above to be trained to take part in performances of a dangerous nature.[62]

---

[60] The Children (Performances) Regulations 1968.

[61] Regulations also provide for the variation and revocation of a licence and a power of appeal to a magistrates' court against the refusal to grant or against the imposition of a condition in the licence.

There is an absolute prohibition on the employment of children under the age of 12 years in such enterprises. The authority must make due inquiry into the fitness of the child, his or her willingness to be trained and that proper arrangement have been made to secure the child's health and kind treatment. Anyone causing, procuring or allowing a child to be trained without a licence or in breach of its terms is liable on summary conviction to a fine of up to £1,000.

Performances abroad

There is a legal prohibition on allowing a child to go abroad for the purpose of performing for profit unless a licence has been issued for the purpose.[63] The licence may only be granted by a justice of the peace in accordance with section 25 Children and Young Persons Act 1933. The licence may be conditional and may in time be amended or revoked. A licence may be granted in respect of a child under the age of 14 years if:

- the engagement is for acting and is accompanied by a declaration that the part cannot be taken except by a person of about the child's age; or
- the engagement is for dancing in a ballet; or
- the engagement is for taking part in a performance the nature of which is wholly or mainly musical or which consists only of opera or ballet.

The District Judge must be satisfied that:

- the application is made with the full consent of the child's parent or guardian
- the child is going abroad to fulfil a particular engagement
- the child is fit for the purpose and that proper provision has been made to secure his or her health, kind treatment and adequate supervision while abroad, and his or her return from abroad at the expiration or revocation of the licence; and
- there has been furnished to the child a copy of the contract showing the terms and conditions of his or her engagement in a language understood by the child.

The chief officer of police on whom notice of the application and the contract must be served is required to report in writing to the magistrate to assist his or her determination of the application. The maximum period of such a licence is three months although it may be extended on

---

[62] A term which includes acrobatics and contortionism and other acts should be construed *ejusdem generis*. It would seem that neither a licence nor any other permission or authority would in fact absolve a parent or other person with responsibility for a child from criminal or other responsibility for serious injury or death.

[63] Section 25(1) Children and Young Persons Act 1933.

application.[64] Anyone acting in violation of the provisions governing child performances abroad is liable on summary conviction to a fine of or imprisonment, and on indictment up to two years imprisonment. Section 26 Children and Young Persons Act 1933 makes detailed provision as to the procedure.

The licensing system ensures that the child performer's welfare is properly respected and allows a judicial or administrative agency to interpose and make provision for the child's safety and well-being so as to ensure he or she is not exploited in the employment. Where a child is employed the duty of the employer to take care of the child and to ensure a safe working environment is in practice greater than it would have been in the same situation with regard to an adult capable of making relevant judgements for himself or herself concerning the degree of risk – and assuming that other offences are not being committed by requiring a person, of whatever age, to perform a given task.[65]

Training schemes

Children in their final year at school may be able to take part in certain training schemes. Sixteen and 17-year-olds who are not of compulsory school age or have left full-time employment but are unable to find work are guaranteed a Youth Training place. Whilst this is neither employment nor welfare work the regime allows children to be engaged in a range of activities for the purpose of education and training. Certain allowances are payable: see the beginning of this chapter.

A young person of 17 registered under such an initiative or under an approved apprenticeship scheme can be engaged to work in licensed premises notwithstanding the general prohibition on the employment of young people in licensed premises.

---

[64] Unless the District Judge considers it unnecessary the applicant for a licence will usually be required to give such security by way of recognisance or otherwise to observe the terms and conditions of the licence.

[65] See, e.g. *Crocker v. Banks* (1888) 4 TLR 324.

Index

Grendon Tales

STORIES FROM A THERAPEUTIC COMMUNITY

'A breathless personal slide through her year talking to some of Britain's most dangerous prisoners': *Community Care*

'A work of intimacy and frankness ... Concrete evidence that therapy does help expose the failures of the past whilst offering hope for the future': *Prison Service News*

As featured on BBC Radio 4's Woman's Hour

For anyone trying to understand what 'drives' people to commit serious and unspeakable crimes the first-hand 'tales' in this book deserve intimate reading.

For over 40 years Grendon Prison in Buckinghamshire - with its 'Therapuetic Communities' of high security 'residents' - has remained unique.

In 2000 Ursula Smartt was allowed to mix with some of Britains most disturbed offenders and the staff who deal with them. The result is *Grendon Tales,* a fascinating - and at times shocking - description of life inside this world famous establishment.

Grendon Prison houses dangerous, disturbed and disruptive criminals (armed robbers to paedophiles, rapists and murderers). It is 'the last chance saloon' – a final opportunity for an offender to alter thinking and behaviour and maybe convince the authorities that his release back into the community should be considered.

The approach remains unique - as can be seen from the author's comparisons with Europe and a new therapeutic regime which opened in July 2001 at Dovegate Prison – Britain's newest and state-of-the-art prison establishment.

Ursula Smartt found some stories she heard overwhelming. Ultimately her captivating style, eye for detail and sensitivity to victims of crime win the day as she writes powerfully – often controversially - about matters which might otherwise be too raw and distressing.

With a Foreword by Lord Avebury

ISBN 1 872 870 96 1 £18 plus £2 p&p

The Magic Bracelet

TECHNOLOGY AND OFFENDER SUPERVISION **Dick Whitfield**

In Europe, over 30,000 criminal offenders were electronically tagged in 2000, and over four times that number elsewhere in the world. With over 20 countries now either starting new schemes or developing existing ones, these figures are expected to grow dramatically over the next few years - and the availability of satellite tracking and voice verification systems will also mean a wider variety of options as technology is increasingly used to supervise offenders.

But how effective is it? Can it have any real impact on growing crime figures and on preventing offending, or does tagging simply provide a short-term answer and an increasingly alienated criminal underclass? Is it just another 'quick fix' which will go the same way as so many penal initiatives? *The Magic Bracelet* is an up-to-date picture - a global jigsaw - of the very different ways in which new technology is being used, the known results to date and the lessons for criminal justice policy.

Separate chapters cover the history and development of tagging, experience in North America, the UK and Europe and elsewhere – as well as operational issues, human and civil rights implications and future possibilities.

ISBN 1 872 870 17 1 £12 plus £2 p&p (UK only; Europe £3; rest of the world £6)

Women, Drugs and Custody

The Experiences of Women Drug Users in Prison **Margaret Malloch**

The approach of HM Prison Service and the Scottish Prison Service to drug users in prison outlined, focusing on the direct experiences of women drug users in particular. A welcome addition to the expanding literature on drugs and offenders, the book looks at three strands - 'Women', 'Drugs' and 'Custody' – often with their conflicting issues and agendas. This book joins a number of innovative Waterside titles dealing with such issues (including *Drug Treatment in Prison* by Carol Martin and Elaine Player, *Drugs, Trafficking and Criminal Policy* by Penny Green and *Invisible Women: What's Wrong With Women's Imprisonment* by Angela Devlin) - to shows how drugs present doubly complex problems in an environment where security and control take priority.

May ISBN 1 872 870 91 0 1 £16 plus £2 p&p

www.watersidepress.co.uk

Waterside Press *QualityPublications* www.watersidepress.co.uk

Visit our enhanced web-site for **latest UK legal news** and details of other titles

'Simply the best book I have ever read on criminal justice'

As featured in *The Times* and *The Daily Telegraph*

Crime, State and Citizen
A FIELD FULL OF FOLK

David Faulkner

This is simply the best book I have ever read on criminal justice; it is quite possibly the best one ever written. It is wide-ranging, comprehensive, detailed, analytical and authoratative. It is also bang up-to-date . . . It is a book that should be read and kept by anyone and everyone who has a finger in the criminal justice pie. It will be a long time before it is excelled: *Justice of the Peace* (September, 2001)

Crime, State and Citizen is a wide-ranging and authoritative appraisal of the factors which sustain the fragile balance between effective government and individual rights and obligations in modern-day Britain. It is about: how Britain governs itself today; the rights and responsibilities of its citizens; the character of its public services and their relations with the state. Writing at a time when issues such as the Rule of Law, human rights and cultural and human diversity are to the fore, David Faulkner examines these and similar questions by focusing on the politics and policies, and the professional standards and day-to-day arrangements, for dealing with crime and criminal justice - thereby touching on issues of immediate concern to Parliament, the Government, the courts, the other criminal justice services and individuals. He also explores the underlying aims and principles of justice, social inclusion, public safety (including matters of concern to victims of crime), accountability and legitimacy before suggesting how they should be applied and inescapable conflicts resolved.

With a Foreword by Lord Windlesham   ISBN 1 872 870 98 8 **£22.50**

Restoring Respect for Justice

Martin Wright

A leading work on restorative justice – A must for anyone concerned about victims of crime

'Should be compulsory reading': *The Magistrate*. 1999 ISBN 1 872 870 78 3 £18 plus £2 p&p

Order from **WATERSIDE PRESS** • DOMUM ROAD • WINCHESTER • SO23 9NN
Full catalogue /Orders ☎ Tel/fax 01962 855567 E-mail: watersidepress@compuserve.com
Or visit www.watersidepress.co.uk where you can order via the Internet in secure conditions